Henry Richard Fox Bourne

The story of our colonies

With sketches of their present condition

Henry Richard Fox Bourne

The story of our colonies
With sketches of their present condition

ISBN/EAN: 9783741160837

Manufactured in Europe, USA, Canada, Australia, Japa

Cover: Foto ©ninafisch / pixelio.de

Manufactured and distributed by brebook publishing software (www.brebook.com)

Henry Richard Fox Bourne

The story of our colonies

THE STORY OF OUR COLONIES.

THE
STORY OF OUR COLONIES:

WITH

SKETCHES OF THEIR PRESENT CONDITION.

BY

H. R. FOX BOURNE,

AUTHOR OF "ENGLISH SEAMEN UNDER THE TUDORS," "FAMOUS LONDON MERCHANTS,"
ETC., ETC.

LONDON:
JAMES HOGG & SON, YORK STREET, COVENT GARDEN.
MDCCCLXIX.

ALL RIGHTS RESERVED.

TO

THE RIGHT HONOURABLE

EARL GRANVILLE, K.G.

HER MAJESTY'S PRINCIPAL SECRETARY OF STATE FOR THE
COLONIAL DEPARTMENT,

THIS VOLUME,

BY HIS LORDSHIP'S PERMISSION,

IS RESPECTFULLY DEDICATED.

PREFACE.

PERHAPS the title of this book sufficiently explains its purport. Of the history of the British possessions—a theme large enough for several volumes—it does not pretend to give a complete account, or even a comprehensive epitome. If it succeed in showing what were the virtues and the vices, the designs and the accidents, which led to the formation and development of our Colonial Empire, what are its present value and prospective importance, and how these may be increased by proper cultivation of the emigration-fields that are open to our over-crowded country, its object will be attained.

H. R. F. D.

LONDON, *October 1863*.

CONTENTS.

CHAPTER I.

OUR EARLIEST COLONIES.

Introduction—The Cathayan Fables—Discovery of America by John Cabot—His "New-found-lands"—The First Efforts of the English in Colonizing America—Sir Humphrey Gilbert and Sir Walter Raleigh—The Rise of English Colonization—The Establishment of the United States—England's other Colonies. [1490-1776.] ... 1

CHAPTER II.

OUR FIRST WEST INDIAN COLONY.

The First English Settlements in the West Indies—The Exploits of Sir John Hawkins and his Successors—The Colonization and Early History of Barbados—Lord Willoughby of Parham—The Civil War in Barbados—Lord Willoughby and Sir George Ayscue—The Progress of the Island during the Seventeenth Century—Its Trade and Population—The Slaves and their Sufferings. [1562-1700.] ... 15

CHAPTER III.

JAMAICA AND THE BUCCANEERS.

Columbus in Jamaica—Its Government by the Spaniards—Cromwell's Conquest—The Maroons—The Buccaneers—The Exploits of Sir Henry Morgan—The Connection of Jamaica with the Buccaneers—Its Early Progress—The Earthquake of 1692, and Subsequent Disasters. [1605-1694.] ... 29

CHAPTER IV.

JAMAICA AND SLAVERY.

The Progress of Jamaica—Its Value to England—Slavery—The Slave Insurrections—The Rising of 1760—The Condition of the Slaves—The Insurrection of 1832—The Abolition of Slavery in 1834. [1604-1834.] . . . 43

CHAPTER V.

OUR WEST INDIAN POSSESSIONS.

The Bermudas—The Bahamas—Other West Indian Islands—British Guiana—Trinidad—Barbados—Jamaica—The Present Condition of our West Indian Colonies—The Causes of their Deterioration and the Means of their Improvement. [1593-1869.] 53

CHAPTER VI.

NEWFOUNDLAND.

The Beginning of the Newfoundland Fisheries—The Growth of Newfoundland as a Colony—English Neglect of it—The Fishers and the Colonists—Its Troubles during War with France — Its Subsequent Development — Seal-Hunting and Cod-Fishing. [1497-1867.] . . . 68

CHAPTER VII.

FRENCH NORTH AMERICA.

The French in North America—The Colony of New France—Samuel Champlain—The Progress of the Colony—Wars with the Indians and the English—The Contests between the English and French Colonists—The English Conquests of Nova Scotia, Cape Breton, and Canada. [1524-1700.] 81

CHAPTER VIII.

NOVA SCOTIA AND NEW BRUNSWICK.

The French Settlers in Nova Scotia—Their Banishment in 1755—Progress of Nova Scotia, Cape Breton, and New Brunswick under the English—A Fire in New Brunswick --Prince Edward's Island. [1755-1861.] . . . 97

CONTENTS.

CHAPTER IX.
CANADA.

The History of Canada under British Rule—The First American War—Internal Troubles—The French and English Canadians—The Second American War—Fresh Domestic Difficulties—The Rebellions of 1837 and 1838—Lord Durham's Services to the Colony—Its Later History—The Canadian Confederation. [1760-1867.] . . 106

CHAPTER X.
THE HUDSON'S BAY TERRITORY.

The Hudson's Bay Company and its Territory—Rivalry in the Eighteenth Century—The Character and Working of the Company—Its Servants and Subjects—The Red River Settlement—Vancouver Island and British Columbia—Dissolution of the Hudson's Bay Company. [1070-1869.] 128

CHAPTER XI.
BRITISH NORTH AMERICA.

A General View of the British North American Colonies—Prince Edward's Island—Cape Breton—Nova Scotia—New Brunswick—Canada—The Western Territories—British Columbia and Vancouver Island. [1869.] . 139

CHAPTER XII.
WEST AFRICA.

The West African Settlements—Sierra Leone—Gambia—Cape Coast Castle—Lagos. [1600-1869.] 158

CHAPTER XIII.
CAPE COLONY.

The Dutch Settlement on the Cape of Good Hope—Early Quarrels with the Hottentots and Cruel Treatment of them—Transfer of the Colony to England—Its Progress under British Rule—The Kaffir Wars and Other Troubles—The Present Constitution of the Colony—Its Natural Advantages. [1648-1869.] 156

CONTENTS.

CHAPTER XIV.
NATAL.

The Kaffirs—First English Visits to the Eastern Coast of South Africa—The Settlement of Port Natal—Its Early Troubles and Later Progress—The Present Condition and Resources of the Colony. [1663-1869.] . . . 175

CHAPTER XV.
BRITISH INDIA.

The Progress of British Trade and Conquest in India—Its Present Condition. [1600-1869.] 184

CHAPTER XVI.
OUR ASIATIC COLONIES.

Ceylon—Its Early Civilization—Its Subjection to the Portuguese, the Dutch, and the English—Its Present Condition—The Straits Settlements: Penang, Malacca, and Singapore—Hong Kong—Borneo and Labuan—The Achievements of Sir James Brooke. [1795-1869.] . . 187

CHAPTER XVII.
EARLY AUSTRALASIAN DISCOVERIES.

Portuguese and Dutch Discoveries of Australia—Tasman—English Voyagers—Dampier in Australia—Captain Cook in New Zealand and Australia—French Expeditions. [1601-1788.] 198

CHAPTER XVIII.
THE FIRST AUSTRALIAN COLONY.

The Convict Settlement in New South Wales—Its First Troubles—The Evil Habits of the Colonists—The Beginning of Better Ways—Governor Macquarie—Australian Discoverers: Flinders and Bass—Inland Expeditions—The Progress of New South Wales. [1787-1821.] . 208

CHAPTER XIX.

OLD NEW SOUTH WALES.

Progress of New South Wales as a Free Colony—Services of Reformed Convicts—John Macarthur and the Wool-Trade—Sydney in 1820—Cruel Treatment of the Convicts—Growth of Free Institutions—Sir Richard Bourke—Development of the Colony—Explorations in the Interior—The Aborigines of Australia. [1821-1839.] . . 219

CHAPTER XX.

TASMANIA.

The Offshoots of New South Wales—The Early History of Tasmania, or Van Dieman's Land—Its Establishment as an Independent Colony—Its Convicts and Bush-Rangers—Extermination of the Aborigines—Its Best Governors: Sir George Arthur and Sir John Franklin—Its Greatest Prosperity — Its Deterioration and Present State. [1797-1869.] 233

CHAPTER XXI.

NEW SOUTH WALES AND THE PORT PHILLIP DISTRICT.

The Discovery of Port Phillip—Captain Collins's Attempted Settlement on its Coast—Later Enterprises—Henty, Batman, Fawkner, and Mitchell — Buckley's Adventures among the Aborigines—Establishment of the Port Phillip Settlement — The Progress of New South Wales — The Squatters and their Work—Melbourne between 1838 and 1850—Sydney in 1848. [1802-1851.] . . 243

CHAPTER XXII.

SOUTH AUSTRALIA.

The Discovery and Colonization of South Australia — The Wakefield Scheme and its Failure—Early Troubles of the Colony—Their Speedy Removal—The Copper Mines—The Effect of the Gold Discoveries in Victoria—Later Progress of the Colony; Copper, Wool, Wheat, and Wine—Its Present Condition. [1822-1869.] . . . 260

CHAPTER XXIII.

VICTORIA.

The Establishment of Port Phillip as an Independent Colony, under the Name of Victoria—The Australian Gold Discoveries—The Ballarat Gold-Fields—The Consequences of the Discovery—The Progress of Victoria—Melbourne in 1856—The Ballarat Outbreak—Political Changes in Victoria. [1851-1869.] 276

CHAPTER XXIV.

NEW SOUTH WALES AND QUEENSLAND.

The Later Progress of New South Wales—Its Gold-Fields and their Fruit—Squatter-Extensions—The Rise of the Moreton Bay District, and the Opening up of Central Australia—The Fertility of this Region—Establishment of the Colony of Queensland—Its Rapid Growth—The Present Condition of New South Wales—Its Coal-Fields. [1851-1869.] 289

CHAPTER XXV.

WEST AUSTRALIA AND WASTE AUSTRALIA.

Origin of the Swan River Settlement, or Western Australia—Early Misfortunes of the Colony—Its Present Condition—Explorations in the Interior of the Australian Continent—The First Discoverers—Sturt, Murray, Eyre, Leichhardt—Sturt again—Stuart—Burke and Wills—The Character of the Interior. [1827-1865.] . . . 299

CHAPTER XXVI.

PAKEHA NEW ZEALAND.

The New Zealand Islands and their Inhabitants—First Intercourse with Englishmen—The Massacre of the Crew and Passengers of the *Boyd* in 1809—The Missionaries and their Work—The Pakeha Traders—Articles of Trade—Traffic in Human Heads—Other Debasing Employments of the Pakehas—Progress of English Influences—Spread of Civilization—The Character of the Maoris. [1809-1839.] 323

CHAPTER XXVII.

NEW ZEALAND COLONIZATION.

The Old Pakeha Population—The New Zealand Company—Establishment of British Sovereignty in New Zealand, and its Construction as a Regular Colony—Its Progress—Land-Quarrels with the Natives—Their Attempted Protection by the Government—The Influence of the Missionaries—Later Growth of the Colony. [1839-1867.] . 338

CHAPTER XXVIII.

NEW ZEALAND WARFARE.

The Rival Races in New Zealand—The Maori Wars of 1843 and the Following Years—The Subsequent Condition of the Maoris—Their Civilization—Their Numbers—The Renewal of Hostilities—The King-Movement and its Issue—Hostilities in 1860 and 1861—The War of 1863-1865—Nature of the Strife—Later Guerilla Warfare—The Pai-Marire, or Hau-Hau Superstition—The Future of New Zealand. [1843-1869.] 348

CHAPTER XXIX.

ENGLISH AUSTRALASIA.

The Relative Advantages of our Australasian Colonies—Western Australia—Queensland—New South Wales—Victoria—South Australia—Tasmania—New Zealand . . 364

CHAPTER XXX.

THE END OF THE STORY.

The Value of our Colonies—The Political and Commercial Advantages Derived and Derivable from them—Their Importance as Fields of Emigration 868

APPENDIX.

	PAGE
I. *Area and Population of the British Colonial Possessions,*	881
II. *Our Emigration Fields:*—India—Canada—New Brunswick—Nova Scotia—Newfoundland—British Columbia and Vancouver Island—Cape Colony—Natal—Queensland—Victoria—New South Wales—South Australia—Tasmania—New Zealand—Table of Colonial Public Lands Alienated and remaining for Alienation at the Date of the last Returns—Summary of Modes of Sale, and Prices, in the principal Land-Selling Colonies—Price of Food and Rates of Wages in the principal Colonies,	882
III. *Our Colonial Gold-Fields,*	896
INDEX,	401

THE STORY OF OUR COLONIES.

CHAPTER I.

OUR EARLIEST COLONIES.

INTRODUCTION—THE CATHAYAN FABLES—DISCOVERY OF AMERICA BY JOHN CABOT—HIS "NEW-FOUND-LANDS"—THE FIRST EFFORTS OF THE ENGLISH IN COLONIZING AMERICA—SIR HUMPHREY GILBERT AND SIR WALTER RALEIGH—THE RISE OF ENGLISH COLONIZATION—THE ESTABLISHMENT OF THE UNITED STATES—ENGLAND'S OTHER COLONIES. [1490-1776.]

"FOR the last seven years the people of Bristol have sent out every year two, three, or four light ships in search of the island of Brazil and the Seven Cities." So wrote the Spanish ambassador in London to his sovereigns, Ferdinand and Isabella, in 1498; and in his brief, bald sentence there is echo of a whole volume of romance.

The island of Brazil—the island of the Seven Cities; these were themes of eager talk and bold speculation throughout Europe four hundred years ago, when Europe comprised nearly all the known world of civilization. A few daring travellers, most of them friars, among whom Marco Polo was chiefly famous, had in previous centuries gone into the far

east, there to hear marvellous tales of places and
people supposed to exist yet farther east. Cathay,
the modern China, and the Japanese and other
islands beyond it—then known by a score of different
names, like the Seven Cities and Brazil, or the
"place of red dye"—were the subjects of countless
fables. Vast palaces of solid gold; pearls and precious
stones; spices and dyes, such as no gold in
Europe could buy; horses with six legs a-piece, and
two-headed ostriches; giants twenty feet high, and
dwarfs not two spans long; fountains of perpetual
youth, and trees bearing fruit of heavenly wisdom:
these and a thousand other priceless treasures were
said to be found in those shadowy regions; and as
the travellers' tales were repeated with ever fresh
exaggerations, the adventurous youth of Christendom
yearned more and more to make them their own.
But barren deserts peopled by savage races, and vast
tracts of lands which, in the old-fashioned ways of
travelling, it took years to cross, were between the
world of civilization and this fabled world of something
better than civilization; and therefore few
attempted, and none thoroughly achieved, the enterprise,
until wise men remembered the speculation
of the ancients, that the earth was a round globe
instead of a flat surface, and considered that Cathay
and Brazil could be reached much more easily by
ships sailing out into the west, than by eastward
travelling on land.

The first who put that speculation to effective
proof, as all the world knows, was Christopher
Columbus. But while he was urging his bold project
upon Ferdinand and Isabella of Spain, and

before the good queen had pawned her jewels in order that he might set out upon his famous voyage to the West Indies in 1492, other brave men were turning their thoughts, and actually venturing on the sea, in the same direction. While we take from Columbus none of the great honour that is his due, we must render honour as great to certain merchants of Bristol, whose wonderful exploits have hardly been recorded, and whose names even have almost passed out of memory.

Four hundred years ago Bristol was, with the exception of London, the busiest and most prosperous trading town in England. In pursuit of their calling, its merchants guided their little vessels to every known haunt of commerce, and to some which they alone frequented. With Iceland and the most northern parts of Europe they traded, and their traffic also took them down to the rich cities of the Mediterranean, and the pirate-troubled shores of the Levant. It is very likely that in Iceland they heard of the early expeditions of Scandinavian voyagers to the coasts of Labrador, which are supposed to have influenced Columbus in his adventurous schemes. It is certain that in Venice, Genoa, and other Italian towns, they heard of the Cathayan fables, and the supposed marvels of the island of Brazil and the Seven Cities. And, as is shown by the sentence with which our story opens, they were the first who actually sailed out to the west in search of those marvels.

But of their doings unfortunately very little is recorded. All that we know of what seems to have been their first enterprise is told in two sentences of

4   OUR EARLIEST COLONIES.

a contemporary narrative. In 1490,[1] it is there said, "a ship of John Jay, the younger, of 800 tons, and another, began their voyage from the King's-road, Bristol, to the island of Brazil, ploughing their way through the sea to the west of Ireland; and Thlyde, the most scientific mariner in all England, was the pilot of the ships. News came to Bristol that the said ships sailed about the sea during nine months, and did not find the island, but, driven by tempests, they returned to a port on the coast of Ireland, for the repose of themselves and their mariners." The Bristol merchants were not discouraged by that failure; but of their further exploits in the ensuing years, until 1497, we have no details at all. All we know is that, in spite of failure, they tried again and again, and thus prepared the way for the success of others.

The success was first achieved by Englishmen, under the leadership of John Cabot, a Venetian by birth, who had settled as a merchant in Bristol, and who, if he was not himself partly the cause of it, was an eager follower of the project in which John Jay, the younger, first adventured. Therein he was mainly encouraged by the recent discoveries of Christopher Columbus, "whereof," as Cabot's son Sebastian afterwards said, "was great talk in all the Court of King Henry the Seventh, insomuch that all men, with great admiration, affirmed it to be a thing more divine than human to sail by the west into the east, by a way that was never known before." From King Henry,

[1] The date given in the manuscript is 1480, but this is evidently an error. The year 1490 coincides with the Spanish ambassador's statement.

Cabot, in 1496, obtained permission to go out on a more systematic voyage of discovery than Englishmen had yet attempted, and this he did, with very memorable results, in 1497.

With his expedition begins the history of English colonization. "In two stout ships, manned by three hundred of the ablest mariners that he could find," it has been said, "John Cabot sailed out of Bristol waters, near the beginning of May. He went first to Iceland, and sailing thence almost due west reached the district now known as Labrador, but called by him and his successors New-found-land, on the 24th of June 1497. It was at five o'clock in the morning that, from the prow of his ship, the *Matthew*, Cabot first saw the mainland of America, just a year before Columbus, passing the West Indian Islands among which his two earlier voyages had been spent, first set eyes on the continent. No counterpart to the tropical beauty, and wealth of gold and pearls and precious stones, which rewarded Columbus and his comrades for their daring enterprise, was seen by Cabot and his hardy followers. Instead, they found a bleak and rocky country, on which very few trees appeared to them to grow, and of which bears and white antelopes seemed to be the chief inhabitants. Some groups of men and women they saw, all clothed alike in the skins of beasts, and with little other furniture than the bows and arrows, pikes, darts, wooden clubs, and slings which helped them in their frequent quarrels with one another. Black hawks, black partridges, and black eagles, as they reported, were all the birds that they could find; and the place would have seemed to them altogether inhospitable but for its wonderful supply of cod and other fish."[1] Cabot discovered not only the part of the American continent which he called New-found-land, but also the island now known by that name. Then he sailed northward, hoping thus to reach the fabled region of Cathay, for which these barren districts offered him but a poor substitute. He was driven back, however, by snow and fogs and icebergs, which so frightened his sailors that they refused to proceed farther; and he was in Bristol again early in August.

Cathay was never reached by John Cabot, nor by any of his brave comrades and successors; but out of this first voyage to America issued its colonization by Englishmen, who have turned the desolate regions into a source of wealth almost rivalling that described in the Cathayan fables. For several years after 1497 visits were paid by the Bristol merchants and their messengers to Labrador and its neighbourhood. A few of them settled there, and established a rude traffic with the natives, sending home such rarities as they could find. In 1505 Henry the Seventh paid 13s. 4d. for "wild cats and popinjays of the New-found-islands," conveyed to his palace at Richmond. Other importations were of kindred sort.

Even at this early period Englishmen began to see the use of those abundant supplies of cod and other fish, which Cabot regarded as the only welcome product of the Newfoundland district, and which later adventurers have found to be a constant source of wealth. Fishing expeditions began at a very early date, and became more and more numerous and profitable in every succeeding generation. In 1578,

[1] Bourne, "English Seamen under the Tudors," vol. i. pp. 32, 33.

eighty years after Cabot's first voyage, the English fishing fleet so employed comprised fifty sail, and contributed greatly to the prosperity of Bristol and the other towns engaged in the trade.

Neither then nor for long after, however, was Newfoundland or any adjoining district colonized by the English. One memorable attempt in that direction was made by Sir Humphrey Gilbert in 1583. Four ships, laden with followers intended to establish a settlement on the island, were guided by him to Saint John's Harbour; but his colonists proved mutinous, and he was unable to bring them into subjection. He had hardly spent a fortnight in his new home when he found it necessary to turn back towards England, and on his way thither he perished by shipwreck. His project died with him.

Failure also attended the colonizing efforts of Gilbert's famous half-brother, Sir Walter Raleigh. Raleigh sought to build up another England in America, and though his own work was unsuccessful, he must ever be honoured as one of the founders of the great Anglo-Saxon commonwealth on the other side of the Atlantic. Having in 1584 obtained from Queen Elizabeth a charter as successor to Sir Humphrey Gilbert, he organized several expeditions to the coast of what is now the state of North Carolina, called by him Virginia, and there a colony was established under the governorship of Ralph Lane. A hundred Englishmen went out in 1585, to spend a year in rude attempts to make for themselves a home, and in cruel treatment of the Indian natives whom they reduced to slavery, and to be themselves so harshly used by these Indians that they were glad on the first opportunity to return to England. In 1587, a second party of colonists, a hundred and fifty in number, with Captain John White for their leader, went to take their place. But they were even more unfortunate than their predecessors. Abandoned by their friends at home, all were killed by the natives, except a few who wandered inland and gave up their English habits to share the life of the red men who afforded them shelter.

The disastrous issue of Gilbert's and Raleigh's projects, however, offered no serious obstacles to the progress of English colonization. These were only the first pulsations in a movement which was to result in a wonderful extension of English power and influence, and to effect a social revolution to which modern history presents no parallel.

England was behind-hand in the planting of colonies. Spain had begun a century before to take possession of the most attractive portions of the vast American continent. Portugal, Germany, and France had followed the example before anything of importance was done by England. But at length she entered on the work with unrivalled energy, an energy that has had no abatement down to the present day. The early delay and the subsequent eagerness resulted from the same cause. During the sixteenth century England was too busy with her internal affairs and with European politics to enter upon any sustained work in distant quarters. Protestantism, taking deeper root and having healthier growth in our little island than almost in any other state, had a hard battle to fight both at home and abroad. Its first great work was in overthrowing the old system of feudalism which, strengthened in past centuries by Catholicism, was now its main source of strength, and in building up those foundations of religious freedom which have become the bases of the political, and, in a measure, the social freedom that have made England a great and powerful nation. That work induced an apparently overwhelming force of opposition from the far greater powers of France and Spain, which, not content with open warfare, sought to gain their end by fostering internal dissension and stirring up hatred and rebellion among the classes who, on religious or other grounds, were most in sympathy with the great Catholic nations. Warfare, open and secret, was the grand business of Englishmen during the long reign of Queen Elizabeth. The men who, in other circumstances, would have become great leaders of colonization, with Sir Francis Drake for their most illustrious representative, expended all their wit and strength in resistance of the great enemies of their country. But that resistance, wholly patriotic, though it was not in all respects praiseworthy, was in the end very helpful to the progress of colonization. Drake and his fellows, urged thereto by their opposition to Spain, swept the seas, both near and distant, that were traversed by the ships laden with the fruits of the Spanish colonies. They became the terror of the European coasts. Their pirate-ships also scoured the West Indian waters, and even made their way to the more distant haunts of Spanish commerce on the Pacific shores of America and in the Indian archipelago. Thus

English seamen learnt to ply their craft with unmatched daring, and, when the proper time arrived, to plant their colonies in the most favoured quarters of the world, and in other quarters, less favoured by nature, which were made propitious by the wisdom and the perseverance of the colonists themselves.

Concerning the first great outcomes of this commercial and colonizing spirit this volume has not to treat in detail. The wonderful history of the East India Company, started near the end of Queen Elizabeth's reign, by which, in the course of two centuries and a half, our vast Indian empire has been established, is rather a history of trade and conquest than of colonization, and to it brief incidental reference in a future page will suffice. The no less wonderful history of the great colonial work in which Englishmen were engaged in America during the seventeenth century—a theme so wide and eventful that more than a volume would be needed for its separate handling—is precluded from our plan, because the colonies thus founded, no longer British possessions, have become themselves a powerful nation as the United States of America.[1] A few paragraphs, therefore, will serve for summing up all that here needs to be told concerning them.

The work, begun with Raleigh's luckless experiments, was first successfully entered upon by two companies of "knights, gentlemen, and merchants"

---

[1] Another reason for not recounting this story is that it has been so often told before. An especially concise and interesting account of it will be found in pp. 180-384 of Miss Elizabeth Cooper's "Popular History of America."

—the one party belonging to London, the other to the west of England—to whom jointly a charter for the colonization of America, under Raleigh's name of Virginia, was granted by James I. in 1606. Three small ships full of emigrants left England for that purpose near the end of the year, and the difficult task of planting the little colony was achieved by Captain John Smith, whose tact in making friends with the Indians by help of the native king Powhatan and his daughter Pocahontas, has been often described in history and romance. The settlement was steadily recruited by fresh arrivals from England, and directed with tolerable success by later governors, who followed to some extent in the course marked out by Smith. Its first important trade was in tobacco, which, sold in Europe, enabled the colonists to supply themselves with all needful commodities from the mother country. A great resort of cavaliers and their dependants during the times of civil war and Commonwealth rule in England, it became the most aristocratic of the American settlements, the centre of agriculture and slavery.

On the northern part of the district originally assigned to Virginia was founded the colony of Maryland, so named in honour of Queen Henrietta Maria, in 1632, with Lord Baltimore for its originator. Designed by him as a settlement especially for fugitive Catholics, it soon fell into the hands of persecuting Protestants, yet under them attained great prosperity.

Still more prosperous were the colonies founded and developed during the same period by the Puritans. "The land is weary of her inhabitants," said the Pilgrim Fathers who quitted England in the *Mayflower* in 1620, "so that man which is the most precious of all creatures is here more vile and base than the earth we tread upon; so as children, neighbours, and friends, especially the poor, are accounted the greatest burthens, which, if things were right, would be the highest earthly blessings. Hence it comes to pass that all arts and trades are carried on in that deceitful manner and unrighteous course as it is almost impossible for a good, upright man to maintain his charge in any of them." Driven thus from old England, they set up their new England on the western shores of the Atlantic, and, as tide after tide of emigrants crossed the ocean, one city after another was founded, until in 1643 there were four goodly groups of settlements, known as Plymouth, Massachusetts, Connecticut, and Newhaven, which organized themselves as the United Colonies of New England, the first germ of the United States. The Puritan plantations grew mightily. But Milton has said that "new Presbyter is but old Priest writ large," and so it proved with the champions of religious freedom in the New World. The liberty which they claimed for themselves was denied to all who differed from them, and persecution was as rife in America as in England. One great benefit, however, sprang therefrom. Not only did fresh streams of emigration flow from England, but hardly-used members of the established colonies branched off to establish younger colonies for themselves; and thus the entire coast-line was rapidly peopled with enterprising settlers, who, seeking their own wealth and comfort, turned the whole region, from

Maine down to Georgia, into a scene of unrivalled wealth and comfort.

When in 1776 the thirteen colonial states in America resolved to throw off their allegiance to Great Britain, their population comprised about two million white men, and nearly half a million slaves; and in the ensuing eighty years the inhabitants of the United States, increased to thirty-four, with eight associated territories, have become more than twelve times as numerous. This mighty group of English colonies has grown into a nation larger than the mother country in the number of its residents, and fourteen times as large if measured by the extent of land which it occupies.

Yet the colonial possessions still subject to Great Britain, the most striking features in whose history have now to be set forth, comprise an area nearly four times as great, and a population nearly four times as numerous, as those of the United States. The extent of territory is not likely to be very much augmented. But the number of inhabitants may be increased almost without limit—

     "As the element of air affords
An easy passage to the industrious bees
Fraught with their burthens; and a way as smooth
For those ordained to take their sounding flight
From the thronged hive, and settle where they list
In fresh abodes—their labours to renew;
So the wide waters, open to the power,
The will, the instincts, and appointed needs
Of Britain, do invite her to cast off
Her swarms, and in succession send them forth,
Bound to establish new communities
On every shore whose aspect favours hope

Or bold adventure; promising to skill
And perseverance their deserved reward.
Change wide and deep, and silently performed,
This land shall witness; and, as days roll on,
Earth's universal frame shall feel the effect,
Even till the smallest habitable rock,
Beaten by lonely billows, hear the songs
Of humanized society, and bloom
With civil arts that shall breathe forth their fragrance,
A grateful tribute to all-ruling Heaven."[1]

[1] Wordsworth, "The Excursion," Book ix.

CHAPTER II.

OUR FIRST WEST INDIAN COLONY.

THE FIRST ENGLISH SETTLEMENTS IN THE WEST INDIES—THE EXPLOITS OF SIR JOHN HAWKINS AND HIS SUCCESSORS—THE COLONIZATION AND EARLY HISTORY OF BARBADOS—LORD WILLOUGHBY OF PARHAM—THE CIVIL WAR IN BARBADOS—LORD WILLOUGHBY AND SIR GEORGE AYSCUE—THE PROGRESS OF THE ISLAND DURING THE SEVENTEENTH CENTURY—ITS TRADE AND POPULATION—THE SLAVES AND THEIR SUFFERINGS. [1562-1700.]

F the colonies now in the possession of Great Britain, the oldest are the West Indies. They were, indeed, the scene of frequent fighting between English and Spaniards, out of which grew the subsequent colonization, long before there was any permanent settlement of our countrymen upon the American continent.

It was an island of the Bahama group that Christopher Columbus, believing he had thus attained his project of discovering a western passage to Cathay, first visited on the 12th of October 1492; and at San Domingo, in Hispaniola, or Hayti, he soon afterwards organized the centre of Spanish government, whence proceeded countless expeditions for conquering and colonizing the adjoining islands and mainland, all of which were then known as the West Indies. For some time the Spaniards were left in undisputed possession of these regions. To the King of Spain they were assigned by a Papal bull, which none dared to dispute until Protestantism was powerful enough to set at defiance the authority of Rome; and by the Spaniards they were cruelly despoiled without hindrance, until the native Indians, reduced to bitter slavery by their conquerors, were almost exterminated.

England, in fact, was first brought into important relations with the West Indies by a memorable plan —the successful working out of which cannot be looked back upon without shame—to supply the need occasioned by the rapid dying out of these Indian slaves. The originator both of the negro slave-trade and of our West Indian colonization was Sir John Hawkins, one of the most eminent of the great seamen under Queen Elizabeth. In his youth, says his old biographer, "he made divers voyages to the isles of the Canaries, and there, by his good and upright dealing, being grown in honour of the people, informed himself of the state of the West Indies; and being amongst other things informed that negroes were very good merchandise in Hispaniola, and that store of negroes might easily be had upon the coast of Guinea, he resolved within himself to make trial thereof."[1]

This he did in 1562. With three little vessels he proceeded from England to Guinea, where he captured three hundred negroes, and, crossing the Atlantic, he sold his cargo at good profit to the Spaniards in San Domingo. His only purpose in so doing was the adoption of a lucrative and, in his

[1] Prince, "Worthies of Devon," p. 389.

eyes, a harmless trade. King Philip II. of Spain, however, regarded any English interference with his colonial possessions as an offence to himself, and a source of danger to those possessions. He confiscated a portion of Hawkins's return cargo which found its way to Cadiz, and sent out strict injunctions to the West Indies, that if Hawkins came again no dealings were to be had with him. Hawkins did not choose to be so thwarted.

In 1564 he fitted out a larger fleet of trading ships, five in number, and, having collected a larger cargo of negroes on the western coast of Africa, went to sell them to the Spanish colonists. King Philip's orders prevented his going again to San Domingo, but he disposed of his slaves on the Spanish Main, and was able to take home a wonderful store of "gold, silver, pearls, and other jewels," which yielded a profit of sixty per cent., after all the expenses of the voyage had been paid. Queen Elizabeth rewarded him with a baronetcy, and the addition of a negro, "in his proper colour, bound and captive," to his coat-of-arms; and King Philip complained loudly of his insolent conduct in again interfering with the colonial trade of Spain.

Those complaints, however, only induced Sir John Hawkins to make a third expedition, greater and more eventful than either of its predecessors. Upon this he started, with young Francis Drake for one of his captains, at the head of six vessels and fifteen hundred men, in 1567. The voyage was to him and his followers wholly unfortunate. He could only obtain a scanty supply of negroes on the African coast, and of these he had difficulty in disposing on the Spanish Main. Returning to England he was forced to seek shelter from bad weather, and the water of which his ships were in great need, by entering the Spanish port of San Juan de Ulloa, in Mexico. There, after a terrible fight with the Spaniards, he was utterly defeated. Great numbers of his comrades were slain. A few escaped with him to England. A hundred were taken prisoners and made slaves of by their enemies. "All our business," wrote Hawkins after his return home, "hath had infelicity, misfortune, and an unhappy end. If I were to write of all our calamities, I am sure a volume as great as the Bible will scarcely suffice."

Those calamities, however, furnished even a stronger motive for continuance of the work begun by Hawkins than sprang from his earlier successes. Bitter hatred of Spain was growing up among all Englishmen, and the hatred was increased in the hearts of many by these West Indian disasters. A desire to punish the Spaniards for the injuries they had inflicted on the English, and forcibly to wrest from them a share of that wealth of trade which they were forbidden to obtain in peaceable ways, actuated many, and none so keenly or with such famous consequences as Sir Francis Drake, who had himself suffered and lost much by the failure of Hawkins's third expedition. Drake started on a warfare of his own against Spain. Over and over again he made what would now be called piratical voyages to the West Indies and the Spanish Main, and in the course of these he captured much and destroyed much more. Others joined with him or followed in his track after

he had entered upon nobler pursuits in the legitimate
service of his country, which service had the same
great end, the injuring of Spain and the seizure of the
wealth she was acquiring in the West Indies and on
the neighbouring mainland. Actual conquest of the
Spanish possessions was not then thought of. The
one thing aimed at was the spoliation of the enemy.[1]
But when that spoliation had been to a great extent
effected, conquest and colonization naturally and
easily ensued. Thus it was that the West Indies
began to pass from the hands of Spain into those of
England.

The islands first seized by England, however, only
nominally belonged to Spain, which, while laying a
claim to the whole group by virtue of Columbus's
discovery, colonized none but those most conveniently situated in relation to Hispaniola, and most
serviceable as places of resort for the fleets and
armies engaged in the conquest and government of
the great territories on the continent that were owned
by Spain, from Mexico down to Chili. Many islands
were never actually appropriated by her, although
on that account she looked none the less jealously
upon attempts at their appropriation made by other
nations.

So it was with Barbados and all the Caribbean
group. To Barbados—thus named by some Portuguese, who, first visiting it, were struck by its pro-
fuse store of luxuriant fig-trees, from whose branches
hung down masses of foliage resembling "barbudos," or
beards—the Spaniards only went to capture the fierce

---

[1] The story of this work has been told at some length in the
second volume of my "English Seamen under the Tudors."

Indians who there resided, and who proved such sturdy slaves that within a short time they were all kidnapped and the island was utterly deserted. It was uninhabited when, in 1605, the crew of the *Olive Blossom*—a vessel fitted out by Sir Olive Leigh, "a worshipful knight of Kent"—chanced to land on its shores. They took possession of the island, planting in a prominent locality a cross, with the inscription, "James, King of England and this island," but quitted it as soon as they had replenished their ship with a supply of pigs, pigeons, and fish, with which it abounded. Its colonization was not attempted till twenty years later, when another vessel, belonging to Sir William Courteen, the famous London merchant, having sought in its harbour shelter from bad weather, attention was again called to its beauty and fertility. In 1625 Lord Ley, afterwards Earl of Marlborough, obtained from King James I. a grant of the island for himself and his heirs, and by him Courteen was commissioned to establish thereon the first English colony in the West Indies. This was done by a party of about forty, who in the same year went out and began to build James-town around the cross that had been set up in 1605. Its progress was delayed by quarrels at home. In spite of the first patent, the island was in 1627 granted by Charles L to the Earl of Carlisle, who proposed to organize "a large and copious colony of English, to be named the Carlisle province," embracing all the Caribbean Islands, from St Christopher down to Trinidad. Lord Carlisle had most influence at Court, and, after a temporary withdrawal of his patent, obtained its renewal. In 1628 he sent out sixty-four colonists, who, under the governorship of Sir William Tufton, formed a rival power to that established by the earlier settlers. An angry feud, often leading to bloodshed, prevailed between the two factions, known as the windward-men and the leeward-men, until a further arrival of two hundred persons made Lord Carlisle's party strong enough to compel the submission of the others; and after that Barbados very quickly rose to importance, both as itself a prosperous plantation, with nearly two thousand inhabitants, reinforced each year by fresh arrivals, and as a centre for the capture and colonization of the neighbouring islands.

The details of this capture and colonization need not here be given. Some of the islands were only seized and abandoned, not to be permanently occupied by Englishmen until many years later. Others, of which St Christopher was the principal, became prosperous settlements for a time, but, for various causes, passed out of English hands, only to be recovered long afterwards. Barbados was the only one of the eastern group of West Indian Islands which greatly flourished during the seventeenth century, and in even its progress there were disturbing, though hardly restraining, influences. The main cause of turmoil within it was also an important cause of its advancement. The strife of parties at home under Charles I. and the Commonwealth leaders, inducing many Englishmen to seek peace in the second England that was growing up on the American continent, drove many also to the fertile little island. "These adventurers," says the Earl of Clarendon, "planted without anybody's leave, and without being opposed or contradicted by anybody." In 1650, only twenty-five years after the first party of settlers had arrived, the population comprised twenty thousand white men, with a goodly number of negro slaves. It had already grown too large to be managed by the Earls of Carlisle or the agents whom they sent out as governors on their behalf. Accordingly, in 1647, the second Earl effected an arrangement with Lord Willoughby of Parham, to whom he assigned half the property of the whole Caribbean group for a term of twenty-one years, on condition of his going out as lieutenant-general, "for the better settling and recovering of the islands." That treaty had memorable consequences. Lord Willoughby, till then a Parliamentarian, was at this time beginning to sympathize with the Cavalier party. Shortly before the execution of Charles I. he was impeached for high treason, and his estates were confiscated. He escaped to Holland, where he openly took up the Royalist cause, and thence, in 1650, he proceeded to Barbados, intending to make of the West Indies a stronghold for Charles II. In the island civil war was already waging, and Lord Willoughby organized troops, set up forts, and equipped vessels for the overthrow of the colonial Roundheads.

He was so successful that Lord Protector Cromwell despatched a fleet, with two thousand soldiers on board, under Sir George Ayscue, to oppose him. Ayscue arrived on the 15th of October 1651, and on the following morning made an easy capture of fifteen vessels lying in the harbour. He lost no time in informing Willoughby that the Parliament of England desired that the people of Barbados should be sharers in the liberty "which had been purchased at the expense of so much blood and treasure," and that he was commissioned to demand the surrender of the island. Willoughby's answer was, that he acknowledged no authority but that of King Charles, and that he should expect reparation for the injuries inflicted on the loyal forces of the sovereign. Ayscue then attempted to effect a landing, but the resistance offered to him was too formidable. On the 26th of October he sent on shore a manifesto to the inhabitants, calling on them to accept the free trade and protection offered by the Commonwealth, urging them to avert the destruction of their "long-laboured-for estates," which must result from their continued obstinacy, and promising forgiveness for their past misdeeds if they would now submit. The Representative Body of the island replied, on the 5th of November, that its good people were proof against the arguments of "those loose and scandalous papers industriously scattered up and down the island to poison their allegiance," and that neither fear of future sufferings nor hopes of reward would weaken their loyalty, "to which their souls were as firmly united as to their bodies." Willoughby also wrote to Ayscue, acknowledging the "civility" of his conduct, and averring that he did not "serve the King so much in expectation of his majesty's prosperous condition as in consideration of his duty," and that "he would never be a means of increasing the King's affliction by delivering up the island." "If there be such a person as the King," answered Ayscue, "the keeping of Barbados signifies nothing to the King's advantage. God will own us in our attempts against you as He has hitherto done." There was a little further parleying, which led to nothing, and in the middle of December Ayscue effected a landing with a loss of ninety of his men, against fifty of the enemy slain and a hundred captured. The fort taken by him, however, could not be held, and he had to return to his ships, where he tended his wounded prisoners with a "courtesy" for which Willoughby wrote to thank him. Willoughby continued to hold the island for a month longer, but one of his regiments, a thousand strong, at length declared for the Parliament, and, with this increase to Ayscue's strength, he was unable to resist it, although three thousand soldiers were still faithful to him. He proposed a dignified surrender, not because he himself was willing thereto, but, as he said, " seeing that the fire is now dispersed in the bowels of the island, and that what may be done in a few weeks would turn the face of a country so flourishing, and so great an honour to our nation, into desolation and sadness." Favourable terms were granted to him by Ayscue, who declared himself " proportionately desirous to save Barbados from further ruin;" and, by a treaty signed on the 12th of January 1652, he and his followers were allowed to proceed to England without confiscation of their property, and the island and its dependencies quietly submitted to the dominion of the Commonwealth.[1]

The peace thus honourably effected was followed by a new period of prosperity, although the rapid growth of the population was not altogether due to peaceable and willing colonization. In 1657, between seven and eight thousand Scots, taken prisoners

[1] Record Office MSS., Colonial Series, vol. xi.

at the battle of Worcester, were "sold as slaves to the plantations of the American isles," many of them being consigned to Barbados; and, among others of like sort, seventy persons detected in the Salisbury plot of 1666, including divines, officers, and gentlemen, were sold to Barbados for 1500 pounds of sugar a-piece. These unfortunate captives, it was said, were "bought and sold from one planter to another, or attached like horses or beasts for the debts of their masters, being whipped at the whipping-posts as rogues, and sleeping in styes worse than hogs in England."[1] The white slaves naturally resented such treatment, and more than one insurrection was organized between them and their black fellow-sufferers in the hope of securing a more humane policy. These were easily quieted, but the laws of humanity were gradually recognised as far as the English bondsmen were concerned. They were admitted to share the freedom of their neighbours, and then the whole brunt of persecution fell upon the negroes, towards whom the civilization of those days accorded no more generosity than was needed to keep them alive and make them profitable chattel.

A vigorous trade existed between Barbados and the mother country during the time of the Commonwealth and afterwards. In the middle of the seventeenth century about a hundred vessels came to the island every year, laden with emigrants, slaves, cattle, tools, clothing, and European produce of all sorts; and their homeward cargoes consisted of indigo, cotton, wool, tobacco, sugar, and other commodities raised

[1] "Barbados Merchandize, a Petition to Parliament, printed in the eleventh year of England's liberty, 1659."

by the industry of the inhabitants. These inhabitants, reduced to submission by Sir George Ayscue, proved willing subjects of the Commonwealth. They even in 1652 sought permission to send two representatives to sit in the English Parliament, and, though this was not granted, their interests were well looked after by the authorities at home. Soon after the Restoration, Lord Willoughby was sent by Charles II. to resume his governorship of an island that had thriven mightily during his absence.

With Willoughby's return began a new period in the history of Barbados. From 1663 it and the other Caribbean Islands were taken out of the hands of the old proprietors, and placed under the direct authority of the Crown. The original patentees were grudgingly compensated, and the planters were established as independent proprietors, subject to their paying a tax of $4\frac{1}{2}$ per cent. upon the value of all their exports. As this tax yielded more than £6000, the prosperity of the island is apparent.

Lord Willoughby's second government of Barbados, wise and generous, was brief. In 1666 he conducted a fleet of seventeen vessels to punish the French and Dutch, who had made numerous aggressions upon the Caribbean Islands claimed by Great Britain; but a terrible hurricane overtook him off Guadeloupe. He and the crews of fifteen of the ships were lost.

These hurricanes and the attendant storms of rain were the chief hindrances to the full development of the resources of Barbados. In 1675, a storm of unexampled magnitude devastated nearly half the island. A century later, in 1780, another brought death to more than four thousand persons, and destroyed more than a million pounds' worth of property. Huge guns were carried through the air by the force of winds and waves. It is recorded that one twelve-pounder thus travelled a hundred and forty yards. The fertility of the soil, however, and the industry of the inhabitants, augmented by a steady importation of slaves, caused the periodical injuries of this nature to be easily retrieved. In 1676 the island contained twenty thousand whites and thirty-two thousand negroes. The English population has never greatly surpassed that limit; but the black and coloured population has been nearly always on the increase, and this in spite of the excessive loss of life which is a necessary result of slavery. Through more than a century about four thousand slaves were imported every year. Of these, some three thousand supplied the place of predecessors killed before their time. The actual increase of the black population was something less than a thousand a year.

Those figures alone, if such evidence was needed, would suffice to show the evil work of slavery. This, the great blot in the history of our West Indian possessions, and perhaps the chief cause of their deterioration in modern times, will receive fuller illustration in later pages. In Barbados it seems, during the seventeenth century, to have assumed its worst and most degrading forms. The early colonists, whether going out by their own choice, or as exiles by decree of the Parliamentary authorities, were mainly of the Royalist party. Imbued with aristocratic and domineering tendencies at home and in their relations with other Englishmen of meaner birth, they were unable to make generous use of the power which they possessed over their negro bondsmen. Down to 1805, the utmost punishment assigned by law to the murder of a black man was a fine of £11 sterling, and so many difficulties were in the way of conviction, even if the murder was sudden and patent to all, that the law was hardly ever enforced. No penalty at all was allotted to slower and more cruel modes of killing by overwork, and castigation for failure in completing it. The slave's only defence against the ill-treatment of his master was in his value as a beast of labour, and so long as new victims could be easily and cheaply procured from the coast of Africa, it was often most economical to work the old ones to premature death. It was poor consolation to the negroes to reflect, if they were not too ignorant for even this reflection, that the cruelties heaped upon them reacted upon their masters and produced their own degradation.

Those masters, however, reaped great profits; and during the seventeenth century Barbadoes, hardly larger than the Isle of Wight, was, after the settlements on the continent of America, the most important colonial possession of Great Britain. The wise rule inaugurated by Lord Willoughby, and carried on for the most part by other governors, under whose administration there occurred no special incidents that need to be recorded, aided it in the path of wealth, and rendered it alike famous as a resort of adventurers and as a source of profit to the mother country.

CHAPTER III.

JAMAICA AND THE BUCCANEERS.

COLUMBUS IN JAMAICA—ITS GOVERNMENT BY THE SPANIARDS—CROMWELL'S CONQUEST—THE MAROONS—THE BUCCANEERS—THE EXPLOITS OF SIR HENRY MORGAN—THE CONNECTION OF JAMAICA WITH THE BUCCANEERS—ITS EARLY PROGRESS—THE EARTHQUAKE OF 1692, AND SUBSEQUENT DISASTERS.
[1603-1694.]

THE early history of Jamaica, including matters of more varied interest, differs widely from that of Barbados. This island, being about a twentieth of the size of Great Britain, is nearly forty times as large as its eastern rival. It was discovered by Columbus in 1494, and in it, being driven thither by a storm in 1503, he took refuge for more than a year from the ingratitude of King Ferdinand of Spain and the cruelty of his agents, barely supported by the charity of the gentle Indians upon whom his great exploit was to bring misery and extermination. "Let the earth, and every soul in it that loves justice and mercy, weep for me," he wrote from his place of exile; "and you, oh glorified saints of God, that know my innocence and see my sufferings here, have mercy! For, though this present age is envious or obdurate, surely those that are to come will pity me, when they are told that Christopher Columbus rendered greater services than ever mortal man did to prince or kingdom, yet was left to perish, without being charged with the least crime, in poverty and misery, all but his chains being taken from him, so that he who gave to Spain another world, had not safety in it, nor yet a cottage for himself. And surely," he added, with prophetic truth, "such cruelty and ingratitude will bring down the wrath of Heaven, so that the wealth I have discovered shall be the means of stirring up mankind to revenge and rapine, and the Spanish nation hereafter suffer for what envious, malicious, and ungrateful people do now."

Jamaica, not having the gold which the Spanish adventurers chiefly sought, was not troubled by them for a few years after Columbus's return to Spain; and when in 1509 his son Diego began to colonize it, the governor whom he appointed, Juan de Esquimel, proved more merciful than most of his countrymen. "The affairs of Jamaica went on prosperously," says the historian Herrera, "because, Juan de Esquimel having brought the natives to submission without any effusion of blood, they laboured in planting cotton and raising other commodities which yielded great profit." His successors, however, were of different disposition. They practised in Jamaica cruelties as harsh as those by which the neighbouring islands were depopulated, and with like result. When Columbus visited the island its inhabitants, supposed to be more than sixty thousand in number, were "a tractable, docile people; equal to any employment; modest in their manners; of a quick and ready genius in matters of traffic, in which they greatly excelled the neighbouring islanders; more devoted also to the mechanic arts;

more industrious; and surpassing them all in acuteness of understanding."[1] By 1558 they were nearly all killed out, and what might have been a thriving possession of Spain, had for its only tenants a scattered population of degraded negroes and of enervated Europeans, idle in everything but the exercise of their evil passions. Sir Anthony Shirley, with a small force, pillaged the island in 1605, and about forty years afterwards it was treated in the same manner by Colonel Jackson. In 1655 it contained only some twelve or fourteen hundred Spaniards, and about an equal number of negro slaves.

In that year it was captured, almost without a blow, by a force of seven thousand Englishmen sent out by Cromwell. Many Puritans resorted to it, both from England and from Virginia and the other settlements in America, during the Commonwealth and after the restoration of Charles II.; but its progress was not at first very rapid. Placed by Cromwell under military rule, the soldiers refused to become colonists. The other residents quarrelled with them, with one another, and with the authorities at home; and all were harassed by the guerilla warfare kept up by the negro slaves of the Spaniards, who, taking refuge in the mountains, and there organizing themselves into a fierce body of lawless warriors, came to be known as Maroons. "Their sudden and unlooked-for emancipation," it has been said of these Maroons, "bestowed by no generous impulse or deliberate act of high principle, but simply resulting from circumstances over which neither slaves nor slave-holders had any control,

[1] Long, "History of Jamaica," vol. iii. p. 951.

produced its natural results. The inestimable prize of freedom they resolved to hold at all hazards, and though a portion of them accepted the offers of pardon made by the English, the majority viewed all friendly overtures in the light of treacherous endeavours to entrap them again into bondage. They and their descendants maintained for nearly a century and a half their position among the mountain fastnesses, whence, with occasional intervals of peace, they harassed the settlers by their predatory expeditions, often attended with bloodshed, undeterred by the cruel punishment which attended them if captured in open hostilities, or tracked to their caves by bloodhounds. These latter auxiliaries were frequently employed in chasing the original Maroons, as well as runaways from the negroes imported by the new colonists, by whom their numbers were subsequently augmented." [1]

Another race of lawless warriors was connected at this time with Jamaica, and, while hindering its peaceable development, helped to make it an important possession of Great Britain. These were the Buccaneers, successors to the piratical adventurers in the West Indies, of whom Sir Francis Drake was the first great leader. Drake's piracy was prompted by patriotic zeal for the overthrow of Spain and Spanish tyranny, even more than by mere desire of gain. Gain, much more than patriotism, actuated those who followed his example.

The buccaneers [2] began to make a new trade for

[1] Montgomery Martin, "The West Indies," p. 22.
[2] The term buccaneer was adopted from the Carib Indians, who called the flesh which they prepared boucan, and gave to the hut

themselves, or to give a new form to the old trade of smuggling and piracy, early in the seventeenth century, by making organized depredations upon the Spanish islands of Cuba and Hispaniola, and the yet richer territories of Spain on the mainland of America. Principally English, they received numerous recruits from France and Holland. Nationalities were abandoned in the commonwealth which they formed under the name of Brethren of the Coast, in which the customs necessary to their calling induced the formation of something like a special code of laws. "Property," we are told, "so far as regarded the means of sustenance, whether obtained in the chase or by pillage, was in common among this hardy brotherhood; and, as they had no domestic ties—neither wife nor child, brother nor sister, being known among the buccaneers—the want of family relations was supplied by strict commdeship, one partner occasionally attending to household duties while the other was engaged in the chase. Their chief virtue was courage, which, urged by desperation, was often carried to an extreme unparalleled among other warlike associations. The fear of the gallows, which has frequently converted a thief into a murderer, made the buccaneer a hero and a savage. Hardihood, the habit and power of extreme endurance, might also, if exerted in a better cause, be reckoned among the virtues of the buccaneers, had not their

in which it was slowly dried and smoked on wooden hurdles the same appellation. To the title by which the desperadoes of England were known, the French preferred Flibustier, said to be a corruption of the English word *freebooter*.—" Lives and Voyages of Drake, Cavendish, and Dampier, including the History of the Buccaneers " (1832) p. 230.

long seasons of entire privation been always followed
by scenes of the most brutal excess. Their grand
principle, the one thing needful to their existence,
was fidelity. As their associations were voluntary,
their engagements never extended beyond the cruise
or enterprise on hand, though they were frequently
renewed. The ablest, the most brave, active, fortunate, and intriguing of their number was elected
their commander; but all the fighting men appear
to have assisted at councils. The same power which
chose their leader could displace him, and this was
frequently done, either from caprice or expediency.
They sometimes settled personal quarrels by duel;
but offences against the fraternity were visited by
different punishments, as, in extreme cases, death,
abandonment on a desert island, or simply banishment from the society. A party having agreed upon
a cruise, the day and place for embarkation was
fixed, and every man repaired on board the ship
with a specific quantity of powder and shot. The
next concern was to procure provisions, which consisted mostly of pork. Many of the Spaniards raised
large herds of swine for the supply of the planters,
and from their yards abundance was procured with
no trouble save that in which the ferocious buccaneers delighted, robbery often accompanied by
murder. Turtle slightly salted was another article
of the food which they stored, and for beeves and
wild hogs they trusted to their fire-arms. Bread
they seldom tasted, and at sea never thought about.
Of this food every man ate generally twice a day, or
at his own pleasure, and without limitation, there
being in this respect no distinction between the com-

mander and the meanest seaman. The vessel fairly victualled, a final council was held, which determined the destination of the cruise and the place of operations; and articles were generally drawn up and subscribed, which regulated the division of the spoils. The carpenter, the sail-maker, the surgeon, and the commander, were in the first place paid out of the common stock. Wounds were next considered, the value of the right arm, the most useful member of the buccaneer's body, being reckoned equal to six slaves: the eye and finger had the same value, which was one slave. The remainder was equally shared, save that the captain had five shares, and his mate two. The first maxim in the code of the buccaneer, dictated by necessity, was, 'No prey, no pay.' In their cruises, the freebooters often put into remote harbours to careen or refit their ships, to obtain fruits and fish, to lie in wait for the Spanish traders, and to plunder either natives or Spaniards. The former they sometimes carried away, selling the men as slaves, while the women were compelled to labour among those of the buccaneers who followed the chase. Their dress consisted of a shirt dipped in the blood of the cattle hunted and killed; trousers prepared in the same rude manner; buskins without stockings; a cap with a small front; and a leathern girdle, into which were stuck knives, sabres, and pistols. The bloody garments, though attributed to design, were probably among the hunters the effect of chance and slovenliness." [1]

Of that sort were the strange adventurers who first made Jamaica a profitable place of resort for

[1] "Lives of Drake," &c., pp. 236-239.

Englishmen. At first they pursued their lawless calling in little bands, which were independent of one another, and made their homes, in which to pass their times of leisure and prepare their *boucan*, or preserved meat, in any nooks and corners of the Spanish Main or West Indian Islands that were least likely to be visited by the Spanish warships which vainly sought to put them down. As they grew in numbers and found it important to make more organized resistance to the enemy that came to attack them in organized ways, they entered into closer associations with one another, and secured one or more centres of action. The little island of Tortuga, between Cuba and Florida, was first chosen by them. There for many years they built their huts and spent their gains in every kind of wild excess, and there a sort of colony was formed by the irregular traders and attendants who crowded to supply their wants. But at length a formidable attack was made by Spain upon the settlement while the bravest of the buccaneers were at sea, and all its rude civilization was wasted amid terrible bloodshed; and soon after that, the island was seized by France, which refused to countenance any but French freebooters. The English rovers had to seek another haunt, and, while they were seeking, Cromwell's force, under General Venables, took possession of Jamaica. Thither a great many of the buccaneers at once went, and it was mainly by their assistance that two powerful attempts to recover the island for Spain, made in 1657 and 1658, were rendered utterly futile. It was partly in gratitude for their aid, partly because their further protection might be valuable, and partly because he secretly sympathized with their pursuits, that Colonel D'Oyley, the English governor, allowed them, from that time, to make Jamaica a regular place of resort. Their crowd of satellites came with them, and the island was at once depraved and enriched by their booty. We are told by Exquemelin, the historian of the buccaneers, himself one of their number, how one especially used to delight in placing a pipe of wine in the streets of Port Royal, and then, with a pistol in his hand, compel every passer-by to drink with him. "At other times he would do the same with barrels of ale and beer; and very often with both his hands he would throw these liquors about the streets, and wet the clothes of such as passed by, heedless whether he spoilt their apparel or not, were they men or women."

The greatest of the English buccaneers was Captain Henry Morgan. The son of a Welsh yeoman, he had gone out in his youth to settle in Barbados. There he was forced into slavery for some years, until, on his escape, he joined the buccaneers. By his wit and daring he soon became a favourite among them, and in the end he was recognised leader of a large section of the fraternity. By Colonel D'Oyley he was encouraged in his marauding expeditions, and as most of the treasure acquired in those expeditions was spent in Jamaica, the island derived as much profit as could result from the extravagance and debauchery of the buccaneers.

Morgan's most famous exploits were in 1670 and 1671. With nine vessels, and less than five hundred men, he proceeded, in the first summer, to surprise

the rich and strongly fortified Spanish city of Porto
Bello, near the Isthmus of Panama. In this he was
successful, and after a fortnight's brutal riot in the
captured town, he took back a great store of money,
and vast quantics of silks, cloths, and other articles
for sale in Jamaica. With so much of the proceeds as
were not needed for the further revels there enjoyed,
he equipped a fleet four times as strong for a bolder
raid on the Spanish possessions. He sacked several
smaller towns, and then, with half his men, advanced
by land to Panama, the centre of Spanish colonial
wealth, defended by a garrison nearly four thousand
strong. He took no food with him, and little was to
be found upon the way. "Happy was he," we read,
"who had reserved since morn any small piece of
leather whereof to make his supper, drinking after it
a good draught of water for his greatest comfort."
But the buccaneers knew how to fast as well as how
to feast. After ten days of hungry marching they
reached Panama. A short night's rest was secured
before they were detected by the enemy, and before
the next night came the Spaniards were routed, and
half the assailing force—the other half having
been killed in the battle—had gained possession of
the city. Most of the inhabitants fled from it, and,
by design or accident, its cedar houses were set on
fire, so that a part of the treasure was lost; but
enough remained to satisfy the rapacity of the leader
and those who were not tricked out of their share.
It was conveyed to Jamaica, and there squandered
like the previous booty.

After that Morgan played the buccaneer no more.
Peace between England and Spain had been made

during his absence, and it was strictly enforced by a new governor, Lord John Vaughan, who had been sent out. Morgan settled down as a planter, until, having won the favour of Charles II., he was knighted and made deputy-governor of Jamaica. A younger planter, then in the island, destined to become in turn a buccaneer, was the famous William Dampier. But his great exploits have very little to do with our present subject.

During the thirty years following the appointment of Colonel D'Oyley as governor of Jamaica, and the conferment of its constitution by Charles II., in 1661, the island made rapid progress. In 1662 it contained 3653 English inhabitants, and 552 negro slaves. In 1673 the white population had risen to 7768, the black to 9504. And it continued to increase almost as quickly, although the tide of English immigration was by no means equal to that occasioned by the working of the slave-trade. Planters settled in nearly every district of the beautiful and fertile colony, and towns arose as marts for its produce, and still more as haunts for the traders who profited most by the achievements of the buccaneers. Spanish Town—as the old capital of the Spaniards, known by them as St Jago de la Vega, was called—continued to be the centre of government; but the busiest seat of commerce was Port Royal, built on the edge of a coral reef which, with the neighbouring mainland, formed the splendid bay that is now termed Kingston Harbour. "Jamaica," says one of its historians, "had at this time made marvellous progress in respect to population and agricultural resources; but, in a moral point of view, its condition was truly deplorable. The strife, vice, and misery attendant on slavery became early manifest. The attempts of the wretched captives to regain their freedom, and the predatory incursions of the Maroons, even then scourged the colonists. Port Royal itself united to more than regal opulence the worst vices and the lowest depravity that ever disgraced a seaport; nor could anything else be expected in a city whose most honoured denizens were buccaneers, whose most welcome visitors were slave-traders."[1]

A terrible earthquake brought retribution upon Port Royal and the whole island, which furnishes a tragic close to the story of its connection with the buccaneers. "On the morning of the 7th of June, 1692," says the historian just cited, "the governor and council were met in session, the wharves were laden with bales of the richest merchandise, the markets and stores displayed the glittering spoils of Mexico and Peru, and the streets were thronged with people, when the clear and serene sky became overshadowed by partial darkness, broken by faint gleams of red and purple, and a tremendous roar, like that of distant thunder, broke from the base of the mountains, and reverberated through the valleys to the beach, while the sea, impelled by the same mighty convulsion, rose in a few minutes five fathoms high over the houses of the devoted town. The scene was appalling beyond description. Shrieks and lamentations rent the air. Mangled corpses floated on the waters, or were flung upwards by the violence of the shocks. Although there was no wind, billows rose and fell with such violence that the vessels in the

[1] Montgomery Martin, p. 28.

harbour broke from their moorings. One of them, the *Swan* frigate, was forced over the tops of the sunken houses, and afforded a means of escape to many persons. Several individuals were wonderfully preserved, being swallowed up during the awful concussion, and thrown back again through an aperture quite distinct from that which had yawned to receive them, without sustaining any material injury. Of the whole three thousand houses, about two hundred, with the fort, remained uninjured. The whole island felt the shock, and shared the disastrous effects of a visitation which happily stands alone in the annals of Jamaica; no other, before or since, having been known to compare with it. Chains of hills were riven asunder. New channels formed for the rivers. Mountains dissolved with a mighty crash, burying alive the people of the adjacent valleys. Whole settlements sank into the bowels of the earth. Plantations were removed *en masse*, and all the sugar-works destroyed. In fact, the whole outline was drawn afresh, and the elevation of the surface considerably diminished. The sentence of desolation, however, was yet but partially fulfilled. A noxious miasm, generated by the shoals of putrifying bodies that floated about the harbour, or lay in heaps in the suburbs, slew three thousand of the survivors. That so fearful a warning might not be forgotten by posterity, the sunken houses of Port Royal are, in calm weather, still visible beneath the surface of the ocean; while, in striking contrast, relieving the deep melancholy of the scene, is a monument erected at Green Bay, on the opposite side of the harbour, which commemorates the preservation of Louis Caldy, a native of Montpelier, in France, who left his country on account of the Revocation of the Edict of Nantes, and, after having been swallowed up during the earthquake, was, by the great providence of God, flung into the sea by a second shock, where he continued swimming until rescued by a boat, and lived forty years afterwards."[1]

The tale of misery does not end there. A new Port Royal was being built up by the survivors, when, in 1693, a hurricane swept over the town and destroyed a great part of the work; and before their fresh injuries were repaired, in June 1694, a powerful fleet, with fifteen hundred soldiers on board, commanded by General Du Casse, the governor of Hayti, came to spread further desolation over the southern and eastern parts of the island. They plundered and destroyed a vast number of plantations, and, though ultimately driven off with a loss of more than seven hundred of their number, the residue escaped with considerable spoil, and about thirteen hundred slaves.[2]

[1] Montgomery Martin, p. 24.
[2] Bryan Edwards, vol. i. p. 127.

CHAPTER IV.

JAMAICA AND SLAVERY.

THE PROGRESS OF JAMAICA—ITS VALUE TO ENGLAND—SLAVERY—THE SLAVE INSURRECTIONS—THE RISING OF 1760—THE CONDITION OF THE SLAVES—THE INSURRECTION OF 1832—THE ABOLITION OF SLAVERY IN 1834. [1094-1834.]

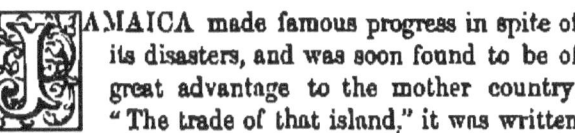AMAICA made famous progress in spite of its disasters, and was soon found to be of great advantage to the mother country. "The trade of that island," it was written in 1728, "employs three hundred sail of ships, and about six thousand seamen, and the very duties on the imports from thence amount to near £100,000 per annum. There are eight fine harbours in it, besides many coves and bays, where ships may safely ride. There are also eighty-four rivers which discharge into the sea, and seven times as many lesser rivers and springs which run into them. Its principal productions, besides sugar, are cotton, ginger, pimento, mahogany-wood, logwood, and indigo. Very little of the four last-named commodities are imported from the rest of the British plantations, so that, but for Jamaica, we should be obliged to purchase them of the French, Dutch, and other nations. The cotton is necessary to work up with wool in many of our manufactures. The ginger is chiefly exported, though great quantities are likewise used at home. Their pimento lessens the consumption of spices, which are

only to be had of the Dutch at their own rates. Indigo, logwood, and fustick, are used by dyers, and are absolutely necessary in many of our manufactures; and before we had those commodities of our own, we paid five times the prices for them that we now do, and for some of them more. Before our West India plantations were settled, we paid the Portuguese from £4 to £5 per cwt. for sugar, now sold from 22s. to 35s.; and above £5 per cwt. for ginger, now commonly sold at 22s. 6d. Our dyers' wares were bought of the Spaniards, to whom we paid for logwood from £100 to £130 per ton, which may now be had at £9 per ton, and other goods proportionably. So that, by having these plantations, we not only save so much as was formerly paid for those commodities to foreigners, but we are also able to furnish other nations therewith; and our manufacturers, by having them at less prices than formerly, are enabled to sell their commodities proportionably cheaper, which is undoubtedly a great advantage to the nation."[1]

Though losing much of its profit from buccaneering exploits, the island advanced steadily in wealth and importance as an agricultural colony and a great centre of trade between Europe and the states of North and South America; and there was as steady an increase of its population. In 1734, when it sent home £540,000 worth of goods, and received from England £150,000 worth, it contained 7644 whites and 86,534 blacks. In 1746, the whites numbered about 10,000 and the blacks 112,428. In 1768 there were 17,947 whites, 3408 free persons of colour, and 176,914 slaves. In 1788 the creoles were

[1] Boyer, "Political State of Great Britain," vol. xxv.

THE GROWTH OF THE COLONY. 45

23,000 in number, the slaves 256,000; and in 1800 the island contained 30,000 whites, 10,000 coloured persons, and 300,000 slaves.

That rapid increase of population shows how rapidly the resources of the colony were increased. But there was a dark as well as a bright side to the picture of its growth. "A faithful description of our provincial governors and men in power," says the most painstaking local historian of Jamaica, "would be little better than a portrait of artifice, duplicity, haughtiness, violence, rapine, avarice, meanness, rancour, and dishonesty ranged in succession, with a very small portion of honour, justice, and magnanimity here and there intermixed, to lessen the disgust which otherwise the eye must feel in the contemplation of so horrid a group."[1] Many of those painful details are of no value to the general reader, and therefore need not here be referred to; but it is necessary to set forth some of the most painful of them in illustration of the character, the working, and the effects of slavery in the British West Indies.

The first Englishmen in Jamaica, finding it impossible to bring back the savage Maroons to the bondage from which they had escaped when their Spanish masters were driven out, straightway began to import new slaves from Africa. All through the hundred and eighty years in which slavery was maintained there were about ten blacks to every white man. Between 1655 and 1787, it is said that there were imported in all 676,276 negroes, and the new arrivals were at the same rate, about 4000 a year, for the ensuing twenty years. In 1807,

[1] Long, "History of Jamaica," 3 vols., 1744.

when the importation of new slaves was prohibited, the blacks in the island only numbered 360,000, and after that, until the emancipation in 1834, the negro population decreased by nearly 2000 a year, whereas, according to the ordinary laws of population, it ought to have been increased by nearly half as much, and, had those laws prevailed all through the time, it should have been at least four times as great as it was. These statistics show that, during the hundred and eighty years, about 3000 negroes were each year killed before their time by hard usage, which was often murder in its cruellest form. "The early West Indian planters," says the historian, himself a champion of slavery, though in more humane shape, "thought it no greater sin to kill a negro than to knock a monkey on the head;" and he thus sums up the law of the island on the subject: "If a white man murders a white man, he ought to die for it; but if a white man murders a black man, he ought to be acquitted."[1] If a black man murdered a white man, no punishment severe enough could be inflicted.

Those murders, however, were frequent. The presence of the Maroons, who often came down from their mountain fastnesses to despoil the English plantations, was a constant incentive to the slaves to seek a like lawless freedom, and they used it in retaliations upon their former masters, concerning which the only wonder is that they were not more vindictive. "Many hundreds of them," it was written by a traveller in 1722, "have at different times run to the mountains, where they associate and commit little

[1] Long, vol. ii. p. 488.

robberies upon the defenceless and nearest plantations, and which I imagine they would not have done but for the cruelty of their usage, because they subsist very hard and with danger, by reason of parties continually sent out by Government against them, who have £5 a-head for every one killed, and their ears are a sufficient warrant for the next justice to pay it. If the negro be brought in a prisoner, he is tormented and burnt alive."[1]

During more than a century and a half an irregular warfare was constantly maintained between the colonists and the Maroons, recruited every year by fugitives from the plantations; and few years passed without some outburst of insurrection among the slaves, in which they were generally aided by their kinsmen of the mountains. Between 1678 and 1832 twenty-eight conspiracies of special importance are enumerated.

The insurrection of 1760 will serve to illustrate their nature and the way in which they were suppressed. It was begun by about a hundred slaves newly imported from the Gold Coast, at a plantation some twenty miles north of Kingston. "Having collected themselves in a body about one o'clock in the morning," we are told, "they proceeded to the fort at Port Maria, killed the sentinel, and provided themselves with as great a quantity of arms and ammunition as they could conveniently dispose of. Being by this time joined by a number of their countrymen from the neighbouring plantations, they marched up the high road that led to the interior parts of the country, carrying death and desolation as they went.

[1] Atkins, "Voyage to the West Indies," p. 245.

At one estate they surrounded the overseer's house, in which eight or ten white people were in bed, every one of whom they butchered in the most savage manner, and literally drank their blood mixed with rum. At other estates they exhibited the same tragedy, and then set fire to the buildings and canes. In one morning they murdered between thirty and forty whites, not sparing even infants at the breast."[1] About sixty white men in all were slaughtered by them; and the blood of those sixty was paid for by the death of about four hundred, killed in action, or afterwards executed, while six hundred more were transported to Honduras. "The records of crime and punishment," says one historian, "can hardly equal or excuse the horrible barbarities and exquisite tortures which were inflicted by and upon these condemned criminals. Some of them were burned, some were fixed alive on gibbets. One of them lived two hundred and ten hours, suspended under a vertical sun, without any sustenance or even a drop of water. Yet they all behaved to the last moment," adds the writer, a clergyman, "with a degree of hardened insolence and brutal insensibility, which drowned compassion and almost authorized their doom."[2] The "hardened insolence and brutal insensibility" of one of the sufferers is described by another historian. "The wretch was made to sit on the ground, and, his body being chained to an iron stake, the fire was applied to his feet. He uttered not a groan, and saw his legs reduced to ashes with the utmost firmness and composure; after which, one of his arms by some

[1] Edwards, vol. ii. p. 64.   [2] Bridges, vol. i. p. 99.

means getting loose, he snatched a brand from the fire that was consuming him, and flung it in the face of the executioner."[1]

It is small extenuation of cruelties like that to say that the sufferers had been subject to yet greater cruelties in their barbarous African homes, and that they were schooled to them by the lesser pains inflicted on them by their overseers on the plantations. Some mitigation of their condition was effected, under the influence of English opinion, by the Consolidated Slave Act of 1792, which made the murder and mutilation of negroes offences in the eye of the law, and regulated their food and working time. Before as well as after the passing of that act, of course, those slaves who chanced to be under kind masters and overseers were treated with some consideration. They were not flogged or branded with unbearable severity, were allowed some of the pleasures of domestic life, and were even permitted on Sunday to cultivate small parcels of land for themselves, and to apply the proceeds in ministering to their coarse tastes. But at best they were slaves, treated like chattel, and especially debarred from the elevating influences of education. Secular teaching was not tolerated, and religious instruction was grudgingly accorded to them.

Their state was to some extent ameliorated by the English law of 1807, which prohibited the further importation of slaves. Those already in the island thus became more valuable, and common-sense selfishness generally prompted the masters to abstain from ill-treatment so great as to render them use-

[1] Edwards, vol. ii. p. 65.

less servants. Missionaries came, too, who instilled into them new views as to their dignity and destiny. Those views, crude and violent, as was to be expected from the degraded condition of the negroes, wrought mischief as well as benefit. Many who had before been quiet beasts of labour, became idle and turbulent men, and a new hatred sprang up between them and their masters, by which their sufferings were often increased, until a terrible crisis occurred in the insurrection of 1832. Yet that insurrection helped materially in bringing about their liberation.

The insurrection began near Montego Bay, in the north-west of the island. The manager of an estate met a black woman who had in her hand a piece of sugar-cane, which he supposed she had stolen. He flogged her on the spot, and then took her back to the estate to be flogged again by the head-driver. The driver chanced to be her husband, and he refused to obey the manager's orders. Another driver was called; but he also refused to inflict the punishment, and so much sympathy was shown by the other slaves that the manager rode off to obtain the aid of the militia. Before he returned with the necessary force, the chief offenders had escaped. The news of this over-reaching of the authorities spread over the adjoining districts, and induced great numbers of slaves to resolve that on a given day they would refuse to work unless free men's wages were paid to them. Before the day came, some drunken negroes set fire to an estate, and that act so excited the others that within a short time the whole district was in flames. The flames lit up the angry passions of the multitude. Desolation spread over all the western portion of the island, and for a few days the blacks gave vent to their long pent-up fury without hindrance. An armed force soon brought them under subjection again; but the planters were not satisfied by the temperate action of the military. After the slaves had returned to their estates under a promise of pardon, they found that they had only come back to be slaughtered. Martial law being proclaimed, they were shot and hung indiscriminately. At Montego Bay negroes were often tried, sentenced, and hung, all within the space of an hour and a half, the corpses being soon cut down in order that fresh use might be made of the gibbets; and in the evening carts came round to collect the heaps of dead bodies that they might be thrown into a huge pit dug for the purpose. In the country districts no burial at all was given to the victims. Where they were shot down, there they were left to rot or become the prey of carrion.[1] About a dozen white men had been murdered. For this more than fifteen hundred negroes were executed, and many others died under the lash of their enraged masters. The persecution lasted long, and fell especially upon those slaves who had dared to listen to the teaching of the Baptist missionaries, although those missionaries appear to have in no way instigated the turmoil.

The insurrection was quelled; yet the thrill of horror which rang through England quickened all men's ears to the arguments that had long been

[1] Parliamentary Papers, Jamaica, 1832.

urged by Clarkson, Wilberforce, and others, and in 1834 slavery was abolished throughout the dominions of Great Britain. But the blight which it had spread over some of the most fertile portions of the earth could not be removed by Act of Parliament.

CHAPTER V.

OUR WEST INDIAN POSSESSIONS.

THE BERMUDAS—THE BAHAMAS—OTHER WEST INDIAN ISLANDS—
BRITISH GUIANA — TRINIDAD — BARBADOS — JAMAICA — THE
PRESENT CONDITION OF OUR WEST INDIAN COLONIES—THE
CAUSES OF THEIR DETERIORATION AND THE MEANS OF THEIR
IMPROVEMENT. [1593-1869.]

OLDER than any of the West Indian Islands as British possessions are the curious coral rocks, said to be as numerous as the days of the year, though only a few of them are large enough for human habitation, which have been named the Bermudas, after Bermudez, the Spaniard, who discovered them in 1527. On one of them, Henry May, an Englishman, was wrecked in 1593, and there he and his twenty-five companions passed five months while they built a bark in which to return home. Among the same group Sir George Somers, going out to serve as deputy-governor of Virginia, was also wrecked in 1609. He took possession of them for the Crown of England, and having gone back in 1611, died in the one known as St George's Isle. In the same year a small colony was founded here by his brother, and since then "the still-vexed Bermoothes" of Shakespeare, previously only the terror of voyagers to other parts, have been occupied by Englishmen. Their convenient position in the Atlantic

Ocean, lying about six hundred miles to the east of Virginia, and somewhat farther north of the West Indies, made them a valuable halting-place both for traders and for war-ships proceeding to the other colonies; and during the last century and a half they have contained 10,000 or more inhabitants, half white and half black.

The genial climate has long been famous for its nourishment of arrowroot, onions, and potatoes; but the chief value of the little colony has been in its military advantages. Formerly a dependency of Virginia, its annexation to the United States was desired by Washington, who saw that it could be made "a nest of hornets to annoy the British trade." To save it from that use, it was furnished with almost impregnable fortifications and a great naval dockyard.

South-west of the Bermudas and very near to Florida is the larger island-group of the Bahamas. New Providence, one of the number, was settled by the English in 1629; but it and the neighbouring islands were throughout the seventeenth century a frequent battle-ground between English, Spaniards, and French, and a yet more frequent field for the depredations of the buccaneers; and not much peaceable use was made of them till after the American War of Independence, when they became the undisputed possession of Great Britain. Less hospitable than most of the West Indies, they are still but thinly peopled. About 40,000 inhabitants, three-quarters black, are spread over an area of some 3500 square miles.

The most important of the early acquisitions

of England in the West Indies, after Jamaica and Barbados, was Antigua. Sir Thomas Warner colonized it in 1632. In 1666 it was desolated by the French from Martinique; but the colony was re-established in the following year by Lord Willoughby, who sent thither some of his Barbadian subjects, and its excellent facilities for sugar-cultivation soon made it a favourite place of resort. The atrocities of slavery had begun to be mitigated as early as 1723. "Several cruel persons," it was stated in the preamble of an Act then passed by the local legislature, "to gratify their cruel humours, against the laws of God and humanity, frequently kill, destroy, or dismember their own and other person's slaves, and have hitherto gone unpunished, because it is inconsistent with the constitution and government of this island, and would be too great a countenance and encouragement to slaves to resist white persons, to set slaves so far upon an equality with the free inhabitants as to try those that kill them for their lives; nor is it known or practised in any of the Caribbee Islands that any free person killing a slave is triable for his life."[1] So great an "inconsistence with the constitution of the island" was not now attempted; but a penalty of not less than £100 was placed upon the murder of a black, and £20 was charged for his dismemberment; and thereby more tenderness towards the negroes was induced. In 1732 Moravian missionaries came to the island, and great good came from their teaching, and still more from their actual example. In 1834, when slavery was abolished, Antigua, alone of all

[1] Southey, "History of the West Indies," vol. ii. p. 235.

the West Indian Islands, chose at once to give full
liberty to the blacks, instead of passing them through
the stage of apprenticeship allowed by law. "Here,
as in other islands," said the governor of Antigua in
1846, "the material condition of the emancipated
race is most satisfactory. They are abundantly supplied with all the necessaries and most of the comforts of life. They are well fed, well housed, and
well clothed. Through the aid of friendly societies,
which are in active and beneficial operation, the
poorest can command good medical attendance, and
other privileges seldom enjoyed by persons in a
similar rank of life in other countries. The number
of labourers withdrawing from estates, and settling
in detached villages, continues to increase. There
appear to be seventy such settlements formed, containing about 3300 houses, and a population of
about 9300. These village communities are not
peculiar to Antigua; but, owing to the transition
which took place here direct from slavery to
freedom, without the intervention of apprenticeship,
they have made greater progress in this island, and
from them may spring the germ of a middle class
which must exercise considerable influence over the
future destinies of the colony."[1] About 37,000 inhabitants, black, white, and coloured, are now in the
island, rather more than half of whose area of 183
miles is under cultivation.

Other islands of the West Indies were annexed by
Great Britain during the seventeenth and eighteenth
centuries, but in none of them was much progress
made until recent times. During the long and costly

[1] Blue Book, 1846.

wars which England carried on with the European
powers and her former colonies on the continent of
America, now the United States, she fought desperately for the possession of those West Indian colonies
which had not previously been greatly thought of,
and of others which had not hitherto been hers. In
1814, when peace was restored, she found herself
mistress of nearly every important island, with the
exception of Cuba, Hayti, and Porto Rico, from the
Bahamas down to Trinidad; and Honduras and
British Guiana also belonged to her.

Guiana had long been coveted by adventurous
Englishmen. Sir Walter Raleigh had gone thither
in 1595, believing that thus he could gain possession of the apocryphal El Dorado. "He, like every
other Englishman, had been attracted by the fables
of the Golden City of Manoa and the Golden Lake
of Parina. Columbus had started the fables, or at
any rate had favoured the traditions out of which
they grew. Vasco Nuñez de Balboa had first been
led by them in quest of the glittering phantom, and
Pizarro had, in following it, won the empire of Peru.
Two generations of daring and bloodthirsty adventurers had hunted the phantom from place to place,
until all the northern parts of South America had
been brought under the dominion of Spain. Raleigh
hoped that where others had failed he might succeed;
and he knew that, whether there was failure or success, he could offer no greater insult, and work no
heavier injury to Spain, than by planting the English
standard in this most sacred scene of Spanish bigotry
and tyranny, whence most of the gold employed by
Philip II. in persecuting Netherlanders and annoying

Englishmen, and troubling the whole of Christendom, was being extracted with the help of cruelties that thrilled every honest looker-on with horror."[1] Raleigh failed, and suffered terribly for his project at the hands of James I.; and, though other Englishmen made small expeditions and even brief settlements, most of Guiana became the property of the Dutch, and under them it was a vigorous colony, and a scene of some of the vilest atrocities of slavery, during nearly two centuries. Its three great provinces of Demerara, Essequibo, and Berbice were seized by Britain in 1796, and, though restored in 1802, were recaptured in 1803, and confirmed as British possessions at the peace of 1814. They comprise an area of 76,000 square miles, over the greater part of which a few Indian tribes roam undisturbed. About 12,000 whites and ten times as many blacks cultivate most of the coast land, which extends for some 200 miles, and the sugar and rum produced by them yield a flourishing trade to George Town, the capital. The vast resources of the interior, rich in timber, dyes, and other natural productions, have yet to be utilized.

Trinidad, the nearest West Indian island, with an area of 1754 square miles, was worthless Spanish property till 1797, when it was captured for England by Sir Ralph Abercrombie. Its population, then 17,000, is now nearly 90,000, and in sugar, rum, arrowroot, and other articles it has a flourishing trade, although that trade seems to be yet only in its first stage of progress. Its most remarkable feature is a great pitch lake, to which attention was

[1] Bourne, "English Seamen under the Tudors," vol. ii. p. 298.

first called by the late Earl of Dundonald, who visited it as admiral of the West India squadron in 1850. "We arrived at La Brea," he wrote, "and before daybreak on the following morning were on the road to the lake or rather stream of bitumen, now indurated, which in former ages overflowed the lake. Indeed, the bitumen beneath this road seems still to be on the move, as is shown by curvilineal roads on its surface, like waves receding from a stone thrown into water. The appearance of the lake is most extraordinary. One vast sheet of bitumen extends until lost amidst luxuriant vegetation. Its circumference is full three miles, exclusive of the creeks, which double the extent. The bituminous surface is of a dark brown, waxy consistence, except in one or two places where the fluid still exudes. Obviously this spring is in full vigour beneath, for the whole surface of the lake is formed into protuberances, like the segments of a globe pressed together, having hollows filled with rain-water, which, except in the immediate vicinity of the bituminous springs, is inodorous and without taste—an extraordinary fact, showing that this bitumen is of a nature quite different from that of pyrotechnic mineral and vegetable tar." The value of this article Lord Dundonald showed to be almost without limit. " Used as a mastic, it is peculiarly suited to unite and insure the durability of hydraulic works. It renders the foundations and superstructure of buildings impermeable to humidity. It is admirably adapted, by its resistance to decomposition by the most powerful solvents, to the construction of sewers, and, being tasteless, it is an excellent coating to water-pipes, aqueducts, and reservoirs. When masticated and prepared, it is a substitute for costly gums as applied to numerous purposes. Combined with a small portion of ligneous matter, it constitutes a fuel of greater evaporating power than coal, and, when pulverized and scattered over growing potato-plants or other vegetables, it prevents their destruction by insects or blight, and acts also a fertiliser of the soil. Essential and viscid oils are obtained by various well-known processes from bituminous substances, but from none in such abundance and possessing such valuable properties as the oils extracted from the bitumen of the lake of Trinidad."[1]

Those sentences are quoted in evidence of the still unused resources of Trinidad. Similar resources, wholly or mainly neglected, exist in nearly all of our West Indian possessions. Those possessions comprise, in the aggregate, an area of about 175,000 square miles, being twice the size of Great Britain and Ireland. Their population hardly exceeds a million, and of these more than half are within the narrow limits of Jamaica and Barbados.

Barbados is the only one of the colonies which has prospered in any adequate degree. In its 166 square miles there are about 160,000 residents, whose imports are about £1,000,000 a year, and their exports about £1,250,000.

Jamaica, twenty times as large and thrice as populous, imports hardly more and exports slightly less than Barbados. And yet, in natural endowments, it is the richest of the whole West Indian group. Every stranger who has visited it, since Christopher Columbus, has spoken in admiration of its splendid

[1] "Life of the Earl of Dundonald," vol. ii. pp. 310, 333, 334.

harbours, its beautiful mountains, its luxuriant valleys, and its fertilising streams. Ceylon and Java alone, among the islands of the world, can rival "the Queen of the Antilles" in external attractions. "On the northern side," says one, "the country at a small distance from the shore rises into hills, which are more remarkable for beauty than boldness; being all of gentle acclivity and commonly separated from each other by spacious vales and romantic inequalities; but they are seldom craggy, nor is the transition from the hills to the valleys oftentimes abrupt. In general the hand of nature has rounded every hill towards the top with singular felicity. The most striking circumstances attending these beautiful swells are the happy disposition of the groves of pimento, with which most of them are spontaneously clothed, and the consummate verdure of the turf underneath, which is discoverable in a thousand openings, presenting a charming contrast to the deeper tints of the pimento. As this tree, which is no less remarkable for fragrance than for beauty, suffers no rival plant to flourish within its shade, these groves are not only clear of underwood, but even the grass beneath is seldom luxuriant, the soil in general being a chalky marl, which produces a close and clean turf, as smooth and even as the finest English lawn, and in colour infinitely brighter. Over this beautiful surface the pimento spreads itself in various compartments. In one place we beheld extensive groves, in another a number of beautiful groups, some of which crown the hills, while others are scattered down the declivities. To enliven the scene, and add perfection to beauty, the bounty of nature has copiously watered the whole district. No part of the West Indies that I have seen abounds with so many delicious streams. Every valley has its rivulet, and every hill its cascade. In one point of view, where the rocks overhang the ocean, no less than eight transparent waterfalls are beheld in the same moment. Those only who have been long at sea can judge of the emotion which is felt by the thirsty voyager at so enchanting a prospect. Such is the foreground of the picture. As the land rises towards the centre of the island, the eye, passing over the beauties that I have recounted, is attracted by a boundless amphitheatre of wood, ' cedar and branching palm,' an immensity of forest, the outline of which melts in the distant blue hills, and these again are lost in the clouds. On the southern side of the island the scenery is of a different nature. In the former landscape the prevailing characteristics are variety and beauty; in that which remains the predominant features are grandeur and sublimity. When I first approached this side of the island by sea, and beheld from afar such of the stupendous and soaring ridges of the blue mountains as the clouds here and there disclosed, the imagination, forming an indistinct but awful idea of what was concealed by what was thus partially displayed, was filled with admiration and wonder. Yet the sensation which I felt was allied to terror rather than delight. Though the prospect before me was in the highest degree magnificent, it seemed a scene of magnificent desolation. The abrupt precipice and inaccessible cliff had more the aspect of a chaos than a creation; or rather, seemed to exhibit the effects of some dreadful convulsion

THE BEAUTIES OF JAMAICA. 63

which had laid nature in ruins. Appearances, however, improved as we approached; for, amidst the thousand bold features, too hard to be softened by culture, many a spot was soon discovered where the hand of industry had awakened life and fertility. With these pleasing intermixtures the flowing line of the lower range of mountains, which, crowned with woods of majestic growth, now began to be visible, combined to soften and relieve the rude solemnity of the loftier eminences, till at length the savannahs at the bottom met the sight. These are vast plains, clothed chiefly with extensive cane-fields, displaying, in all the pride of cultivation, the verdure of spring blended with the exuberance of autumn; and bounded only by the ocean, on whose bosom a new and ever-moving picture strikes the eye, for innumerable vessels are discovered in various directions, some crowding into, and others bearing away from, the bays and harbours with which the coast is everywhere indented."[1]

Those sentences were written in 1793, when Jamaica was almost at the height of its prosperity as a slave colony, and when none but the very wisest understood that the grand and beautiful island was being wasted by the unholy means that were being used for its development. Men admired the luxuriant cane-fields, and rejoiced at the wealth which they produced, not heeding that the wealth and the beauty were obtained for the profit of a few through the degradation of the many. Slavery being the rule in all the British colonies, Jamaica progressed as rapidly as any of the others. Since free-

[1] Edwards, vol. L. pp. 180-188.

dom has been established, its actual progress has continued, though, relatively with other and better governed dependencies, that progress is really deterioration.

All the institutions of the island were offshoots of slavery, and planned in accordance with it: they have proved worse than useless under the freer atmosphere that now prevails. The traveller entering the noble harbour of Kingston, which was founded in 1693 after the destruction of Port Royal, and is now the capital of the island, expects to see man's work in some accordance with nature's. He finds a mean and squalid haunt of poverty and vice. "The distant beauty of the varied buildings vanishes before the sight of streets without a plan, houses without the semblance of architecture, lanes and alleys without cleanliness and convenience."[1] "During the heavy rains in May and October, the water finds its way by broken and irregular channels into the gullies on the east and west sides of the town, but much of it pours down the steep streets, forcing along a broad and muddy stream a foot or more in depth. As none even of the leading thoroughfares are paved, nor provided with any artificial channels for the water, and the soil is generally loose and sandy, their surface has become ploughed up with deep ruts and broken hollows, while, from the quantity of gravel, stones, and bricks strewed about, they present more the appearance of river courses than of streets in an inhabited city. The cross streets are in some respects still worse, being often flanked by dilapidated buildings, and

[1] Madden, "Twelve Months in the West Indies," vol. i. p. 98.

filtered over with rubbish. Nor is it only by inanimate objects that the senses of sight and smell are offended. Lean, mangy dogs are at all times to be seen rolling about in the noisome puddles, while others are wandering here and there, grubbing up the rubbish for food. Besides the swine and goats constantly moving about, Kingston has always been noted for its number of half-starved dogs. It is no uncommon thing to see the carcase of one of these unfortunate brutes lying in the middle of a street, with a troop of the vulture crows which are ever wheeling about the city tearing it to pieces, while the air all around is tainted with the most baneful effluvia."[1] And the dirt and disorder of Kingston too truly indicate the neglect and mismanagement that pervade the whole island. The same indolence and incompetence that prevail in parochial matters are displayed in all the administration of the colony, whether by central authorities or by local managers.

The abolition of slavery, moreover, has not abolished the old antipathy between the negroes and their former masters. It has only found for it new ways of development. The planters expect that the blacks will work for them with the same energy that was formerly forced from them by terror of the lash. The blacks, rejoicing in their liberty, and willing to punish, now that it is in their power, a race which has treated them so badly, are idle, or at any rate prefer to toil on their own little farms, all whose profits come to themselves. Thus a jealousy has arisen, and even been intensified, during the past generation, which finds vent in numberless disputes, and out of

[1] Martin, "West Indies," p. 77.

which arose the so-called insurrection of 1865, and its vindictive suppression.

The prevalent absenteeism increases this evil. The real owners of West Indian estates seldom live on their property, which is intrusted to subordinates schooled in all the vicious influences of slavery, who make no honest effort to bring about a better state of things by educating the negroes, and caring for them in matters concerning which they are too ignorant to care for themselves. All the traditions, and most of the present associations of the negroes, incline them to be thoughtless, stubborn, and jealous, and these characteristics are alike injurious to themselves and their employers. So long as they can secure for themselves a home, in which cleanliness and European comfort are no necessaries, enough cheap food to live upon, and enough gaudy clothes to wear, they have no inducement to improve their state, or to consult the interests of their masters.

Perhaps the amelioration of this gloomy condition of affairs is not difficult. Philanthropy, though often misguided, has done much to put worthier thoughts into the negro mind. Black settlements have been formed, in which gradually a higher self-reliance and a worthier spirit of independence have found expression in the happiness and comfort of the settlers. These must be encouraged, if only to get rid of the indolence and discontent of a great part of the negro population, which help to stagnate the whole condition of the island. Nobler motives, also, which are only the best phases of self-interest, must actuate the white residents in their relations with one another and their dependants. A generous master does not often find his trust betrayed. If he consults the interests of those under him, he generally finds that his own interests are not neglected.

Moreover, in Jamaica, and nearly all the West Indian colonies, there is room, and even need, for new settlers. Men and women to whom the more stirring life of most of our younger dependencies is not attractive, who care to make their homes in a temperate climate which makes agricultural life easy and delightful, if not convenient for the rapid accumulation of wealth, can find it in most of the islands of the West Indies, and perhaps best in what travellers describe as—where man's hand has not marred the beauty and luxuriance—a modern Garden of Eden.

CHAPTER VI.

NEWFOUNDLAND.

THE BEGINNING OF THE NEWFOUNDLAND FISHERIES—THE GROWTH OF NEWFOUNDLAND AS A COLONY—ENGLISH NEGLECT OF IT—THE FISHERS, AND THE COLONISTS—ITS TROUBLES DURING WAR WITH FRANCE—ITS SUBSEQUENT DEVELOPMENT—SEAL-HUNTING AND COD-FISHING. [1497-1867.]

THE vast district now known as British North America, to which John Cabot led the way in his famous voyage of 1497, and which then, so far as the bare discovery could make it, became the property of England, was not at first duly valued by its claimants. Cabot's visit to Newfoundland and Labrador was followed by many voyages conducted by his son Sebastian and other Englishmen; but their object was rather to find a northern passage to India than to make good use of the source of wealth already found. Gradually these districts came to be frequented by fishing-vessels in search of cod, but even in that work foreigners took a greater part than Englishmen. The older fishing-trade with Iceland, carried on by merchants of Bristol, Hull, and other ports, was preferred to what was thought the more hazardous commerce with Newfoundland. Those who courted danger generally went elsewhere. Yet the North American fisheries were not altogether neglected. In 1544 there were many English fishing-ships in Newfoundland waters, and "in 1578 Anthony Parkhurst, an intelligent merchant of Bristol, reported that he had been annually to Newfoundland in the four years past, that during that time the English fishing-fleet had increased from thirty to fifty sail, and that, although the French sent about a hundred and fifty boats, the Spaniards about a hundred, and the Portuguese some fifty, the English, by reason of the greater strength of their vessels, were masters of the trade."[1]

Soon after that, in 1583, Sir Humphrey Gilbert made the attempt, which has been already referred to, to turn Newfoundland from a mere fishing-station into an organized English colony, but it failed; and failure also befell a kindred effort of his brother, Sir John Gilbert, more than twenty years afterwards. Later Englishmen went farther south, especially after Henry Hudson had gone to the district of New York; and Newfoundland continued to grow only as an irregular home of fishermen and their families. The share taken by the French in this work is apparent by the number of foreign names yet existing in the island. Point Enragée, Isle aux Morts, Bonne Bay, and Petit Fort Harbour, contrast oddly with such blunt English titles as Old Harry, Piper's Hole, Hell Hill, Seldom-come-by, and Come-by-chance.

Not much thought was given by statesmen or rich adventurers to Newfoundland until the Stuart troubles made it necessary for the violent members of every party to take refuge in the New World. There, however, while the Pilgrim Fathers were

[1] Bourne, "English Seamen under the Tudors," vol. i. p. 187.

establishing themselves on the mainland, Sir George Calvert, afterwards Lord Baltimore, took the lead of the Catholic emigrants. In 1623 he obtained a charter, assigning to him and his heirs a large part of the island, and a promising colony was founded, which fared none the worse because its leader, eleven years later, procured a new grant and organized the Catholic settlement of Maryland, on the Continent. Before long another little colony, consisting of Irishmen, was despatched by Lord Falkland, the Lord-Lieutenant of Ireland; and in 1654 Sir David Kirk conducted a second body of Irishmen to the island. The total winter, or resident, population of Newfoundland then numbered three hundred and fifty families, in fifteen distinct settlements. Besides this, there was in the summertime a floating population of some thousands, consisting of the fishermen who came for the cod-season.

As these fishermen were of all nations, and as they thought it their interest to oppose with all their power the permanent occupation of the island by English subjects, great confusion necessarily arose. For a long time the country was hardly governed at all. The traders laboured in all sorts of lawless ways to drive out the settlers; but the settlements grew every year, though also in lawless ways. "As they were made of scarcely any account by the Government, they grew up without authoritative regulations, each man being a law to himself, and doing what seemed good in his own eyes."[1] In 1667 they petitioned King Charles II. for a governor

[1] Pedley, "History of Newfoundland."

and proper legislative arrangements for their well-being, but no answer was given to them. In 1674 they petitioned again; when they were told by the Lords of the Committee for Trade and Plantations, which was in the place of a Colonial Secretary under the Stuarts, that all plantations in Newfoundland were objectionable, and that, if they were not satisfied with their position, they had better come home. An agent, Sir John Berry, was even sent out "with orders for the deportation of the settlers, the destruction of their houses, and in fact the entire uprooting of the thriving colony which had been reared at the heavy cost of the energies, treasure, and life-blood of several of England's bravest sons."[1] Sir John Berry was too humane to obey his instructions, but all he could do was to leave the colonists as they had been when they sought the protection of the English Crown. In 1676 the threat of extermination was withdrawn, but strict injunctions were issued by Charles II. against the conveyance of any fresh emigrants to Newfoundland.

In that unpropitious way the colony grew into importance. Even the wise statute of William III., published at the close of the seventeenth century, and regarded as the first charter of Newfoundland liberties, contained the singular provision, that the master of any fishing-vessel from England, Wales, or Berwick-upon-Tweed, who, in each year, first entered any harbour or creek in the island, should during the fishing-season be admiral of the harbour or creek, and should have full power to decide all differences between the fishermen and the inhabitants. The

[1] Montgomery Martin, "The British Colonies," vol. L p. 293.

visitors were to have their own way in everything during the summer, and there was to be no magistrate of any sort in the winter. "When it is considered," says the historian, "that, according to the testimony of a credible witness, the island had become at this time 'a sanctuary and refuge for them that broke in England,' it may readily be imagined that during these wintry, unoccupied intervals, disorder and wrong must have prevailed to a frightful degree."[1]

At length a better state of things was brought about, though only by help of a war which nearly deprived England altogether of the possession of her neglected colony. The French had persevered in their North American fisheries, for which their great possessions in Canada and the adjacent parts had given them special facilities, and the settlement of Placentia, which they had established in Newfoundland, had, under careful management, grown to be a source of serious danger to the English. William III., at the outbreak of war with France, made it a special subject of complaint, "that of late the encroachments of the French upon Newfoundland and his Majesty's subjects' trade and fisheries there, had been more like the invasions of an enemy than becoming to friends who enjoyed the advantages of that trade only by permission." Louis XIV. answered that his right to Newfoundland was as good as that of the King of England, and that from Placentia he intended to govern the whole island. Thereupon William resolved that he should have no share at all in its government. The resolution was hardly contested.

[1] Pedley.

Placentia was attacked in 1692, but only slightly injured, and in 1696 the French attacked and desolated all the British stations except those in Conception Bay. The Peace of Ryswick in 1698 only restored matters to their former condition, and enabled the French to increase their force in the island in anticipation of the greater struggle that began in 1702.

Eleven years of varying fortune and constant trouble then befell the Newfoundlanders. "On the declaration of the famous War of the Succession," we read, "Sir John Leake was immediately despatched by Queen Anne with a small squadron to take possession of the whole island, which he failed in doing, although he succeeded in destroying several French settlements and capturing a number of vessels, with which he returned to England at the close of the year. In August 1703, Admiral Graydon was sent with a fresh fleet off the coast of Newfoundland, but, owing to a fog which continued with great density for thirty days, his ships were dispersed, and could not be brought together till the 3d of September. He then called a council of war as to the practicability of attacking the stronghold of the French at Placentia, and it was decided that it would not be prudent to do so with the force at his disposal; on which he returned to England, where his conduct was severely censured. In 1705 the garrison of Placentia, reinforced by five hundred men from Canada, attacked the British colonists, and attempted to become sole masters of the island by assailing the harbour of St John's, where they were repulsed; but they succeeded in gaining possession of several settlements, destroyed Fort Forillon, and spread their rav-

ages as far as Bonavista. In 1706, the British again
expelled them from their recent conquests, and Captain Underdown, with only ten ships, destroyed several
of the enemy's craft in the harbours along the coast,
notwithstanding that the French had as many as
ten armed vessels on that station. Although Parliament earnestly entreated the Queen 'to use her royal
endeavours to recover and preserve the ancient possessions, trade, and fisheries of Newfoundland,' little
attention was paid to their address, the whole disposable force being assigned to the Duke of Marlborough, at that time in the midst of his victorious
career. The French, however, notwithstanding their
repeated disasters in Europe, still found leisure to
persevere in their endeavours for the expulsion of
the English from Newfoundland; and accordingly St
Ovide, the French commander at Placentia, having
effected a landing, without being discovered, within
five leagues of St John's, attacked and completely
destroyed it on the 1st of January 1708. The French
then seized on every English station except Carbonier, which was bravely defended by the fishermen.
The news of this misfortune produced great excitement in England, as the possession of the fisheries
had ever been considered a point of immense importance. An expedition was ordered to attempt to dispossess the French; but little was done beyond the
destruction of a few fishing-stations. The British
Government, being fully occupied with the events
then occurring on the Continent, was unable to take
any immediate measures for the recovery of Newfoundland; but, at the close of the war, England
demanded its restitution which Louis XIV. was no

longer in a condition to refuse, and by the Treaty of Utrecht, in 1713, Louis conceded the exclusive sovereignty of Newfoundland and the adjacent islands to Great Britain."[1]

After that, its possession by England was only disputed on one occasion, during the turmoil in which France lost all her American colonies; and better care began to be taken of a colony whose value was at last discovered. In 1728, Captain Henry Osborne, R.N., was sent out as its first governor and commander-in-chief, with authority to appoint justices of the peace, and to build a court-house and a prison. For these there was much need. There was hard work to be done in rooting up the lawless institutions that had been allowed to gain ground for generations. Mutinies and insurrections, incendiarisms and private feuds, had to be overcome before either the governors or the governed had any peace. In the end this was secured, and during the last century the career of Newfoundland has been one of almost steady progress, though the progress has perhaps been less rapid than it ought to have been. The resident population, which at the beginning of the eighteenth century was only 3506, had in 1785 risen to 10,224. In 1806 it was 26,505; in 1822, 52,157; in 1836, 73,705; in 1845, 96,506; and in 1862, 122,638.

The great wealth of Newfoundland has always been in its fish. "Other colonies," quaintly said the Abbé Raynal, "have yielded productions only by receiving an equal value in exchange. Newfoundland alone hath drawn from the depths of the waters

[1] Martin, vol. i. pp. 294, 295.

riches formed wholly by nature, and which furnish
subsistence to several countries of both hemispheres.
How much time hath elapsed before this parallel hath
been made ! Of what importance did fish appear
when compared with the gold which men went in
search of in the New World ? It was long before it
was understood that the representation of a thing is
not greater than the thing itself, and that a ship filled
with cod and a galleon are vessels equally laden with
gold. There is even this remarkable difference, that
mines can be exhausted, but never fisheries. Gold
is not reproductive; the fish are so incessantly."

The value of the fisheries was thoroughly appreciated in early times, and especially during the first half of the seventeenth century. It was this, indeed, that, under a mistaken view, led statesmen and merchants at home to use all the means in their power to discourage permanent settlement in the island. They desired that all the waters round about should be used only for fishing, and that the whole coast should be nothing but a curing-ground. In 1615, five thousand seamen, in 15,000 tons of shipping, collected 15,000 tons of fish. In 1644 the trade employed twice as many men, and was twice as profitable. In 1677 it was less than it had been in 1615, and in 1684 it had sunk very much lower. This decline was attributed to the evil influences of steady colonization. It was really due to the greater care taken of the trade by the French Government, and the facilities provided by it for the disposal of the produce. This has continued, and further hindrance has come to the exclusive use of the fisheries by England through the later competition of the

United States. Fishers from England and the inhabitants of Newfoundland carry on the trade with advantage; but their French and American rivals pursue it with yet greater zest under the encouragement of bounties which the English Government refuses to give.

The same causes have hindered the development of the other resources of Newfoundland. Until near the beginning of the present century, the internal wealth of the island was almost entirely neglected, and its agricultural and manufacturing pursuits are capable of very much further extension, in spite of all that has hitherto been done. Having an area of 40,200 square miles, its coast-line is almost the only part that has as yet been put to use.

That coast-line, indented by numberless bays, harbours, coves, and creeks, has not much beauty to recommend it, and St John's is the only important town to be seen along the whole of its rugged course. The other towns are chiefly haunts for the collection, preparation, and re-shipment of the cod, seal, and herring, that furnish a livelihood to most of the inhabitants. Cod, and its oil, form more than half their exports; and most of the other half consists of seal-oil and seal-skins.

Seal-hunting is the most hazardous pursuit of the people. "The vessels," we read, "are from 60 to 150 tons, with crews of from sixteen to thirty men each, provided with firearms to kill the seal, and poles to defend the vessels from the pressure of the ice. In the beginning of March the crews of the vessels collect on the ice with hatchets and saws, and cut two lines in the frozen surface, wide enough apart to allow their schooners to pass. After the thick flakes have been sawn or cut through, they have to be pushed beneath the firm ice with long poles. The vessels then get out to sea, if possible, through the openings, and work their perilous way to windward of the vast fields of ice, until they arrive at one covered with the animals of which they are in quest, and which is termed a seal-meadow. The seals are attacked by the fishers, or, more properly speaking, hunters, with firearms, or generally with short, heavy batons, a blow of which on the nose is instantly fatal. The hooded seals sometimes draw their hoods, which are shot-proof, over their heads. The large ones frequently turn on the men, especially when they have young ones beside them, and the piteous cries and moans of the latter are truly distressing to those who are not accustomed to the immense slaughter which is attended with so great a profit. The skins, with the fat surrounding the bodies, are stripped off together, and the carcases left on the ice. The pelts or scalps are carried to the vessels, whose situation, during a tempest, is attended with fearful danger. Many have been known to be crushed to pieces by the ice closing on them. Storms during the dark night, among vast icebergs, can only be imagined by a person who has been on a lee shore in a gale of wind; but the hardy seal-hunters seem to court such hazardous adventures."[1]

Less perilous is the calling of the cod-fisher. This is of two sorts. The deep-sea fishery is conducted chiefly by vessels from Europe which come for the season. The shore-fishery is in the hands of the

[1] Martin, vol. i. p. 333.

resident population. "An immense number of boats of different descriptions are engaged in the shore-fishery; punts, skiffs, jacks or jackasses, western boats and shallops, employing from one to seven men each, according to their size and the distance they may have to sail before they reach their respective fishing-grounds. The punts and small boats are generally manned by two persons, and employed in fishing within a very short distance of the harbours or circles to which they belong. The skiffs, carrying three or four hands, proceed to more distant stations, sometimes twenty or thirty miles. The western boats are larger than skiffs, and usually fish off the entrance of St Mary's Bay. The shallops are still larger craft. The punts and skiffs, constituting what is termed a 'mosquito fleet,' start at the earliest dawn of day, and proceed to the fishing-grounds, where the cod are expected in great abundance, for at certain seasons they congregate and swim in shoals. These boats generally land their cargoes at the 'stage' at least once a day. The western boats and shallops split and salt their fish abroad, and return to their respective harbours when they have expended all their salt or loaded their craft. The 'stage' is erected on posts, and juts out into the sea, far enough to allow the boats to come to its extremity, for the ready discharge of their cargoes. On the same platform is the salt-house, which is provided with one or more tables, around which are placed wooden seats and leathern aprons for the cut-throats, headers, and splitters. The fish having been thrown from the boats, a man is generally employed to pitch them with a pike from the stage on to the table before the cut-throat, who rips open the bowels, and, having also nearly severed the head from the body, passes it along the table to his right-hand neighbour, the header, whose business is to pull off the head and tear out the entrails. From them he selects the liver, and in some instances the sound. The head and entrails being precipitated through a trunk into a flat-bottomed boat placed under the stage, and taken to the shore for manure, the liver is thrown into a cask exposed to the sun, where it distils itself into oil, and the remaining blubber is boiled to procure an oil of inferior quality. After having undergone this operation, the cod is next passed across the table to the splitter, who, in the twinkling of an eye, cuts out the backbone as low as the navel. For the next process the cod are carried in hand-barrows to the salter, by whom they are spread in layers upon the top of each other, with a proper quantity of salt between each layer. In this state the fish continue for a few days, when they are again taken in barrows to a square wooden trough, full of holes, which is suspended from the stage head in the sea. The washer stands up to his knees in this trough, and rubs the salt and slime off the cod with a soft mop. It is then taken to a convenient spot and piled up to drain. On the following day or two it is removed to the fish-flakes, and there spread in the sun to dry, being piled up in small faggots at night. When sufficiently dried, the cod are stored up in warehouses, ready for exportation."[1] In 1867, 815,038 quintals of cod-fish, thus cured, were exported.

[1] Martin, vol. I. pp. 334, 335.

CHAPTER VII.

FRENCH NORTH AMERICA.

THE FRENCH IN NORTH AMERICA—THE COLONY OF NEW FRANCE—
SAMUEL CHAMPLAIN—THE PROGRESS OF THE COLONY—WARS
WITH THE INDIANS AND THE ENGLISH—THE CONTESTS BE-
TWEEN THE ENGLISH AND FRENCH COLONISTS—THE ENGLISH
CONQUESTS OF NOVA SCOTIA, CAPE BRETON, AND CANADA.
[1524-1760.]

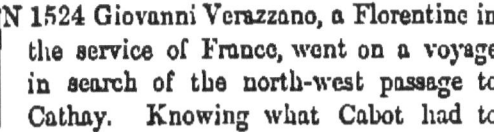

IN 1524 Giovanni Verazzano, a Florentine in the service of France, went on a voyage in search of the north-west passage to Cathay. Knowing what Cabot had to find out for himself, that America stood in the way, he sailed across the Atlantic to the west of Carolina, intending thence to follow the northward course of the shore. This he did, making curious acquaintance with the natives whom he passed, until he reached Nova Scotia. There, rightly judging that he had already made discoveries of sufficient importance, he abandoned his first intention, and, passing the eastern side of Newfoundland, he returned to France. His proposal that all this great territory should at once be appropriated by King Francis I. was not adopted; but ten years afterwards, in 1534, Francis sent out another exploring expedition under Jaques Cartier. Cartier first visited Newfoundland, and nearly circumnavigated it; and then passed through the Gulf of St Lawrence into Chaleur Bay, so named by him because of the summer heat which he found there. On its shore he erected "a fair high cross," from which was suspended a shield marked with a fleur-de-lys, and the words, "Vive le Roi de la France," in token that the country was henceforth the property of his master. Going home in the autumn, he was next year sent to prosecute his discoveries. He entered the St Lawrence river, and, passing the site of Quebec, proceeded to a hill from which he had so fair a prospect of the surrounding country that he called it Mont-Royal, now Montreal. Hearing the natives talk of their "canada," or huts, he supposed that to be the name of the country. On his return to France he urged its immediate colonization. To that, however, Francis I. did not consent, and after two feeble efforts made by a French nobleman, the Seigneur de Roberval, Canada was undisturbed by Europeans for more than fifty years.

But it was not forgotten. In 1598 Henry IV. sent a party of convicts, under the Marquis de la Roche, to explore and colonize New France, as Canada was then styled. They seem not to have gone so far, but, halting at Sable Island, near Nova Scotia, to have there lived miserably, until seven years afterwards, when, in pity for their state, the survivors, twelve in number, were allowed to go back to France. Before that, in 1600, King Henry had granted a patent for the more orderly colonization of the North American continent, and in 1603 an expedition was sent out under the guidance of the famous Samuel Champlain. That expedition was only planned for exploring the country. Champlain proceeded to the St Lawrence river and tracked its course as far as

Montreal, whither Cartier had gone long before, and went home with a report of his observations in the same year. In 1604 he went out again with a small colonizing party, of which the Sieur de Monts was appointed governor; "all New France," says the chronicler, "being contained in two ships."

They went, not to the mouth of the St Lawrence, but to the districts a little south of it, now known as Nova Scotia, and there they wandered about for some time, exploring all the country and making a place which they called Port Royal, now Annapolis, the centre of their investigations. A simple little colony grew up under the wise management of Champlain, who, while De Monts was in France, to which he returned to arrange for extension of the colony, was its chief director. The task of providing food for the company was each day assigned in turn to one of the number. "We had ordinarily," they said, "as good cheer as we could have at La Rue aux Ours of Paris, and at far less charges, for there was none but two days before his time came was careful to go a hunting and fishing, and brought some dainty thing besides that which was our ordinary allowance. When March came, the best disposed among us did strive who should best till the ground, and make gardens to sow in them. It was a marvellous pleasure to see them daily grow up, and yet greater contentment to use thereof so abundantly as we did."[1]

After four years thus pleasantly spent in exploration and deliberation, the site of Quebec—the Indian name of a strait—was fixed upon as the chief station. Champlain went home for two more ship-loads of

[1] Churchill, "Collection of Voyages."

people and stores, and returned, as lieutenant-governor of the colony, in July 1608. His first care was to divide the land, to see that it was suitably cleared and built upon, and to make sure of provisions for the winter; his second, to be friends with the neighbouring Indians. This policy led him to assist the Algenquins in war with the Iroquois, when he won a battle with a single gun-shot. The shot killed two chiefs and wounded another; whereupon, terrified by the new sight and sound, and by the instant falling of the leaders, the enemy fled. Slowly and steadily the colony advanced under the wise oversight of Champlain. Missionaries and more settlers came. Some of the idle colonists showed an inclination to mutiny, and made violent efforts to bring Champlain into disgrace with the French king. Though these were unsuccessful, they led to embarrassment by causing the appearance of a rival party of colonists. But Champlain quickly overcame all difficulties. He succeeded in amalgamating the two parties. He sent back to France those settlers who refused to work. He formed alliances with the friendly native tribes. Hostile tribes he checked by his firm dealing, at the cost of very little blood. On one occasion he was offered, by way of hostage, three young girls to bring up as he chose. He accepted the gift, and they became almost the first Indian converts to Christianity. One of them soon died; but the other two he carefully educated, and learned to love as daughters.

In that prudent way the colony of New France, or Acadie, the first European settlement in the northern parts of the American continent, was begun. But troubles soon arose to hinder its progress, although by them fresh attention was attracted to the work, and thus it was ultimately helped on.

Many of the first colonists were Huguenots. In 1627 the whole enterprise was intrusted to a new and Catholic association, styled the Company of One Hundred Partners, which, under the direction of Cardinal Richelieu, Louis XIII.'s great minister, made its first great object the conversion of the North American Indians to Christianity; its second, the extension of commerce, and especially of the fur trade. Jesuits were sent out as spiritual guides of the enterprise, and "Protestants and other heretics and Jews" were rigidly excluded.

Champlain had only commenced to reorganize his colony in accordance with these arrangements, when a much greater embarrassment arose. The proceedings of the French in North America were jealously regarded by the English, who, though they had hitherto been content with prosecuting the Newfoundland fisheries, regarded the whole region as their own by right of John Cabot's discovery. In 1614 the governor of Virginia sent a force to Nova Scotia, and there captured and destroyed the little settlement at Port Royal, which Champlain had first established. As nothing more was done at that time, and as the French colonists were then prospering in their new home at Quebec, they were not much disturbed by that action. But in 1621, Sir William Alexander obtained from James I. a grant of the whole peninsula in which Port Royal had been constructed, and which, as it was to be colonized by Scotchmen, was now for the first time styled Nova

Scotia, and, to aid his project, a distinct body of gentry, the baronets of Nova Scotia, was organized in 1625 by Charles I., each baronet receiving 16,000 acres of land, and being bound to send out six men to the colony. Alexander at first contented himself with driving out all the French still resident in the peninsula; but in 1628 he sent David Kirk, a French Protestant refugee of Scottish origin, to invade Quebec. He entered the St Lawrence with a small fleet and summoned Champlain to surrender. Champlain replied that "he was sure Kirk would respect him much more for defending himself, than for abandoning his charge without first making trial of the English guns and batteries," and that he would wait his attack. But the failure of supplies, both in food and powder, reduced the garrison of Quebec to such extremities, that, when Kirk returned in the following year, Champlain was forced to abandon the settlement without a struggle. He returned to France, and for three years Quebec was in the hands of the English.

In 1633, however, by the treaty of St Germains, between Charles I. and Louis XIII., Quebec and all the disputed territory, from Cape Breton into the unknown west, was ceded to France, and Champlain went back to the settlement for which he had done so much. He died in 1635, having fairly earned the title, given him by comrades and successors, of Father of the Colony. Acadie, or New France, as the whole territory was again called, then revived, although destined to be the scene of frequent strife between the rival nations for a hundred and fifty years more.

Troubles also came from the Indians, whose rights were by no means so well respected as they had been by Champlain, though even he had at last found it impossible to abstain from mixing in their quarrels, and so, while receiving the friendship of some, meeting with vindictive opposition from others. The fur trade, from which the French settlers derived most of their profit, brought them into intimate relations with the natives, and, besides the legitimate barter, they soon acquired the habit of exacting from those tribes whom they protected, as well as from those they conquered, a heavy tribute in skins. Thus they made for themselves sullen friends and open enemies, ready to use the endless opportunities that occurred for revenging upon individuals the injuries that they received from the whole community.

Gradually encroaching upon the native territories, and, in spite the frequent loss of life and property which they incurred at the hands of the Indians, growing steadily in numbers and influence, the French sought to extend their dominion in a southerly as well as in a westerly direction. With the English settlements on the coast they dared not interfere; but from Montreal, which was founded as an European town in 1644, as well as from Quebec and the intervening forts, they made numerous raids towards the south in the interior, aiming to carry the limits of New France down to the Mississippi. There they over and over again came into collision with the English, who, also seeking to obtain furs from the natives, went westward too, and considered that the St Lawrence and the great lakes connected with it formed the narrowest boundary proper to New

England. Thus the barrier-line became an endless subject of dispute, and a cause of private warfare, to which the peace existing between the two nations in Europe yielded no restraint. A curious instance of the aggressive spirit encouraged among the French colonists by Louis XIV. and his bold ministers, Richelieu and Colbert, is in the charter granted in 1662 to a new West Indian Company, as it was styled, which was to try and win possession of all the best parts of both North and South America, as well as the neighbouring islands, from the Amazon up to Hudson's Bay, and, in fact, of every region and country, "so far as the said Company may be able to penetrate, whether the countries may now appertain to France, as being or having been occupied by Frenchmen, or in so far as the said Company shall establish itself by exterminating or conquering the natives or colonists of such European nations as are not our allies."

The French West India Company did not long have authority over the colonists of Canada; but the colonists readily adopted the policy of "extermination or conquest" on which it was founded. In 1678, one named La Salle started an organized scheme for penetrating south. After two years of preparation, he proceeded westward as far as the Mississippi, and gradually passed down its course till he reached its mouth, in the Bay of Mexico. Of the adjoining country he took possession in the name of his sovereign, in whose honour he called it Louisiana. He also set up a fort in Florida. Soon after that his men mutinied, and put him to death; but others carried on his ambitious project.

Alliances were formed with the Illinois and other Indian tribes near the Mississippi, and a fierce war was waged between these allies and the Iroquois and other tribes, whom the English colonists on the coast befriended. With the Illinois on their side, the French found they had raised up an opposition too formidable to be properly withstood; and when, in 1689, the Illinois made peace with the Iroquois, and all the Indians became partisans of the English interest, they were in imminent danger of themselves falling victims to the "extermination and conquest" which they designed for others. In desperation, Frontignac, then governor of Quebec, planned an expedition for the capture of New York and the neighbouring settlements of the English. As a counter move the people of New York and New England sent an army, under General Winthrop, for the conquest of Nova Scotia. Both expeditions failed, but others were entered upon, until, both French and English being wearied out by their previous strife, there was for a time a cessation of hostilities. The greater strength of the English in America, however, keeping pace with the successes of the mother-country in Europe, caused a serious crippling of the projects of their colonial enemies. By the Treaty of Utrecht, in 1713, besides the abandonment of the French claims to Newfoundland, which has been referred to, Nova Scotia, or Acadie, was given up to the English, and all schemes for the extension of French sovereignty along the Mississippi were declared to be unlawful. New France was thus restricted to the regions then and still known as Canada. The restriction was not permanent, and the lack of any proper definition of the boundaries left room for future quarrel, but for a time there was peace.

New France had suffered greatly from the ambition of its colonists and their governors. During the peace time it made rapid progress. "In 1720," we are told, "Quebec had a population of about 7000, and Montreal of 3000. Nineteen vessels cleared from Quebec, laden with peltries, lumber, tar, tobacco, flour, and pork, and four men-of-war were built in the colony. Part of the upper and lower towns of Quebec had been built, but the adjacent shores and islands were still covered with forests. The society generally was described as gay and sociable, consisting chiefly of military men and the lower order of noblesse, all poor and likely to continue so, being much better adapted for practising the most agreeable ways of spending money than the more laborious methods of making it. They saw their English neighbours steadily employed in accumulating wealth, but consoled themselves with the reflection that they did not know how to enjoy it. Their favourite employment was the fur-trade, the only one indeed at all adapted to their excitable natures and desultory habits; but the little fortunes they occasionally made thereby were compared by the traveller who visited them to the hillocks of sand in the deserts of Africa, which rise and disappear almost at the same moment. Below Quebec the banks of the St Lawrence were laid out in tolerably cultivated seigniories. Trois Rivières then contained only 800 inhabitants. The city of Montreal was rapidly extending, and was in a great degree protected from the incursions of hostile Indians by villages inhabited by friendly tribes. Above Montreal there were only detached stations for defence and barter with the natives. Fort Cataraqui, or Frontenal, on Lake Ontario, appears to have stood in the midst of an uncultivated country, without any settlements in its vicinity. At Niagara a cottage was dignified with the name of a fort, and guarded by a few French officers and soldiers."[1]

That moderate prosperity, and all the care taken by the colonists for their solid advancement in ways of agriculture and commerce, was chiefly due to the wise government of the Marquis de Vaudreuil, who died in 1725, after ruling in Canada for twenty-two years. His successor, the Marquis de Beauharnois, was of more ambitious temperament, and under him new quarrels with the English were provoked. They were of no great importance, until they were aggravated by the outbreak of fresh war between England and France in 1744. In 1745 Cape Breton, a valuable island which had remained in the hands of the French after the surrender of the neighbouring mainland of Nova Scotia, was taken by a naval force from Britain, aided by New England troops; and in 1746 and 1747 the French sought to recover both it and Nova Scotia. By the treaty of Aix-la-Chapelle, in 1748, Cape Breton was restored, and Nova Scotia was left in English hands; but the spirit of opposition thus revived between the rival colonists could not be wholly stayed by European treaties. The old antagonism as to the possession of the basin of the Mississippi, and the adjoining districts, again became formidable, and they were augmented by a new governor of

[1] Martin, vol. i. p. 10.

Canada, the Marquis du Quesne, who arrived in 1752; and the violence of his successor, another Marquis de Vaudreuil, sent out in 1755, led to the final overthrow of his government and of the authority of France in North America.

The Pennsylvanians had carried on a lively trade in furs with the Iroquois who resided between Lakes Michigan and Erie, until the importance of the trade led to the planning of the separate settlement of Ohio. That movement provoked the jealousy of the Canadians, who asserted their right to the territory, and proceeded to maintain their title by force of arms. Thus war began again. Du Quesne built a fort, which bore his own name; and the English erected a Fort Necessity, very near to it, which George Washington, then learning his work as a soldier and a patriot, was sent to defend. This he did, until, in an attack on Fort du Quesne, he was unsuccessful, and then he had to capitulate.

Good came out of this defeat, however, as it helped to arouse English interest in the dispute. A strong force was organized and sent out, in January 1755, under General Braddock, who, detaching a part of his army for work in other quarters, led the rest into Ohio, with Washington as his second in command. There he was mortally wounded and his army defeated. Other defeats followed. The English soldiers, ill adapted for the new ways of fighting in which they had to engage, and often at variance with the colonial militias, proved at first unable to cope with the Canadians, who had been reinforced by a large body of troops from France. Not till 1758, when Pitt had sent out another strong force for the assistance of the colonists, were they able to withstand the encroachments of the enemy.

Then, however, the tide turned. Sir Ralph Abercrombie, as commander-in-chief, found himself at the head of an army of 50,000 men, and able to make three separate and formidable attacks upon the French in Canada, and the outlying districts which they had begun to regard as their own. The first, under General Amherst, with James Wolfe as his chief assistant, was sent to capture Cape Breton, and this was soon done through the skill and boldness of Wolfe. The second, led by Abercrombie against the enemy's forts in the basin of the Mississippi, was less successful, but it served to hinder the French from making any fresh encroachments in that direction. The third, in which Washington was employed, with General Forbes for chief, was directed against Fort du Quesne, which was easily captured, and the whole Ohio district was thus restored to the English.

In these ways the summer of 1758 was well employed. In 1759 yet bolder work was done. Three separate armies were again organized, and each achieved the task assigned to it. By one the Mississippi region was secured; and by another Fort Niagara was captured, and the French were thus driven north of the St Lawrence. But the exploits of the third army were more memorable.

It was commanded by General Wolfe, who, though then only thirty-three years old, had been intrusted with the most difficult work of all. He was to make himself master of Quebec, and thus expel the French from their central stronghold. "Before the city, more strongly fortified by nature than by art, could be attacked," says his biographer, " a vast theatre, exceeding thirty miles in extent, and embracing both sides of a prodigious river, had to be occupied by an army numbering not quite 7000 men. Within view of a much superior force, in a hostile country, and surrounded by prowling savages, it was necessary that distinct operations should be carried on by several detachments; but distant though these detachments were, Wolfe, by his constant presence as well as by his master-mind, so directed them that they acted with all the unity of a single battalion. Between the invaders and the only weak side of the city lay a defensive army, surrounded by impregnable entrenchments, and commanded by a cautious and hitherto successful general; but Wolfe, by his unwearied vigilance and his untiring perseverance, at length beguiled his unwilling adversary to meet him in the open field."[1] " In this contest, with so many difficulties, one may say with nature itself," said Burke, " the genius of the commander showed itself superior to everything, all the dispositions were so many masterpieces in the art of war."

Wolfe, with whom acted a fleet of twenty sail of the line, landed on the isle of Orleans, overlooking Quebec, at the end of June 1759. The French army of about 13,000 men, commanded by the Marquis de Montcalm, was quartered partly in the lower town, on the bank of the river, partly in the upper town, built on a hill to the westward, partly on the fortified heights stretching eastward as far as the Falls of Montmorency. Wolfe occupied Point Levi, on the south side of the St Lawrence, exactly oppo-

[1] Wright, " Life of Major-General James Wolfe."

site to Quebec, with a portion of his army, which he instructed to bombard the town. This was unsuccessful, and he himself failed in an attempt to seize the entrenchments at Montmorency, when 182 of his men were killed, and 650 wounded. Further action was delayed by a fever which threatened to remove him before his work was done, and he had, in July, to transport most of his troops to Point Levi, leaving only a garrison on the isle of Orleans. He was still weak, and no immediate movement was expected by the enemy, when, shortly after midnight of the 12th of September, he stealthily embarked his army in flat-bottomed boats and followed the tide as far as a convenient landing-place on the northern shore, now known as Wolfe's Cove. Thence he marched along a rocky path, and by day-break was on the Plains of Abraham, above Quebec, and in the rear of the army of De Montcalm. The French general, as Wolfe had anticipated, thought that only a part of the English army had thus approached, and went recklessly to punish the impudent intruders. At ten o'clock the armies met, Wolfe's being carefully and compactly arranged for the battle, De Montcalm's in some confusion and widely spread out. No English shot was fired till the nearest French were within forty yards of their assailants. Then volley succeeded volley, while Wolfe himself headed a bayonet charge. Twice he was wounded without abandoning his place as leader of the attack. A third and mortal wound made it impossible for him to hold up any longer. "Support me," he whispered to one near him, "let not my brave soldiers see me drop. The day is ours: keep it!" He was taken to the rear and a surgeon was called. "It is needless," he said, "it's all over with me." They thought it was even then all over with him, when some soldiers were heard shouting, "They run! they run!" Wolfe started up, and asked in a leaden whisper, "Who runs?" "The enemy, sir," was the answer; "they give way everywhere." "God be praised!" he said. "One of you run to Colonel Barton, and tell him to march with all speed down to Charles River, and cut off the retreat of the fugitives. I die in peace."

The exploit by which he died won Canada for Great Britain. Quebec speedily capitulated. The English who had occupied it were feebly besieged by the enemy in the following spring; but an English fleet drove them off, and taking refuge in Montreal, they were there surrounded on the 8th of September 1760 by all the three branches of the British army. On the same day they tendered their submission, and before night-time the whole of New France was formally surrendered to England. That surrender was confirmed by the treaty of peace signed in Paris in 1762.

CHAPTER VIII.

NOVA SCOTIA AND NEW BRUNSWICK.

THE FRENCH SETTLERS IN NOVA SCOTIA—THEIR BANISHMENT IN 1755—PROGRESS OF NOVA SCOTIA, CAPE BRETON, AND NEW BRUNSWICK UNDER THE ENGLISH—A FIRE IN NEW BRUNSWICK —PRINCE EDWARD'S ISLAND. [1755-1861.]

NOVA Scotia or Acadie, as we have seen, having been colonized by the French in 1604, was in 1614 conquered by the English, and in 1621 assigned by James I. to Sir William Alexander and his baronets of Nova Scotia. In 1667 it was given back to France, and in 1713 it was again and finally transferred to Great Britain, although, for nearly half a century more, a frequent source of contest between the two nations.

By General Nicholson, the first British governor, the French residents, then numbering nearly 10,000, were allowed to remain in peaceable occupation of their homes and property, and this notwithstanding the refusal of most of them to abandon their allegiance to the crown of France. Forty years afterwards they had increased to about 17,000 or 18,000, the British settlers being only some 5000. The presence of so great a majority of aliens, all whose sympathies were with the Canadians, who were then attempting to regain the colony, was a not unreasonable cause of alarm to the subjects of George III.; and as, in 1755,

they erected forts, and in various ways sought to aid
their countrymen in a new project for reconquest,
they were in that year violently removed by the
English authorities, and distributed over the colonies
of New England, New York, and Virginia. Only
after the transfer of all the French North American
territories to Great Britain in 1760 were these unfortunate people permitted to return to their homes, and
then solely on condition of their avowing themselves
British subjects. About a sixth of the number availed
themselves of the permission. Their sufferings, for
which, it must be admitted, that they or their leaders
were alone responsible, has been told in the pathetic
poem of "Evangeline," which, if it uses pardonable
licence in concealing the offences of many of the
French settlers, in no way exaggerates the virtues of
some and the troubles of all. Picturesque, and doubtless true, is its portrayal of the homely life of the
more quiet of their number—

"In the Acadian land, on the shores of the Basin of Minas,
Distant, secluded, still, the little village of Grand-Pré
Lay in the fruitful valley. Vast meadows stretched to the eastward,
Giving the village its name, and pasture to flocks without number.
Dikes, that the hands of the farmers had raised with labour incessant,
Shut out the turbulent tides; but at stated seasons the floodgates
Opened, and welcomed the sea to wander at will o'er the meadows.
West and south there were fields of flax, and orchards and cornfields,
Spreading afar and unfenced o'er the plain; and away to the northward
Blomidon rose, and the forests old, and aloft on the mountains
Sea-fogs pitched their tents, and mists from the mighty Atlantic
Looked on the happy valley, but ne'er from their station descended.

There, in the midst of its farms, reposed the Acadian village.
Strongly built were the houses, with frames of oak and chestnut,
Such as the peasants of Normandy built in the reign of the Henries.
Thatched were the roofs, with dormer-windows; and gables projecting
Over the basement below protected and shaded the doorway.
There, in the tranquil evenings of summer, when brightly the sunset
Lighted the village street, and gilded the vanes on the chimneys,
Matrons and maidens sat in snow-white caps and in kirtles,
Scarlet and blue and green, with distaffs spinning the golden
Flax for the gossiping looms, whose noisy shuttles within doors
Mingled their sound with the whirr of the wheels, and the songs of the maidens.
Solemnly down the street came the parish priest; and the children
Paused in their play to kiss the hand he extended to bless them.
Reverend walked he among them; and up rose matrons and maidens,
Hailing his slow approach with words of affectionate welcome.
Then came the labourers home from the field, and serenely the sun sank
Down to his rest, and twilight prevailed. Anon from the belfry
Softly the *Angelus* sounded, and over the roofs of the village
Columns of pale blue smoke, like clouds of incense ascending,
Rose from a hundred hearths, the homes of peace and contentment.
Thus dwelt together in love these simple Acadian farmers—
Dwelt in the love of God and of man. Alike were they free from
Fear, that reigns with the tyrant, and envy, the vice of republics.
Neither locks had they to their doors, nor bars to their windows;
But their dwellings were open as day and the hearts of the owners;
There the richest was poor, and the poorest lived in abundance."

If the Acadians who were exiled in 1755 did not all exhibit that pastoral simplicity and worth, it is clear that they formed, in the main, an estimable community. Their great fault, and a fault which the exigencies of the times made especially disastrous to them, was a keen aversion to the English, who had come to intrude upon their quiet life in "the forest primeval," where

> "The murmuring pines and the hemlocks,
> Bearded with moss and in garments green, indistinct in the twilight,
> Stand like Druids of old, with voices sad and prophetic,
> Stand like harpers hoar, with beards that rest on their bosoms."

Much of the same primitive character appertained to those who in 1761, and the ensuing years, returned to their desolated homes, and was by them bequeathed to their descendants, who still reside in the colony. Different in many respects were the new settlers from Britain. Of these settlers there were about 5000 in 1755. In 1764 they exceeded 10,000, and they continued rapidly to increase, being recruited not only from England, Scotland, and Ireland, but also from the more southern colonies, many of whose people preferred British rule to that of the newly constituted United States of America. In and near the year 1783 some 20,000 of these loyalists, as they were called, migrated to Nova Scotia. Most of the newcomers preferred town life and commerce to agricultural pursuits, and the colony throve greatly through their energy.

Of Acadie, and accordingly of Nova Scotia, during its early government by the English, the province now known as New Brunswick formed a part, and to the colony was added in 1758 the island of Cape Breton, then finally taken from the French. In the same year the military rule that had before prevailed was exchanged for a regular constitution, in which a governor, representing the British crown, presided over a Legislative Council and a House of Assembly, modelled to some extent from the two estates of the English Parliament. This constitution was somewhat modified by increase of the functions of the House of Assembly, and of the number of its members, on the accession of George IV. in 1820.

Before that the limits of Nova Scotia had been curtailed. In 1784 New Brunswick, which then contained about 12,000 inhabitants, was made a separate colony. Cape Breton was also treated in the same way, but in 1629 it was restored to the province of Nova Scotia, of which it still forms a part.

In the subsequent history of the two colonies there is little that need be here recorded. Both have grown steadily in wealth and population. In Nova Scotia, then including New Brunswick and Cape Breton, there were in 1764 only about 13,000 residents, both English and French. In 1772 the inhabitants numbered more than 19,000. In 1783 they exceeded 32,000. In 1807 there were in Nova Scotia, exclusive of both Cape Breton and New Brunswick, about 65,000. In 1817 it contained 85,000, besides 14,000 more in Cape Breton. In 1827 the colonies, again united, contained upwards of 150,000. In 1847 the population amounted to nearly 200,000, and in 1861 it exceeded 330,000. The population of New Brunswick, numbering about 12,000 when it became a separate colony, had risen to 27,000 in 1803, to 35,000 in 1817, to 119,000 in 1834, to 156,000 in 1840, and to 250,000 in 1861.

To the natural resources of these colonies, and the advantages derived from them, reference will be hereafter made. Their progress has been in spite of occasional disasters, of which one striking instance may here be given. "The summer of 1825," said a resident of Newcastle, near Miramichi Bay, on the eastern coast of New Brunswick, "was unusually warm in both hemispheres, particularly in America, where its effects were fatally visible in the prevalence of epidemic disorders. During July and August extensive fires raged in different parts of Nova Scotia, especially in the eastern division of the peninsula. The protracted drought of the summer, acting upon the aridity of the forests, had rendered them more than naturally combustible; and this, facilitating both the dispersion and the progress of the fires that appeared in the early part of the season, produced an unusual warmth. On the 6th of October the fire was evidently approaching Newcastle. At different intervals fitful blazes and flashes were observed to issue from different parts of the woods. Many persons heard the crackling of falling trees and shrivelled branches, while a hoarse rumbling noise, not dissimilar to the roaring of distant thunder, and divided by pauses, like the intermittent discharges of artillery, was distinctly audible. On the 17th of October the heat became very oppressive, and at about twelve o'clock a pale sickly mist emerged from the forest and settled over it. This cloud soon retreated before a large dark one, which, occupying its place, wrapped the firmament in a pall of vapour, and the heat became tormentingly sultry. A stupifying dulness seemed to pervade every place but the woods, which trembled and rustled and shook with an incessant and thrilling noise of explosions, rapidly following each other. The whole country appeared to be encircled by a fiery zone. A little after four o'clock an immense pillar of smoke rose in a vertical direction, at some distance northwest of Newcastle, and the sky was absolutely blackened by this huge cloud; but a light northerly breeze springing up, it gradually distended and then dispersed in a variety of shapeless mists. About an hour after, innumerable large spires of smoke, issuing from different parts of the woods, and illuminated by flames, mounted to the sky. The river, tortured into violence by the hurricane, foamed with rage, and flung its boiling spray upon the land. The thunder pealed along the vault of heaven: the lightning appeared to rend the firmament. For a moment all was still. A deep, awful silence reigned over everything. All nature appeared to be hushed, when suddenly a lengthened and sullen roar came booming through the forest, driving a thousand massive and devouring flames before it. Then Newcastle, and Douglastown, and the whole northern side of the river, extending from Bartibog to the Naashwaap, a distance of more than a hundred miles in length, became enveloped in an immense sheet of flame that spread over nearly six thousand square miles. That the stranger may form a faint idea of desolation and misery which no pen can describe, he must picture to himself a large and rapid river, thickly settled for a hundred miles or more, with four thriving towns, two on each side of it, and then reflect that these towns and settlements were all composed of wooden houses, stores, stables, and barns, and that the barns and stables were filled with crops, and that the arrival of the fall importations had stocked the warehouses and stores with spirits, powder, and a variety of combustible articles, as well as with the necessary supplies for the approaching winter. He must then remember that the settlement formed a long narrow stripe, about a quarter of a mile wide, lying between the river and almost interminable forests, stretching along the very edge of its precincts and all around it, and he will have some idea of the extent, features, and general circumstances of country which, in the course of a few hours, was suddenly enveloped in fire. A more ghastly picture of human misery cannot well be imagined. Nothing broke upon the ear but the accents of distress. The eye saw nothing but ruin and desolation and death. Newcastle, yesterday a flourishing town containing nearly a thousand inhabitants, was now a heap of smoking ruins, and Douglastown was reduced to the same miserable condition. Of two hundred and sixty houses and storehouses in the former, but twelve remained. Of seventy in the latter, only six were left. The confusion on board a hundred and fifty large vessels, then lying in the Miramichi and exposed to imminent danger, was terrible; some burnt to the water's edge, others burning, and the remainder occasionally on fire. Dispersed groups of half-naked, half-famished, and homeless creatures, all more or less injured in their persons—many lamenting the loss of property, children or relations—were wandering through the country. Upwards of five hundred human beings perished. Domestic animals of all kinds lay dead and dying in different parts of the country. Thousands of wild beasts, too, had been destroyed in the woods. Property to the extent of nearly a quarter of a million was wasted."[1]

[1] Martin, vol. i. pp. 222, 223.

Not far from the scene of that terrible conflagration, in the Gulf of St Lawrence and between New Brunswick and Cape Breton, is Prince Edward's Island, which, for a brief period, was also part of the colony of Nova Scotia. It had been little used by the French until the conquest of Acadie by Great Britain, when many settlers crossed the narrow strait. In 1758, however, it also fell into the hands of the English, and its inhabitants, like their brethren on the mainland, were expelled. In 1763 it was incorporated with Nova Scotia; but in 1770 it was made a separate province in fulfilment of a curious plan of colonization. It was parcelled out in sixty-seven townships, and these were distributed by lottery among the creditors of the English Government, each of whom was bound to lodge a settler in every lot of two hundred acres that fell to him. The experiment was not at first very successful, but gradually the shares in the island passed from the original speculators to men who knew how to use the rich soil and unusually healthy climate of the island. In 1802 it contained 20,651 inhabitants, of whom about half were Scotch, and a quarter French. In 1821 the population was 24,600; in 1841 it was 47,034; and in 1861 it was 80,857.

CHAPTER IX.

CANADA.

THE HISTORY OF CANADA UNDER BRITISH RULE—THE FIRST AMERICAN WAR—INTERNAL TROUBLES—THE FRENCH AND ENGLISH CANADIANS—THE SECOND AMERICAN WAR—FRESH DOMESTIC DIFFICULTIES—THE REBELLIONS OF 1837 AND 1838—LORD DURHAM'S SERVICES TO THE COLONY—ITS LATER HISTORY—THE CANADIAN CONFEDERATION. [1760-1867.]

THE surrender of Canada to Great Britain, in 1760, did not bring peace to the colony. Its French inhabitants, about 60,000 in number, with some 8000 converted Indians among them, were allowed to remain; but they were suddenly called upon to submit themselves to English law, as interpreted and perverted by a few regimental officers, and a few traders from Britain and the older colonies. The latter did not then number more than 500, and their efforts to lay violent hands on all the richest portions of the colony, and their harsh treatment of the earlier residents, strengthened the ill-feeling natural in a conquered race. The first step towards the removal of this was made in the "Quebec Bill" of 1774, which confirmed the possessions of the French occupants, and preserved to them their civil rights and customs, on condition of their taking an oath of allegiance to the British Crown, which was framed so as to be no more distasteful to them than could be helped.

Fresh troubles, however, were in store, both for them and for the English settlers among them. Discontent at the policy shown towards them by the Home Government had long prevailed in the minds of the English colonists south of the St Lawrence, and the threatened rupture between them and the mother country, deferred in order that their common force might be exerted against the encroachments of the Canadians, received fresh strength from the new jealousies that sprang up in the course of the Canadian war. No sooner was that war over than the indignant colonists began to claim better treatment from the British Government. The unwise answers given to those reasonable claims led to bolder assertions on the part of the colonists, which were met by more foolish replies from home. Thus the great American War of Independence was brought about, blood being first shed at the Battle of Lexington in 1775, which ended in England's loss of her richest colonies, and their establishment as the United States of America.

The Canadians were asked by the first Congress of the States to join in the revolution, or, at any rate, to be neutral during the war. But the sometime French on the north of the St Lawrence had no sympathy with the sometime English on the south. They welcomed the crowd of loyalists, as they were called, who, crossing the river, came to continue their allegiance to the British Crown in Quebec and Montreal; and prompt measures were taken to renew the defences of the border, and to support the mother-country in her efforts to suppress the revolution. Old Canadians, who had done battle with British troops, now prepared to fight by their side, and colonial loyalists, who had lately taken part with their brethren in the conquest of Canada, now made ready to turn their arms against their former comrades.

Seeing that thus a formidable enemy was growing up, and believing that, if they could get possession of the northern districts, many of its people would be friendly to them, and all could be soon subdued, the champions of independence quickly resolved upon the invasion of Canada. A force of 4000 men, in two divisions, set out upon this enterprise in the autumn of 1775. The main division, under General Montgomery, was at first very successful. Chambly, St John's, and Montreal, in turn attacked by Montgomery, soon yielded to him. But Benedict Arnold, at the head of the other division, fared ill in his attempt upon Quebec. Scant provisions and bad weather caused trouble on the march, and the garrison of Quebec held out till it was reinforced by fugitives from Montreal and the other captured forts. The conquerors of these forts passed down the St Lawrence to aid their comrades; and thus, in December, the whole besieging force was united, under Montgomery, to attack Quebec, in which nearly all the defenders of the colony were congregated. They were not thought very formidable. Only 900 British troops were there, and it was thought that the civilians under arms could easily be turned from their allegiance. But they were firm and brave. On the 8th of December, Montgomery summoned the town to surrender. His flag was fired on, and his messengers were ignominiously expelled. After weaker efforts, Montgomery attempted, on the 31st, to surprise the town in a way similar to that in which, as a subordinate, he had shared with Wolfe sixteen years before. Like Wolfe, he fell a victim to his valour on the heights of Abraham. But there the likeness ended. The assailants, panic-struck at their loss, hastily retreated; and, in spite of the energy shown by Arnold, they refused to repeat the attack. They loitered in Canada and its neighbourhood for several months, and reinforcements came from New England. But reinforcements also came from Old England. The invaders were expelled, one after another, from Montreal and all the other ports which they had taken, and in September 1776 the wreck of the invading army went home to report that the attempt to conquer Canada was hopeless.

Canada also suffered much by this war, but its gains were greater through the increased strength which it received from Britain, and the steady tide of loyalist emigration that arrived from the south. Its defences were augmented and maintained until the close of the American war in 1783, when there was thought to be no further danger of invasion. In that year the population was more than twice as numerous as it had been at the beginning of English rule in 1760. The 60,000 or 70,000 French residents were associated with 60,000 or 70,000 English colonists and refugees from the United States.

Between these different races, however, no great friendship prevailed, and the differences were hardly removed by time. They prevailed almost without abatement, in 1837, when they were vigorously described by the Earl of Durham, then governor of the colony. "Among the people," he said, "the progress of emigration has introduced an English population, exhibiting the characteristics with which we are familiar as those of the most enterprising of every class of our countrymen. The circumstances of the early colonial administration excluded the native Canadian from power, and vested all offices of trust and emolument in the hands of strangers of English origin. The highest posts in the law are confided to the same class of persons. The functionaries of the civil government, together with the officers of the army, composed a kind of privileged class, occupying the first place in the community, and excluding the higher class of the natives from society, as well as from the government of their own country. It was not till within a very few years that this society of civil and military functionaries ceased to exhibit towards the highest order of Canadians an exclusiveness of demeanour which was more revolting to a sensitive and polite people, than the monopoly of power and profit; nor was this national favouritism discontinued until after repeated complaints and an angry contest, which had excited passions that commissions could not allay. The races had become enemies ere a tardy justice was extorted; and even then the Government discovered a mode of distributing its patronage among the Canadians, which was quite as offensive to that people as their previous exclusion." The same difference that prevailed among the wealthier and more high-born residents of Canada, divided the humbler members of society. "I do not believe," continued Lord Durham, "that the animosity which exists between the working classes of the two origins is the necessary result of a collision of interests, or of a jealousy of the superior success of English labour. But national prejudices naturally exercise the greatest influence over the most uneducated; the difference of language is less easily overcome; the differences of manners and customs are less easily appreciated. The labourers whom emigration introduced contained a number of very ignorant, turbulent, and demoralized persons, whose conduct and manners alike revolted the well-ordered and courteous natives of the same class. The working men naturally ranged themselves on the side of the educated and wealthy of their own countrymen. When once engaged in the conflict, their passions were less restrained by education and prudence; and the national hostility now rages most fiercely between those whose interests in reality bring them least into collision. The two races thus distinct have been brought into the same community, under circumstances which rendered their contact inevitably productive of collision. The difference of language from the first kept them asunder. It is not anywhere a virtue of the English race to look with complacency on any manners, customs, or laws which appear strange to them. Accustomed to form a high estimate of their own superiority, they take no pains to conceal from others their contempt and intolerance of their usages. They found the French Canadians filled with an equal amount of national pride, a sensitive but inactive pride, which disposes that people not to resent insult, but rather to hold aloof from those who would keep them under. The French could not but feel the superiority of English enterprise. They could not shut their eyes to their success in every undertaking in which they came in contact, nor to the constant advantage which they were acquiring. They looked upon their rivals with alarm, with jealousy, and finally with hatred. The English repaid them with a scorn which soon also assumed the form of hatred. The French complained of the arrogance and injustice of the English. The English accused the French of the vices of a weak and conquered people, and charged them with meanness and perfidy. The entire mistrust which the two races have thus learned to conceive of each other's intentions induces them to put the worst construction on the most innocent conduct, to judge every word, every act, every intention unfairly, to attribute the most odious designs, and to requite every overture of kindness or fairness as covering secret treachery and malignity. No common education has served to remove and soften the differences of origin and language. The associations of youth, the sports of childhood, and the studies by which the character of manhood is modified, are totally distinct. In Montreal and Quebec there are English schools and French schools. The children in these are accustomed to fight nation against nation, and the quarrels that arise among boys in the streets usually exhibit a division into English on one side and French on the other. As they are taught apart, so are their studies different. The literature with which each is the most conversant is that of the peculiar language of each; and all the ideas which men derive from books, come to each of them from perfectly different sources. The articles in the newspapers of each race are written

in a style as widely different as those of France and
England at present, and the arguments which con-
vince the one are calculated to appear utterly unin-
telligible to the other. It is difficult to conceive the
perversity with which misrepresentations are habi-
tually made, and the gross delusions which find
currency among the people. They thus live in a
world of misconceptions, in which each party is set
against the other, not only by diversity of feelings
and opinions, but by actual belief in an entirely
different set of facts. Nothing, though it will sound
paradoxical, really proves their entire separation so
much as the rarity, nay, almost total absence, of
personal encounters between the two races. Disputes
of this kind are almost confined to the ruder order
of people, and seldom proceed to acts of violence. As
respects the other classes, social intercourse between
the two races is so limited that the more prominent
or excitable antagonists never meet in the same
room. The ordinary occasions of collision never
occur, and men must quarrel so publicly or so
deliberately that prudence restrains them from com-
mencing individually what would probably end in a
general and bloody conflict of numbers. The two
parties combine for no public object. They cannot
harmonize even in associations of charity. The only
public occasion on which they ever meet, is in the
jury-box; and they meet there only to the utter
obstruction of justice."[1]

Efforts were made at a very early date by the
English Government, though not with much beneficial result, to lessen these differences of race and

[1] Canadian Blue Book, 1839.

disposition, or, at any rate, to prevent them from breeding dissensions that might be ruinous to the colony. But the work was not easy. The English, chiefly resident in the western parts, near Montreal, had been accustomed to a certain amount of political power at home, and the loyalists from the United States who associated with them had enjoyed fuller freedom; and to satisfy their demands, as well as to meet the urgent need of better government in the colony, it was in 1791 decided to form a representative assembly, for which every forty-shilling freeholder had the franchise, which should be associated with the governor and a council appointed by the Crown in caring for the legislative and administrative affairs of Canada. But the French settlers in and around Quebec, accustomed to the despotic rule of the House of Bourbon and its deputies, thought this no boon. "It is our religion, our laws relating to property, and our personal security, in which we are most interested," they said in 1778, when the question was first mooted; "and these we enjoy in the most ample manner by the Quebec Bill. We are the more averse to a House of Assembly from the fatal consequences which will result from it. Can we, as Catholics, hope to preserve for any length of time the same prerogatives as Protestant subjects, in a House of Representatives? and will there not come a time when the influence of the latter will over-balance that of our posterity? In this case, should we and our posterity enjoy the same advantages which our present constitution secures to us? Shall we not fear that we may one day see the seeds of dissension created by the Assembly of Representatives, and nourished by those intestine hatreds which the opposite interests of the old and the new subjects will naturally give birth to?"[1] It was partly in deference to those prejudices that, while representative institutions were forced on the French Canadians, they were allowed to use them chiefly among themselves, by the separation of the colony into two provinces, each with its own popular chamber. In 1791, the western district, extending from the borders of Montreal to the River Detroit, and including the whole promontory formed by Lakes Ontario, Erie, and Huron, was defined as Upper Canada; while Lower Canada, mainly peopled by the French natives, stretched eastward, on both sides of the St Lawrence, to Quebec, and thence on to the mouth of the river and the borders of New Brunswick.

Lower Canada, containing both the chief cities, was then and till lately the most populous province. Within an area of 205,860 square miles, nearly four times as large as England, it contained about 113,000 inhabitants in 1784; 423,630 in 1825; 511,922 in 1831; 690,782 in 1844; 890,261 in 1852; and 1,111,566 in 1861. Upper Canada, not quite thrice the size of England, and comprising 141,000 square miles, was almost uninhabited before the close of the eighteenth century. It contained 77,000 inhabitants in 1811; 151,097 in 1824; 320,693 in 1834; 486,055 in 1842; 952,004 in 1852; and 1,396,091 in 1861. Its population has nearly been doubled in each period of ten years, while Lower Canada has required about twenty-four years for a like growth. This has been

[1] Martin, vol. I. p. 16.

mainly due to the circumstance that the western districts were already distributed among the French families, whose vested interests, however much to be respected, were a great obstacle to the free settlements of English emigrants, and that the latter have therefore gone to build their own towns and cities in quarters previously unoccupied.

Differences of race were not the only obstacles to the full development of Lower Canada, but they were sufficiently serious. In spite of the large proportion of French *habitans*, as they were called, in the province, they were outnumbered by English settlers, and, which was worse, they were kept under by the military and civil officers who had most weight with the authorities. Over and over again they had to complain that the representative privileges accorded to them were worse than useless, as the whole government of the colony was in the hands of the Legislative Council, to which none but Englishmen were admitted.

In 1807 there was an open rupture between the House of Assembly and the Legislative Council. The Assembly was dissolved; a French newspaper was suppressed; and six persons were imprisoned without trial. The "reign of terror," as it was styled in Canadian circles, lasted till 1811, when a new governor arrived, whose conciliatory action prevented any serious disturbance. But the *habitans* continued dissatisfied with their position in the colony.

Of this dissatisfaction evil use was sought to be made by the Americans. In 1812 war arose between the United States and England, and the conquest of Canada was again attempted by the Government of the former. "We can take the Canadas without soldiers," said the Secretary at War in Congress. "We have only to send officers into the provinces, and the people, disaffected towards their own Government, will rally round our standard." "It is absurd," said another, " to suppose that we shall not succeed in our enterprise. We have the Canadians as much at our command as Great Britain has the ocean. We must take the continent from her. I wish never to see peace till we do so."[1]

The Americans misjudged the disposition of the French Canadians. They desired justice from England; but they had no wish to swerve from their allegiance, and they had no liking for the republicanism, then violent and offensive, of the United States. Within six weeks they organized and equipped four fine battalions of militia, the Canadian Voltigeurs, and in other ways gave proof of their devotion to the cause of England. An expedition was promptly fitted out for the invasion of Canada; but its inhabitants of both races were no less prompt in preparing to resist it.

On the 12th of July an American force, 2500 strong, entered Upper Canada from Detroit, and took possession of Sandwich; but General Brock, then governor of the province, quickly gathering together a little army, consisting of 330 regulars, 400 militiamen, and 600 Indians, soon drove the enemy back to Detroit, and, crossing the river, invested that fort and compelled its surrender. Two months afterwards a stronger invading army, numbering 6000 men, again crossed the frontier, this time at Niagara, and over-

[1] Martin, vol. i. p. 17.

powered the small garrison that had charge of Queenstown. Again Brock went to meet the enemy. He was killed, and his small force was not successful; but soon some British troops arrived, and by them the Americans were forced to retreat. A third invasion was attempted at Fort Erie; but there 4500 of the enemy were repulsed by Canadian volunteers and a few British troops, 600 in all.

Those were the exploits of the first year of the new Canadian war. In 1813 the Americans, still believing that, if they could only gain a footing in the west, the French in the east would willingly join their side, renewed their attacks on Upper Canada. Herein they were more successful than they had been in the previous year. In April, crossing Lake Ontario, they surprised York, now Toronto, the capital of the province, and destroyed its public buildings. Fort George also fell into their hands after desperate resistance. For some months they were masters of the most populous parts of Upper Canada; and, in October, 14,000 men, in two detachments, taking different routes, were sent against Montreal. The first, however, 6000 strong, was met and defeated by 800 volunteers, chiefly French and Indians, under Colonel de Salaberry; and the other had to yield to the main body of the regular troops in Lower Canada, who were sent out to resist it. The earlier successes of the invaders were thus neutralized.

In the following year Upper Canada was again assailed with some success. Fort Erie was captured, and much injury was done to the neighbouring settlements before the Canadians, nearly exhausted by a contest which they had had to maintain with very scant help from England, could hold their own against the enemy, and then nothing but rare bravery sustained them. On the 25th of July the battle of Lundy's Lane, near the falls of Niagara, was fought. From afternoon till midnight 4000 Americans were withstood by 2800 Canadians and Englishmen. Of their number 878 were killed and wounded before the enemy, with a loss of 854, were driven back to Fort Erie. That fort was then besieged by General Drummond; but in a single attack he lost 905 of his men against 84 of the foe, and after that could do no more than maintain a feeble blockade. The Canadians must have succumbed had not the cessation of England's long European war in 1814 released her troops and ships from yet more urgent work, and enabled her to despatch an adequate force across the Atlantic. This was promptly done, and with a speedy issue. Reinforcements were sent to Canada, but the great scene of the war was transferred to the enemy's own country. Washington was attacked and captured, and the British then retaliated for the destruction of property that had occurred in Upper Canada. The Americans found now that their case was hopeless, and readily agreed to the treaty of peace that was signed on Christmas Eve, in 1814. Canada was henceforth free from invasion, and from serious fear of it, at the hands of the United States.

Before the mischief done by the war had been thoroughly repaired, however, domestic troubles were renewed. The French Canadians in the eastern province were ill repaid for the loyalty which they had shown during the war. Immediately after the restoration of peace, the old insults were revived, and their efforts to assert their claims in the House of Assembly were treated with ignominy by the English party which had supremacy in the governing councils. "For a long time," said the Earl of Durham, in the document which has already been cited, "this body of men, receiving at times accessions to its numbers, possessed almost all the highest public offices, by means of which it wielded all the powers of government. It maintained influence in the legislature by means of its predominance in the Legislative Council, and it disposed of the large number of petty posts which are in the patronage of the Government all over the province. Successive governors, as they came in their turn, are said to have either submitted quietly to its influence, or, after a short and unavailing struggle, to have yielded to it the real conduct of affairs. The bench, the magistracy, the high offices of the Episcopal Church, and a great part of the legal profession, are filled by the adherents of this party. By grant or purchase they have acquired nearly the whole of the waste lands of the province. They are all-powerful in the chartered banks, and till lately shared amongst themselves, almost exclusively, all offices of trust and profit. A monopoly of power so extensive and so lasting could not fail, in process of time, to excite envy, create dissatisfaction, and ultimately provoke attack; and an opposition consequently grew up in the Assembly, which assailed the ruling party by appealing to popular principles of government, by denouncing the alleged jobbing and profusion of the official body, and by instituting inquiries into abuses for the purpose of promoting reform and especially economy. The official party, not being removed when it failed to command a majority in the Assembly, still continued to wield all the powers of the executive government, to strengthen itself by its patronage, and to influence the policy of the colonial governor, and of the colonial department at home. By its secure majority in the Legislative Council it could effectually control the legislative powers of the Assembly. It could choose its moment for dissolving hostile Assemblies, and could always ensure for those who were favourable to itself the tenure of their seats for the full term of the four years allowed by law."

Of that sort was the political feud that existed and seriously hindered the progress of Lower Canada in all ways during more than twenty years following the termination of the war with the United States. In 1831 the British Parliament declared that the House of Assembly should have control over the colonial revenues, thus conceding one point which had long been a source of reasonable complaint; but the official party, forced to yield in this respect, became more tyrannical in others, and the result was that greater discontent than ever prevailed. In 1835 a Royal Commission was sent out to investigate this unfortunate state of affairs and suggest a remedy; but no material benefit resulted from its proceedings.

In the meanwhile a similar and even more violent antagonism had been established in Upper Canada, now a province almost as populous as the other. Here an official party also gained supremacy in the Legislative Council, and set at nought the opinions and decisions of the House of Assembly; but the members of the House of Assembly and those who elected them were not French *habitans*, but rough Englishmen, more out-spoken in their demands, and more determined that those demands should be complied with. Whereas in the eastern provinces none did more than complain, and offer such resistance as was strictly legal, the extreme section of the popular party in the west soon resolved to take the law into their own hands. In December some five or six hundred of this section, headed by a man named Mackenzie, assembled a few miles from Toronto, intending to surprise the city and instigate an insurrection for transferring the whole province to the United States. Sir Francis Head, the governor, however, was warned of this movement in time. By him a strong force of volunteers and militia was quickly mustered for the defence of Toronto, and he called on the rebels to surrender their arms. On their refusing, the volunteers and militia, under Lieutenant-Colonel M'Nab, the Speaker of the House of Assembly, went out to compel them, and this was quickly done, with loss of only a few of the insurgents. The rebellion of 1837, as it was called, only lasted three days, and in it were implicated only a few of the most ignorant and least influential colonists. But it gave reasonable alarm, both in the colony and at home; and its occurrence, together with the long-continued feuds between the Legislative Council and the House of Assembly in each of the two provinces, made it necessary that the utmost efforts should be made to remedy the existing evils. Accordingly, in 1838, the Earl of Durham, a statesman of rare wisdom and ability, was sent out as Governor-General of all the provinces of

British North America, with special functions for "the adjustment of certain important questions depending in the provinces of East and West Canada respecting the form and future government of the said provinces."

Lord Durham's visit to Canada marks a turning-point in its history. He visited all the principal stations in the colony, and in each made careful inquiry as to the state of the people, and the requirements for their good government. In the end he recommended that the two provinces should again be made one, with a single legislative and administrative system, in which the governor should be aided by a Legislative Council in harmony with the people and with its representatives in the House of Assembly; and that that body should have powers of legislation and control over the administration, of like nature to that possessed by the British House of Commons. He also recommended such an union of all the British North American colonies as has lately been inaugurated. "Our first duty," he nobly urged, "is to secure the well-being of our colonial countrymen; and if, in the hidden decrees of that wisdom by which the world is ruled, it is written that these countries are not for ever to remain portions of the empire, we owe it to our honour to take good care that, when they separate from us, they should not be the only countries on the American continent in which the Anglo-Saxon race shall be found unfit to govern itself."

Lord Durham's recommendations had not reached England when fresh evidence of the need of their adoption, or at any rate of some sound remedial measures regarding Canada, was afforded by a second rebellion, small, but larger than the first, which broke out in November 1838. Its forerunner had revived in the United States the hope of annexing the prosperous district north of the St Lawrence; and by some lawless subjects, who received no countenance from the Government, and whose action somewhat resembled that of the supporters of the Fenian agitation in our own day, the second rising was encouraged. It consisted in an attempt, by about four thousand violent persons, to effect a rising in the neighbourhood of Montreal. But within less than a week they were subdued by two hundred volunteers, who, in a contest lasting two hours and a half, had fifteen of their number killed and wounded, the loss of the insurgents being about a hundred.

The most important suggestions of the Earl of Durham were adopted in 1839. The two provinces were reunited, and the machinery of government was reorganized, under the superintendence of Mr Charles Poulett Thompson, who, for the zeal, tact, and good feeling towards all classes with which he did his work, was made Baron Sydenham shortly before his untimely death in 1841. To him Sir Charles Metcalf proved a wise successor; and of the history of the next five and twenty years it is enough to say, that, amid the many obstacles that had grown up during the three-quarters of a century before, rapid progress was made in the establishment of peace and order, and in meeting the requirements not only of the large population then in the colony, but of the rapid in-come of fresh settlers. The history of Canada, as a separate province, ends with the adoption of Lord Durham's other suggestion, the union of all the British North American colonies under one government. In 1865 the Canadian Confederation was proposed, and four delegates from the colony visited England to urge its feasibility, and take counsel as to its details. In 1867 the Confederation was authorized, and it now comprises Canada, New Brunswick, Nova Scotia, and Prince Edward's Island. To it will doubtless be added all the other British possessions in North America.

In spite of its troubles, Canada has during the present century increased more rapidly in population than any portion of the world, except Australia—more rapidly even than the United States; and the tide of wealth has not been very much behind that of population. The comparison between the growth of population in Canada and that in the United States is noteworthy. "Boston," we are told, "between 1840 and 1850, increased forty-five per cent. Toronto, within the same period, increased ninety-five per cent. New York, the great emporium of the United States, and regarded as the most prosperous city in the world, increased, in the same time, sixty-six per cent., about thirty less than Toronto. The cities of St Louis and Cincinnati, which have also experienced extraordinary prosperity, do not compare with Canada any better. In the thirty years preceding 1850, the population of St Louis increased fifteen times. In the thirty-three years preceding the same year, Toronto increased eighteen times. And Cincinnati increased, in the same period given to St Louis, but twelve times. Hamilton, a beautiful Canadian city at the head of Lake Ontario, and founded much more recently than Toronto, has also had almost unexampled prosperity. In 1836 its population was but 2846; in 1854 it was upwards of 20,000. London, still farther west in Upper Canada, and a yet more recently-founded city than Hamilton, being surveyed as a wilderness little more than twenty-five years ago, has now upwards of 10,000 inhabitants. The city of Ottawa, recently called after the magnificent river of that name, and upon which it is situated, has now above 10,000 inhabitants, although in 1830 it had but one hundred and forty houses, including mere sheds and shanties; and the property upon which it is built was purchased, not many years before, for £80. The town of Bradford, situated between Hamilton and London, and whose site was an absolute wilderness twenty-five years ago, has now a population of 6000, and has increased, in ten years, upwards of three hundred per cent.; and this without any other stimulant or cause save the business arising from the settlement of a fine country adjacent to it. The towns of Belleville, Cobourg, Woodstock, Goderich, St Catherine's, Paris, Stratford, Port Hope, and Dundas, in Upper Canada, show similar prosperity, some of them having increased in a ratio even greater than that of Toronto, and all of them but so many evidences of the improvement of the country, and the growth of business and population around them. That some of the smaller towns in the United States have enjoyed equal prosperity can be readily believed, from the circumstance of a large population suddenly filling up the country contiguous to them. Buffalo and Chicago, too, as cities, are magnificent and unparalleled examples of the business, the energy, and

the progress of the United States. But that Toronto
should have quietly and unostentatiously increased
in population in a greater ratio than New York, St
Louis, and Cincinnati, and that the other cities and
towns of Upper Canada should have kept pace with
the capital, is a fact creditable alike to the steady industry and the noiseless enterprise of the Canadian
people. Although Lower Canada, from the circumstance of the tide of emigration flowing westward,
has not advanced so rapidly as her sister province,
yet some of her counties and cities have recently
made great progress. In the seven years preceding
1851, the county of Megantic, on the south side of
the St Lawrence, and through which the Quebec and
Richmond railroad passes, increased a hundred and
sixteen per cent.; the county of Ottawa, eighty-five;
the county of Drummond, seventy-eight; and the
county of Sherbrook, fifty. The city of Montreal,
probably the most substantially-built city in America,
and certainly one of the most beautiful, has trebled
her population in thirty-four years. The ancient
city of Quebec has more than doubled her population
in the same time; and Sorel, at the mouth of the
Richelieu, has increased upwards of four times, showing that Lower Canada, with all the disadvantages of
a feudal tenure, and of being generally looked upon
as less desirable for settlement than the west, has
quietly but justly put in her claim to a portion of
the honour awarded to America for her progress."[1]

[1] Russell, "Canada; its Defences, Condition, and Resources."

CHAPTER X.

THE HUDSON'S BAY TERRITORY.

THE HUDSON'S BAY COMPANY AND ITS TERRITORY—RIVALRY IN THE EIGHTEENTH CENTURY—THE CHARACTER AND WORKING OF THE COMPANY—ITS SERVANTS AND SUBJECTS—THE RED RIVER SETTLEMENT—VANCOUVER ISLAND AND BRITISH COLUMBIA—DISSOLUTION OF THE HUDSON'S BAY COMPANY.
[1670-1868.]

IN 1610 Henry Hudson, who had already made other memorable voyages of discovery both in the far north and along the shores of the American continent, set out on an expedition in search of a north-west passage to India. He perished in the quest; but not before he had explored several coasts and outlets, and especially the great sea called Hudson's Bay in honour of him, and Hudson's Straits, which lead to it. Others followed in his track, and in 1668 Prince Rupert fitted out a vessel designed to form a settlement in the bay, and put to use the vast territories that had hitherto been only nominally subject to the English Crown. The expedition succeeded; and in 1670 the Hudson's Bay Company, with Prince Rupert at its head, was formed for the appropriation of the region, and the development of commerce in it.

This region, known as Prince Rupert's Land, or the Hudson's Bay Territory, comprised, according to the wording of the Company's charter, " all lands and territories upon the countries, coasts, and confines of the seas, bays, lakes, rivers, creeks, and sounds, in whatsoever latitude they shall be, that lie within the entrance of the straits, commonly called Hudson's Straits, that are not already actually possessed by, or granted to, any of our subjects, or possessed by the subjects of any other Christian prince or state." To the Company was also conceded "the whole and entire trade and traffic to and upon all havens, bays, creeks, rivers, lakes, and seas, into which they shall find entrance or passage, by water or land, out of the territories, limits, or places aforesaid, and to and with all the natives and people inhabiting, or which shall inhabit, within the territories, limits and places aforesaid, and to and with all other nations inhabiting any of the coasts adjacent to the said territories, limits, and places which are not already possessed as aforesaid, or whereof the sole liberty and traffic is not granted to any other of our subjects."[1] That was the origin of the Hudson's Bay Company, which, by virtue of its charter, has had, for nearly two centuries, the ownership of more than three million square miles of land, an area nearly half as large as that of Russia, thrice as large as that of India.

The Company lost no time in making use of its privileges, though the extent of its operations was strangely disproportionate to the vastness of its territory. A settlement was promptly formed at Rupert River, near the southern corner of Hudson's Bay, and stations and factories were founded in its neighbourhood for carrying on a trade in furs with the Indian tribes there resident. The trade was

[1] Anderson, "History of Commerce," vol. iii. p. 514.

very profitable, yielding sometimes as much as fifty per cent. profit in a year; and this in spite of the violent opposition offered to it by the French in Canada, who claimed the exclusive possession of these districts. In 1682 and 1686, and again in 1692, 1694, 1696, and 1697, the Company's forts were attacked, and some of them destroyed, by expeditions from Quebec; and in the latter year, by the Treaty of Ryswick, part of the territory was ceded to the French. It was restored to the Hudson's Bay Company, however, by the Treaty of Utrecht in 1713, and after that no serious resistance was offered to its progress. In 1730 the Company brought home more than fifteen thousand beaver-skins, and nearly as many skins of martins, otters, foxes, wolves, and bears. "The Hudson's Bay trade," it was said in 1731, "employs generally three ships from London, carrying thither coarse duffle cloth or blanketing, powder and shot, spirits, &c.; and, in return, brings home vast quantities of peltry of many kinds, bed-feathers, whale-fins, &c. And as that small Company makes a large dividend of eight, or formerly ten, per cent. on their capital of £100,000, besides the employment it gives to our people in fitting out and loading those ships, it may truly be said to be an advantageous commerce."[1]

More than a hundred years ago, however, it was urged in Parliament that this commerce ought to be more advantageous. "The Company's four factories," it was said in 1749 by one of its agents, "contain only one hundred and thirty servants, and two small houses with only eight men in each. There

Anderson, vol. iii. pp. 167, 233.

are incontestible evidences of rich copper and lead mines; yet the Company gives no encouragement for working them, nor for their servants going into the inland countries. If the least evidence had been suffered to transpire that the climate is very habitable, the soil rich and fruitful, fit both for corn and for cattle, rich in mines, and the fisheries capable of great improvements, the legislature would have taken the right into its own hands, and would have settled the country, and laid the trade open for the benefit of Britain. The Company, therefore, have contented themselves with dividing a large profit upon a small capital amongst only about one hundred persons, and have not only endeavoured to keep the true state of the trade and country an impenetrable secret, but have also industriously propagated the worst impressions of them."[1] Parliament, however, decided that the rights of the Hudson's Bay Company were indisputable, and that it must be allowed to carry on its trade as it judged best for its own interests.

But its exclusive privileges were again, and this time successfully, disputed about fifty years afterwards. A North-West Company was founded with powers to carry on its trade in the unused portions of the Hudson's Bay Company's Territory. The Quebec Fur Company, moreover, established even before the Hudson's Bay Company, and which had long confined its operations to commerce with the Indians bordering upon Canada, now became more active. The rivalship of the three Companies led to a great extension of our acquaintance with the distant parts of North America, and intercourse with its natives.

[1] Anderson, vol. iii. p. 271.

The trade in furs, that had hitherto been chiefly limited to the regions about Hudson's Bay, was pursued in the far west. Exploring parties were formed, and by them fertilising rivers and fruitful plains were discovered in quarters never before visited; and in some of these districts valuable factories and strong forts were built. The feuds of the rival Companies, sometimes issuing even in bloodshed, greatly lessened their profits, but caused a vast increase of their operations. The feuds died out, but not the enterprise, with the fusion of the North-West Company in the Hudson's Bay Company in 1821; and by that time the general character of the immense territory was tolerably understood and, to some extent, rightly valued.

In 1847 the Hudson's Bay Company, with a capital of £400,000 in the hands of two hundred and thirty-nine proprietors, had a hundred and thirty six separate establishments, extending east and west from Labrador and the Atlantic Ocean to British Columbia and the Pacific Ocean; and north and south from the boundaries of Canada and the United States up to Baffin's Bay and the Arctic Ocean. Its factors, clerks, and servants, stationed at these settlements, then numbered about fourteen hundred, and their business was to trade with the Indian population, scattered over the vast area, which was supposed to amount to about ninety thousand. "The trade in America," said an impartial and well-informed citizen of the United States, in 1844, "is especially directed by a resident governor, who occasionally visits and inspects all the principal forts. Under him, as officers, are chief factors, chief traders, and clerks, for the most part

natives of North Britain, and an army of regular
servants, employed as hunters, traders, and voyageurs,
nearly all of them Canadians or half-breeds. The
number of all these persons is small when compared
with the duties they have to perform; but the manner
in which they are admitted into the service, and the
training to which they are subjected, are such as to
render their efficiency and their devotion to the
general interests as great as possible. The strictest
discipline, regularity, and economy are enforced in
every part of the Company's territories; and the
magistrates appointed under the Act of Parliament
for the preservation of tranquillity are seldom called
to exercise their functions, except in the settlement of
trifling disputes. In the treatment of the aborigines
of the countries under its control the Hudson's Bay
Company appears to have admirably reconciled policy
with humanity. The prohibition to supply these
people with ardent spirits appears to be rigidly
enforced. Schools for the instruction of the native
children are established at all the principal trading
forts, each of which also contains an hospital for sick
Indians, and offers employment for those who are
disposed to work whilst hunting cannot be carried
on. Missionaries of various sects are encouraged to
endeavour to convert them to Christianity, and to
induce them to adopt the usages of civilized life, so
far as may be consistent with the nature of the labours
required for their support; and attempts are made, at
great expense, to collect the Indians in villages, on
tracts where the climate and soil are most favourable
for agriculture. It is, however, to be observed that,
of the whole territory, only a few small portions are

capable of being rendered productive by agriculture.
From the remainder nothing of value can be obtained
excepting furs, and those articles can be procured in
greater quantities and at less cost than by any other
means."[1] But the "few small portions" of the great
Hudson's Bay Territory comprise districts almost
as large as England, while others have been proved
to be rich in other sorts of wealth, till lately never
dreamt of.

The stations of the Company, most plentiful about
Hudson's Bay, but also distributed over the country
stretching westward for more than two thousand
miles, serve as small centres of civilization in the
midst of wide areas of forest desolation. "They
are built usually in the form of a square, or nearly
so, of about a hundred yards. This space is picketed
in with logs of timber, driven into the ground, and
rising fifteen or twenty feet above it. In two of the
corners is usually reared a wooden bastion, sufficiently
high to enable the garrison to see a considerable distance over the country. In the gallery of the bastion
five or six small guns, 6 or 12 pounders, are mounted,
covered in and used with regular ports, like those of
a ship, while the ground-floor serves for the magazine.
Inside the pickets are six or eight houses; one containing the mess room for the officers of the fort, and
their dwelling-house when the number of them is
small; two or three others—the number of course
depending on the strength of the fort, which seldom
exceeds a dozen men—being devoted to the trappers,
voyageurs, etc. Another serves for the Indian trading store, and one for the furs, which remain in store

[1] Greenhow, "History of Oregon and California."

at the inland forts during the greater part of the year."[1]

Near each station one or two Indian villages are generally to be found. Other villages are far away from English settlements. Of the aborigines, when they have not been maddened by the strong drink which white men have taught them to love, most travellers speak well. "The Indian," we are told by two who, in 1862 and 1863, travelled all across the Hudson's Bay Territory, "is constantly engaged in hunting to supply his family with food; and when that is scarce he will set out without any provision for himself, and often travel from morning to night for days before he finds the game he seeks. Then, loaded with meat, he toils home again, and, whilst the plenty lasts, considers himself entitled to complete rest after his exertions. This self-denial of the men, and their wonderful endurance of hunger, is illustrated by the case of one hunter who, several years ago, narrowly escaped death by starvation. That winter buffalo did not come up to the woods, and moose and fish were very scarce. After killing his horses, one after another, when driven to the last extremity, the family found themselves at length without resource. The hunter, leaving with his wife and son a scanty remnant of dried horseflesh, hunted for two days without success, and at last, faint and still fasting, with difficulty dragged himself home. All now made up their minds to die; for the hunter became unable to move, and his wife and boy too helpless to procure food. After being eight days longer without tasting food,

[1] Mayne, "Four Years in British Columbia and Vancouver Island," p. 117.

and exposed to the fierce cold of winter, they were fortunately discovered by some of the Company's voyageurs, by whose careful attention they were with difficulty brought round."[1]

Different from the other stations of the Hudson's Bay Company is the Red River Settlement, begun in 1813, with Fort Garry for its capital. Here, within easy reach of Canada and the United States, its first experiment of colonization was made, and with considerable success. An agricultural population of five thousand occupied the district in 1843. It is now twice as numerous, being composed chiefly of civilized Indians or half-breeds, with a mixture of Canadians, Englishmen, and colonists from the continent of Europe.

Two other and much more important settlements, the colonies of British Columbia and Vancouver Island, have since grown up on the most western limits of the Hudson's Bay Territory.

Some part of the district now known as British Columbia had been visited by Sir Francis Drake in the course of his famous voyage round the world, and many later adventurers had visited its Pacific coast-line and the neighbouring islands during the two following centuries. But the formidable barrier of the Rocky Mountains deterred the Hudson's Bay Company from making use of this portion of its territory until recent times. In 1804 it established a fur-trading station at Fort George, on Fraser River, in New Caledonia, and soon other factories were opened in the neighbourhood. These proving successful, it extended its

[1] Viscount Milton and Dr Cheadle, "The North-West Passage by Land."

operations and erected a trading fort near the site of Victoria, in Vancouver Island, in 1843, and the great natural resources of the island soon suggested more extensive colonizing work. In 1847 it asked permission of the British Government to pursue this work in an orderly way. The permission was given, and in 1848 Vancouver Island was assigned to the Hudson's Bay Company for ten years. The discovery of the California gold-fields brought many settlers to this quarter of the world, and some of them, preferring the quiet of agricultural life to the turmoil of the district of gold-mines, went northward to Vancouver Island and British Columbia. Thus their colonization was begun, soon to be rapidly augmented. In 1857 British Columbia was also found to be rich in gold, and immediately a tide of immigration set in. Victoria, hitherto a quiet village, became suddenly a busy port, through which, in the course of four months, twenty thousand adventurers passed on their way to the new El Dorado. Both the island and the mainland were then taken out of the hands of the Hudson's Bay Company, which was in no way adapted for the control of settlements promising to become so important, and the separate colonies of British Columbia and Vancouver Island were formed. In 1866 they were united under one administration, designed to meet the requirements of the new England growing up on the northern shores of the Pacific.

The surrender of these youngest colonies of England by the Hudson's Bay Company was only the prelude to its entire dissolution. Started when monopolies were common, if not necessary for the development of British commerce and civilization—

the greatest and most fruitful monopoly of all being the East India Company—it outlived all other institutions of its kind. It did its work as worthily and honestly as could be expected of it. But the same necessities which led to the blending of the various British North American colonies in the Canadian Confederation rendered inexpedient the longer existence of the Hudson's Bay Company. In 1868 an Act was passed by the British Parliament authorizing the transfer of all the vast territories vaguely described in Charles II.'s days as Prince Rupert's Land to the dominion of Canada.

CHAPTER XI.

BRITISH NORTH AMERICA.

A GENERAL VIEW OF THE BRITISH NORTH AMERICAN COLONIES—PRINCE EDWARD'S ISLAND—CAPE BRETON—NOVA SCOTIA—NEW BRUNSWICK—CANADA—THE WESTERN TERRITORIES—BRITISH COLUMBIA AND VANCOUVER ISLAND. [1869.]

F our North American colonies, the elder, grouped on the western side of the continent, have already been united in the Canadian Confederation. Between them and their younger sisters in the distant east, there intervenes a wide tract of land, of which no adequate use has yet been made. When the intervening space has been bridged over, the English possessions in this quarter will form a belt nearly three thousand miles in length, and, at its widest part, about half as broad, occupying about four million square miles, which, whether it be united under one rule or not, will be closely bound together by community of interests, and, amid many differences, by physical resemblances. Of this region, in its natural and artificial aspects, a comprehensive view will here be given.

Excluding Newfoundland, which, as a great fishing-station and not much else, stands alone, British North America begins with the mainland and islands that lie on either side of the Gulf and River of St Lawrence. On the northern side is Labrador, still almost unexplored, but of too barren an appearance to promise much benefit from its use, save as a haunt for fishermen on the coast, and a resort of fur-traders in the interior. On the southern side is the fair Acadian land of the old French settlers, including Cape Breton and Prince Edward's Island, Nova Scotia, and New Brunswick.

Prince Edward's Island, which had in 1866 a population of about 90,000 spread over an area of 2173 square miles, about the size of Norfolk, lies pleasantly in the bay which skirts New Brunswick and Nova Scotia. A narrow and irregular strip of land, it contains numberless small bays, abounding in fish, of which little use is made, and offering convenient harbourage for far more shipping than frequents its shores. The dense forests with which it once abounded have been partly destroyed by fires, and other parts have been cleared to make room for the pastoral and agricultural pursuits which the island especially invites. The forests that remain furnish material for the ship-building that has long been a favourite and lucrative pursuit of the inhabitants. " In few places," it was said twenty years ago, " have there been greater changes of fortune. A person who came from England in the capacity of a cook was employed in a ship-yard, and recently his former master was among the number of his servants. He now owns extensive tracts of land and farms, mills of different kinds, and a great variety of other property. During the past year he has built no less than ten ships, and loaded them with timber for Great Britain. He is a man of influence, and has several times been elected a member of the House of Assembly. There are not thirty words in his vocabulary, yet all his sayings and doings are characterized by sound sense and correct judgment."[1] If some new-comers to Prince Edward's Island, however, lack education, exemplary care is taken to provide it for their children. A fifth of its revenue of about £50,000 is so spent; and in Charlotte-town, the capital, it is said "there are almost more seminaries than roads to them."

Cape Breton, an island about half as large as Yorkshire, divided from Nova Scotia by a narrow channel which is in one part only a mile wide, and nearly parted into two islands by an inlet, which at its end leaves only a few miles of land, lies to the east of Prince Edward's Island. Its northern and larger half is wild and mountainous. The southern part is an undulating plain, crowded with bays and streams, and terminating in high cliffs which form a rocky barrier to the Atlantic Ocean on the south-eastern shore. In it are most of the dwellers in the island. Sydney, the capital, is beautifully situated at the head of a bay which forms a safe harbour for the ships that frequent it, and that will be much more numerous when proper use is made of the resources of the island. Noble forests offer an unlimited supply of timber, which, with agricultural productions, long formed the staple exports of Cape Breton. In later times profit has also been derived from the two coal mines which have been opened at a convenient distance from the capital, both being connected with the vast bed which passes under the sea to the north-eastward and appears in Newfoundland. Besides the two veins that are worked in the island,

[1] Martin, vol. i. p. 240.

twelve others wait to be made use of. Immense deposits of gypsum, and numerous salt-springs, also occur among the red sandstone rock, of which a great part of the island is composed.

Red sandstone and coal also abound, as well as granite, in the adjoining mainland of Nova Scotia and New Brunswick. Nova Scotia, more than twice as large as Wales, having an area of 15,617 square miles, is an oblong, about 200 miles long and some 50 broad, connected with New Brunswick by a narrow isthmus. Its undulating surface, marked by no high hills, is varied by countless bays and creeks along the shore, and inland by numerous lakes and several rivers. The chosen home of the French Acadians, its population has to this day maintained much of the character of those first settlers and their offspring. Agricultural and pastoral employments render life too easy for the other resources of the country to be quickly developed, and still about a fourth of its 300,000, or more, inhabitants are so employed. Other ways of wealth, however, have lately been opened up. The ash, beech, birch, maple, oak, pine, and spruce, that throng its forests, have not only helped to stock the timber market of Europe, but have been extensively employed in ship-building in the colony itself, and especially in the fine harbour of Halifax, chosen by Great Britain as its chief naval station in North America. The discovery of coal and iron has also led both to a quickened foreign trade, and to the establishment of many local manufactories, and a further stimulus has lately appeared in the finding of gold in the colony. This new attraction, if over-estimated in itself, is beneficial in its encouragement of colonization and enterprise of other sorts. Thirty new mining companies were started in Nova Scotia in 1868. The exports, which in 1827 were valued at £267,277, had risen to £831,071 in 1847, and to £1,133,601 in 1868. The imports, which in 1827 were worth £810,819, amounted in 1847 to £1,031,953, and in 1868 to £1,902,341. While both have thus been largely augmented, the greater development of the export trade, being twice as rapid as that in imports, shows that the colony has learnt better how to feed and clothe itself, as well as how to profit by the requirements of other portions of the world. "Prior to 1824," said one of its recent governors, Sir John Harvey, "the foreign trade of Nova Scotia was very limited, but the changes in the commercial policy of the empire opened a wider field for enterprise, of which the North Americans were not slow to avail themselves. Nova Scotia vessels, besides their traffic with the neighbouring states and the West Indies, now trade to the Baltic, the Mediterranean, China, the Mauritius, the East Indies, the Brazils, and Havannah, and our merchants and mariners are fast acquiring an accurate acquaintance with distant seas, and in every part of the world."[1] In 1868, 252,760 tons of coal were exported from Nova Scotia.

New Brunswick, an almost square block of land between Nova Scotia and Canada, containing 27,037 square miles, and nearly as large as Scotland, has not improved as rapidly. Its population, which was 156,162 in 1840, was only 252,047 in 1861. Its magnificent stores of coal, iron, copper, and other

[1] Nova Scotia Blue Book, 1847.

minerals are still but little used, and its chief trade is in the timber that abounds in its vast and rarely traversed forests. Its least used and most beautiful districts are in the north-west, watered by the Ristigouche and its tributaries. "Wherever the eye wanders nothing is to be seen but an almost incalculable number of lofty hills, interspersed with lakes, rivers, and waterfalls, glens, and valleys. Some of the mountains are clothed with the tall and beautiful pine. Others sustain a fine growth of hard wood. Many have swampy summits, and several terminate in rich meadows and plains. Sometimes the precipitous banks of the Ristigouche are three hundred feet above its bed; and at every bend, which is about once in six miles, the voyager is deceived with the appearance of entering a well-sheltered lake. But, at about seventy miles from the sea, the country becomes comparatively level, and all the way to the head of the river is a fine, bold, open territory, consisting of a rich upland, skirted with large tracts of intervale, and covered with a dense growth of mixed wood, in which large groves of pine are very conspicuous."[1]

Of the same wild character is the strip of Canadian land that lies between New Brunswick and the southern bank of the St Lawrence; while so much of the northern shore as is included in Canada shares to some extent the bleak and rugged aspect of Labrador. Neither of these sections of Lower Canada has yet been put to much use, save by the Hudson's Bay Company, some of whose forts have grown into towns or villages along the banks of the river, here a noble estuary, from thirty to forty miles wide.

[1] Martin, vol. i. p. 230.

Busy Canada begins about a hundred miles east of Quebec, near the mouth of the Saguenay. Thence along the banks of the river, on either side, there appears an almost continuous line of villages and towns extending to Lake Ontario, the southern bank, soon after Montreal is passed, being the property of the United States. "The country below and above Quebec, for some distance, presents scenery whose beauty is unequalled in America, and probably in the world. From the eminence over which the post-road passes, or in sailing up the St Lawrence, there are frequent prospects of immense extent and variety, consisting of lofty mountains, wide valleys, bold headlands, luxuriant forests, cultivated fields, pretty villages and settlements, some of them stretching up along the mountains, fertile islands, rocky islets, and tributary rivers; while on the bosom of the St Lawrence, with a breadth varying from ten to twenty miles, ships, brigs, and schooners, with innumerable pilot-boats and river-craft in active motion, charm the eye of the traveller. The scenery on approaching Quebec is truly magnificent; on the left, Point Levi, with its romantic church and cottages; on the right, the western part of Orleans Isle, which closely resembles our own Devonshire coast. Beyond, the lofty mainland opens to view, and the spectator's attention is rivetted by the magnificent falls of Montmorency—a river as large as the Thames at Richmond—which precipitates its vast volume of constantly flowing waters over a perpendicular precipice two hundred and forty feet in height. The eye then runs along miles of richly cultivated country, terminating in a ridge of mountains, with the city and battlements of Quebec, rising in the form of an amphitheatre, cresting, as it were, the ridge of Cape Diamond, and majestically towering above the surrounding country, as if destined to be the capital of an empire."[1]

From Quebec the panorama continues, with less grandeur, for about two hundred miles, when Montreal is reached, a city larger and handsomer than Quebec, though with fewer natural or artificial defences. It stands on an island in the middle of the St Lawrence. Here the river ceases to be navigable by large vessels; but it passes through scenery as grand as is found on the eastern side of Quebec, till it reaches Kingston, where the waters widen into Lake Ontario, to contract again at the famous Falls of Niagara, opposite to which is the noble city of Toronto; and beyond it, fed by the same river, under different names, are Lakes Erie, Huron, and Superior. There Canada ends, and the waters cease to be a boundary between British America and the United States.

Northward of this splendid barrier are lofty mountains and fertile plains, dense forests, and varied lakes and rivers, as far as the shores of Hudson's Bay. Upper Canada, less mountainous than the eastern province, is for the most part a vast plain, diversified by hills, and covered with luxuriant vegetation. Wheat and other grain are cultivated where the noble forests have been removed; but forestland, containing maple, beech, oak, baywood, elm, hickory, walnut, chestnut, cherry, birch, cedar, and pine, all of largest growth, abound. " The autumnal

[1] Martin, vol. i. p. 56.

tints of these forests, even on cloudy days, are so brilliant that the yellow leaves give the impression of sunshine, each leaf presenting a point of sparkling gold. The hues change from day to day, and pink, lilac, vermilion, purple, deep blue and brown, combine to form a gorgeous mass of colouring that surpasses imagination. Even the decay of the aged and fallen trees is concealed by a mantle of geraniums, honeysuckles, foxgloves, and flowers."[1]

Timber, thus furnished in such profusion, is still the staple article of Canadian commerce, being chiefly collected in the far west, and floated eastward along the course of the Ottawa. The pine and other wood exported in the last half of 1866 and the first of 1867, by Canada, Nova Scotia, and New Brunswick, was valued at £2,789,729, half of it being dispatched to Great Britain, and more than twice as much was reserved for use in the colony as material for ship and house building, and as fuel. In the same period the exports of fish and oil from the districts of Ontario and Quebec amounted to £950,000. Very much larger was the value of the wheat, oats, rye, and barley sent abroad. The total exports were worth £12,983,055, of which less than a third reached the United Kingdom, while from it came more than half of the imports, estimated at £16,806,157. The benefits of this trade appertained to a population of over three and a half millions, of whom four-fifths were in the provinces of Canada. In 1861 the population of Montreal was 90,323; of Quebec, 51,109; of Toronto, 44,821; of Hamilton, 19,096; of Ottawa, 14,696; of Kingston, 13,743; and of London, 11,555.

[1] Somerville, " Physical Geography," p. 144.

To the north and north-west of Canada is a vast extent of wilderness, the hunting-ground of the Hudson's Bay Company, gradually becoming more barren and inaccessible as it approaches the Arctic Region. To the west, south of Lake Winnipeg, is the hardly defined and yet feebly developed Red River settlement; and beyond it is a huge prairie-land, comprising some 65,000 square miles, about as large as Great Britain, which is waiting to become another colony. In it, it is reckoned, are at least 40,000,000 acres of the richest soil, well watered, and blessed with a temperate climate. This is the district of Saskatchewan, destined to be nearly useless until brought into communication either with Canada on the east, or with British Columbia on the other side of the Rocky Mountains.

British Columbia, stretching from the Rocky Mountains to the Pacific, and from the United States boundary-line to the territory lately ceded to the United States by Russia, forms something like an oblong block about 600 miles long and nearly 400 broad. With Vancouver Island, which in size and shape nearly resembles Nova Scotia, and in climate and fertility is said to be on a par with England, it comprises about 220,000 square miles. Both the mainland and the island have rapidly acquired importance in recent years through the discovery of gold in the one, and the convenience of the port of Victoria in the other as a halting-place for travellers in search of the glittering treasure. But both, and especially Vancouver Island, are rich in timber, coal, copper, iron, and other natural commodities, and are admirably adapted for agricultural pursuits.

Of the two colonies Vancouver is more interesting than British Columbia. About 250 miles long to 70 broad, and apparently quite covered with pine forests, except where the frequent conflagrations have laid bare surfaces some miles in extent, the island has for the traveller who first approaches it a strange and gloomy interest, which is increased when he proceeds to examine it in detail. Plants and animals are, for the most part, similar to those with which Englishmen are familiar; but their immense number and predominance over the whole district greatly alter the impression made by them. Outside Victoria and the few other settlements the European colonists have as yet set very little of their mark; and the wild Indians, wandering from place to place, or lodging in flimsy huts, in no degree occupy the place proper to man as master of nature.

These Indian tribes have the same high cheek-bones, broad flat faces, long black hair and copper complexion, as their kinsmen on the continent; but the men of some tribes are taller and stronger. They are described by travellers as being nearly all equally barbarous, greater strength of body only coming in aid of the same ferocity of mind. Individuals have deadly strifes with one another; tribes maintain hereditary feuds. "Treachery and artifice," we are told, "constitute the base of their tactics in war. They appear insensible to anything like chivalry or generous feeling, killing and slaying with remorseless cruelty, undeterred by any sentiment of compunction." They build huts with posts and beams, often large and commodious, but always so fitted as to be easily transferred from one place to another. Their dress consists of a blanket tied round the body with strips of bark, and their tattooing is sometimes really ornamental. They are skilful huntsmen and excellent fishermen, and in the art of cooking salmon, of which fish good specimens are everywhere to be met with, they claim to be connoisseurs. "The true Indian method of cooking a salmon consists in putting it into a wooden bowl with water, which is made to boil by dropping in red-hot stones." The canoes, in the manufacture of which they show considerable skill, not only are so much used in lifetime that no Indian when out of them can move his limbs in a graceful way, but also generally serve as tombs for the dead. Often each tribe finds a little rocky island at a short distance from the coast, and thither the canoe, freighted with its owner's corpse and his principal weapons and other articles, is taken, to be dragged on shore, and left. Among some tribes it is the practice to place their dead in boxes upon the branches of trees; and with a few others incremation is said to be the rule.[1]

Victoria, the capital of Vancouver Island, is favourably placed on the south-eastern corner of the island, and seems destined to become a sufficient rival to San Francisco, as a great mart for trade along the shores of the Pacific Ocean, and across it, to China and the East Indies. Its population has increased in ten years from about 500 to considerably more than 5000. Many stories are told of the rapid money-making of its inhabitants. "There is a person," it was said in 1865, "luxuriating in England at the

[1] "Travels in British Columbia and round Vancouver's Island," by Captain C. E. Barret-Lennard.

present moment, who went to the island as a poor ship's carpenter. When the rush of immigration came in 1858, he and his wife were living behind the bar of a small public-house, the resort of sailors. He bought about £40 or £60 worth of property after he arrived, which now brings him the handsome income of £4000 per annum. Another inhabitant brought to the country £60 in 1857, and the land he purchased with that amount now realises to him £80 a month."[1] Esquimault is another thriving town in Vancouver Island, and New Westminster (founded in 1860) is the capital of British Columbia. The revenue of Vancouver Island in 1862 was £24,000; in 1863, £30,000; in 1864, £38,000; and in 1866, £89,000. The revenue of British Columbia, about £18,000 in 1859, was £36,000 in 1861, £56,000 in 1863, and £90,000 in 1866. In the latter year the imports of both colonies amounted to about £900,000; and the exports to more than £1,200,000, of which five-sixths were bullion.

The vast and varied treasures of these youngest colonial possessions of England are still almost wholly undeveloped. The rush of gold-seekers, while leading the way to healthier colonization, has, at the same time, presented obstacles thereto. Reckless adventurers have introduced lawless ways which hinder the progress of quiet settlers. The experiences of travellers and emigrants show that both British Columbia and Vancouver Island offer wonderful advantages for settlers; but neither they nor any other portions of the world can afford comfortable resting-places for those who desire more than may be

[1] Macfie, "Vancouver Island and British Columbia," p. 89.

fairly earned by their own brains and hands. Those who seek for gold have the chance of rapid fortune, but also the chance of starvation and of moral ruin. But the patient and persevering miner will find ample stores of copper, iron, and coal, always surer sources of wealth than the more precious mineral; and to another class of emigrant, the man with manufacturing talent, there is a wide field of prosperity. The plentiful timbers of the island, joined to its other resources, offer strong inducements to the shipbuilder; and when good colonial ships are built, they can never lack cargoes of raw material, for which Asia and Europe will gladly pay in articles of food and clothing, cheaper and better than the native market can produce. That is a state of things not to be brought about in a day, nor in a few years; but if patient industry is employed, it must needs arrive in its due time.

It will be facilitated—and the whole prospects of British North America, bright already, will be brightened—by the opening up of a convenient road, and ultimately of a railway, extending over the whole vast territory from east to west. Thereby free interchange of commodities will be made possible, and our American colonies can vie with the United States in their new and splendid enterprise of constructing a pathway for commerce and civilization, across the great continent and the two great oceans that bound it, between Europe and the Indies.

CHAPTER XII.

WEST AFRICA.

THE WEST AFRICAN SETTLEMENTS—SIERRA LEONE—GAMBIA—CAPE COAST CASTLE—LAGOS. [1600-1869.]

ALMOST the earliest voyages of discovery undertaken by the English were along the African coast, and with the savage tribes of the western shore they very soon began a rude trade, in which cheap trinkets and gewgaws were bartered for ivory and the few other commodities possessed by the natives. But until a century ago there was no attempt at regular colonization, and the inhospitable districts were chiefly frequented in order that their natives and the captives brought by them from the interior might be bought or stolen, and taken as slaves to the West Indian settlements. Sir John Hawkins was the first slave-trader; and Queen Elizabeth, while sanctioning the commerce, is said to have declared that "it would be detestable, and call down the vengeance of Heaven upon the undertakers." Cape Coast Castle was erected as a well-protected haunt for these traders early in the seventeenth century; and soon afterwards James Fort, near the Gambia, became another factory for the English, who long maintained a fierce rivalry with the Spaniards, French, and Dutch. In 1787 it was guessed that up to that time ten million negroes had been thus taken from Africa, the rate of exportation being then a hundred thousand a year. More than a third of the trade was then in the hands of the English. Then it was that Clarkson, Wilberforce, and others began the popular opposition which ended in the suppression of the slave-trade, as far as law and an armed force could suppress it, in 1808. After that the English had more time to attend to their West African possessions, although as colonies there is still little to be said about them.

These possessions are in four groups. Sierra Leone, the district first visited by Hawkins, is, by reason of its unhealthy climate, abandoned by all Europeans who are not actually forced to reside in it. Among its population of some 50,000, half of them being in Free Town, the capital, there are scarcely more than a hundred whites. The hardly less unhealthy district of the Gambia, also, is only visited by the few Englishmen who are required to superintend and make capital out of the growing trade carried on by the black settlers, numbering about 12,000, with the native tribes, in which European commodities are exchanged for ground-nuts and palm-oil. The Gold Coast, with Cape Coast Castle for its centre, alone invites white residents, and these are chiefly missionaries, augmented by a floating population of merchants. An extensive territory is kept under subjection to the British; and, as the name implies, the chief attraction to Europeans is the gold here collected in small quantities. Besides gold dust, there is commerce in palm-oil, gum, and ivory, bartered chiefly for clothing, rum, and gunpowder. A fourth and more hopeful settlement is at

Lagos, in the Bight of Benin, which became a British possession in 1861. Its healthier climate renders it a fitter dwelling-place for Europeans, and it offers advantages for trade in the lead ore, indigo, and camwood that abound in the interior, and for cultivation of cotton along the coast.

The population of all these settlements, including tributary tribes of Africans, was in 1866 about 200,000; and their exports and imports were each valued at about £600,000.

No other colonial possessions of England have so unwelcome a history or offer such few attractions to visitors, save those of travel among barbarous races and effort to improve their state by means of Christianity and civilization. Here, however, there is some encouragement. "After many years' intercourse with the race," said the governor of Gambia in 1866, "I cannot see in the African any incapacity for civilization. On the contrary, I am convinced that the liberated Africans contain in themselves all the elements of a commercial people."[1]

[1] Colonial Governors' Reports, 1867, part II. p. 17.

CHAPTER XIII

CAPE COLONY.

THE DUTCH SETTLEMENT ON THE CAPE OF GOOD HOPE—EARLY QUARRELS WITH THE HOTTENTOTS AND CRUEL TREATMENT OF THEM—TRANSFER OF THE COLONY TO ENGLAND—ITS PROGRESS UNDER BRITISH RULE—THE KAFFIR WARS AND OTHER TROUBLES—THE PRESENT CONSTITUTION OF THE COLONY—ITS NATURAL ADVANTAGES. [1648-1869.]

THE Cape of Good Hope, called by him the Cape of Storms, was discovered by Bartholomew Diaz, a Portuguese, in 1494; and it was from this time often visited by later voyagers, who followed in the track of Vasco de Gama, and sailed round the coast of Africa in their search for the treasures of the East Indies. But its colonization was not thought of till a century and a half later.

In 1648 a Dutch vessel, the *Haarlem*, on its way to India, was wrecked upon the coast. Its crew, forced to reside there for some months, sent home so favourable an account of the district, and so strongly urged the advantage of a settlement at which vessels, passing to and from the east, might halt and gain refreshment, that their suggestion was adopted by the Dutch East India Company. Seventy or eighty soldiers, peasants and convicts, under Jan van Riebeeck, arrived in Table Bay in April 1652, and by them a wooden shed was erected on the site of Cape Town. The natives welcomed them; and, amid many difficulties caused by their appearance in the winter season, when food was scarce and wild beasts roamed over the district, a little colony was formed, which, augmented by fresh arrivals from Holland, numbered in 1858 three hundred and sixty persons.

The first difficulties, however, were soon followed by others of the colonists' own making. With the Hottentot natives they were at first well pleased; but very soon they claimed more from them than they cared to give, and the first "insolence," as it was termed, was fiercely resented. The insolence was in the same sort of cattle-lifting which has been a source of trouble ever since. Van Riebeeck, having caught a man in this act, questioned him as to his motive, and was told by him, as he reported, "that it was for no other reason than because they saw we were breaking up the best land and grass where their cattle were accustomed to graze, trying to establish ourselves everywhere, with houses and farms, as if we were never more to move, but designed to take up our permanent occupation more and more of this Cape Colony, which had belonged to them from time immemorial,—ay, so that their cattle could not get at the water without passing over the corn land, which we would not allow them to do." Van Riebeeck considered that cattle-stealing was "a matter most displeasing to the Almighty when committed by such men as they were;" but saw no harm in the land-stealing resorted to by such men as he. Therefore in 1659 he made war upon the Hottentots with a hundred and thirty of his colonists; and with the help of some bloodshed and "a little torture," punished them for their iniquity.

That first quarrel was the parent of others that need not be detailed. The colony grew steadily but not rapidly. Dutch farmers ploughed the land and sowed and reaped the wheat which it yielded in abundance, and, in spite of the frequent depredations of the natives, made profit out of great herds of sheep and cows; and gradually the Hottentots were driven further and further inland, away from "their birth-place and their own land, full of pure water, after which their hearts longed," as they had said in one complaint against the encroachments of the colonists. In 1759, a century and a quarter after it was started, the Cape settlement contained 9782 Europeans, of whom only 1486 were women, and 8104 slaves.

Of the way in which these slaves were caught and treated, a precise account is given by a Dutch traveller who resided in the colony between 1772 and 1776. "Several persons that are in want of servants join together and take a journey to that part of the country where the Bushmen live. They endeavour to spy out where the Bushmen have their haunts. They are found in societies from ten to fifty or a hundred, reckoning old and young together. On a dark night the farmers set themselves on them, stationing themselves at some distance about the kraal. They then give the alarm by firing a gun or two. By this means there is such a consternation spread over the whole body of these savages that only the most bold and intelligent among them have the courage to break through the circle and steal off. These the captors are glad enough to get rid of in so easy a manner; those that are stupid and timorous, and allow themselves to be carried into bondage, best answering their purpose. If a colonist at any time gets sight of a Bushman he fires immediately, and spirits up his horses and dogs in order to hunt him, with more ardour and fury than he would a wolf or any other wild beast. The slave business is exercised by the colonists towards the nation of Bushmen with a cruelty which merits the abhorrence of every one, though I have been told that they pride themselves in it; and not only is the capture of a Hottentot considered by them as a work of pleasure, but in cold blood they destroy the bonds which nature has knit between husband and wife, and between parents and children. I have known some colonists not only, for a trifling neglect, deliberately flay both the backs and limbs of their slaves by a peculiar, slow, lingering process, but even, outdoing the very tigers in cruelty, throw pepper and salt over the wounds. Many a time have I seen unhappy slaves, who, with the most dismal cries and lamentations, were suffering such punishments, during which they are used to cry, not so much for mercy as for a draught of water; but, so long as their blood is inflamed with the torture, it is said that great care must be taken to avoid allowing them drink of any kind, as experience has shown that in that case they would die in a few hours, and sometimes the very instant after they drank it. I am far from accusing all the colonists of having a hand in these and other cruelties. There are many who hold them in abomination, and fear lest the vengeance of Heaven should, for all these crimes, fall upon their land and their posterity. Government has no other part in the cruelties exercised by its subjects than that of taking no cognizance of them."[1]

Perhaps, however, that was part enough. It was thought well to suffer the Hottentots to be exterminated, in order that the colony might be free from their wicked cattle-stealing ; and if, while that was being done, some of them could be put to use as slaves, their masters must be responsible to a higher power than man's for any harshness that occurred in the work. So the Dutch farmers led on their lazy life, in which the only excitement was in hunting and torturing the Hottentots; and their numbers were slowly increased and their territories rapidly extended, until 1795, when Cape Colony was given to England by the Prince of Orange, then a refugee in London. In 1797 the Earl of Macartney went to take possession of it and found a district of about 120,000 square miles, more than thrice the size of England, peopled by about 20,000 white men, with their slaves, and an abject race of savages in the interior. Little but confusion prevailed, however, the Dutch residents rebelling against their new masters and wreaking vengeance upon their black subjects, until 1803, when, by the Treaty of Amiens, the colony was restored to Holland. Soon after that, the European war been revived, the British Government resolved to seize the district by force of arms. Cape Town, after a gallant fight, surrendered to Sir David Baird in 1806, and military rule was in force, being chiefly directed against the sterner Kaffirs who had advanced from the interior to take the place of the almost ex-

[1] Sparrman, "Voyage to the Cape of Good Hope," vol. i. pp. 53, 202; vol. ii. pp. 143, 342.

terminated Hottentots, until 1815, when the colony was formally and finally ceded to Great Britain.

There was mismanagement on the part of the new owners of the colony, although their chief troubles sprang from a worthy action. In 1808 the making of fresh slaves was forbidden, and laws began to be enforced for improving the condition of those already on the farms. The white inhabitants would have cared little whether they were nominally subject to England or to Holland, but this novel interference with their privileges as slaveholders was indignantly resented by them. Thus a keen spirit of opposition to their new rulers was aroused, and much mischief sprang from it. The boons at first conferred upon the subject Hottentots were too small to win from them any gratitude; and no attempts at all were made to pacify the few Hottentots who yet remained in freedom, and the hordes of Kaffirs in their rear.

These Kaffirs, residing in the eastern part of South Africa, had come into contact with the European settlers, partly by their own encroachments upon the districts held by the now almost exterminated Hottentots, partly by the advances made by the Europeans within their own border lands. It seems as if the new Government of the English might easily have made peace with them. Better able to fight than the Hottentots, they were less disposed to do so, having fewer grudges against the white man. "Some," we are told, "harassed the border colonists by frequent predatory incursions; but a considerable number lived quietly, engaged in cultivating the ground and herding their cattle, and those, together with another class who had entered the service of the colonists at their request, would gladly have pledged their allegiance to the British Crown, had the privileges of British subjects been offered and duly explained to them in return. The chiefs were daily becoming more sensible of the advantages to be gained by civilization, and entreated that missionaries should be sent for the instruction of their young people. Under these circumstances there is little doubt a large body of Kaffirs might, by legalising their tenure of certain lands, and otherwise by judicious treatment, have been incorporated with and rendered useful members of the community. Others might have been bought out with far less expense than they could be driven out; and the really irreclaimable, when proved so, expelled with the consent of the chief and council of the sub-tribes to which they belonged."[1]

Unfortunately this wise and honourable line of action was not thought of. The English, finding that the Kaffirs were the enemies of the Dutch, made them their own enemies—"irreclaimable, barbarous, and perpetual enemies," as they were described in a proclamation issued at this time. In 1809, Colonel Collins, who had been employed as a commissioner for the settlement of the frontier, recommended the expulsion of all Kaffirs from the border, and even the dismissal of all who had become servants in the colony. In 1811 this was begun. "A great commando, comprising a large force of military and burgher militia, was assembled under Colonel Graham; and, though the Kaffirs earnestly pleaded

[1] Martin, vol. iv. p. 50.

the cruelty of including the innocent and the guilty in the same condemnation, all were expelled with unrelenting severity. No warning was given; but they were forced to abandon their crops of maize and millet, then nearly ripe, and so extensive that the troops were employed for many weeks in destroying their cultivations by trampling them down with large herds of cattle, and burning to the ground their huts and hamlets; and much longer time elapsed before they succeeded in driving the whole of the people, to the number of 20,000 souls, over the Great Fish River."[1] No heed was paid to the pathetic appeals of these poor outcasts. "We have been with you fifteen or twenty years," said some of them, as we are told by one who was present. "We are your friends. We have watched your cattle when they were taken away by our countrymen. We have followed them and brought them back to you. Our wives have cultivated your gardens. Our children and yours speak the same language."[2]

The colonial troops then crossed the river after the fugitives, and attacked the Kaffir tribes among whom they took refuge. The land-drost, or magistrate and overseer of the district, Mr Stockenstrom, who had often befriended the natives, now sought to prevent bloodshed. "He was proceeding across the mountains, accompanied by about forty men, when, on approaching one of the kloofs, or passes, of the White River, he beheld numerous bands of Kaffirs assembling on both sides of the narrow ridge connecting two arms of the great mountain-chain along which

[1] Martin, vol. iv. pp. 51.
[2] Parliamentary Papers relative to the Cape, 1835, part L. p. 176.

lay their path. Relying on his great personal influence, and hoping to induce the Kaffirs to leave the country without further hostile operations, he rode straight up to them and dismounted in the midst, followed by a few who, having vainly striven to dissuade their leader from his daring enterprise, determined to share whatever hazard he might incur. The conference began, and continued for some time in the most amicable manner. The chiefs and their counsellors gathered round the venerable magistrate and listened with deference to his arguments, until a messenger arrived with the intelligence that the right and centre divisions of the British troops had attacked the Kaffirs, some of whose principal men had already fallen. The hope of striking a decisive blow by the destruction of a leader so powerful as the laud-drost, combined perhaps with the desire for retaliation, was irresistible. A boor, standing close by Mr Stockenstrom, remarked to him the agitated discussion which had suddenly arisen among a party of Kaffirs who stood aloof in the thicket, but he replied, with a smile, that there was no danger. While yet speaking, his words received a fearful contradiction. The Kaffir war-whoop rent the air, and was re-echoed by barbarian voices from hill and dale for many miles around. In a brief space the land-drost and fourteen of his companions lay dead, pierced by innumerable wounds. The survivors, of whom several were wounded, availed themselves of the fleetness of their horses to escape along the mountain ridge to the camp."[1] The only effect of that conduct towards one of the few European friends of the Kaffirs, was

[1] Martin, vol. iv. p. 52.

increased severity in the unholy exploits of the English. "The Kaffirs," said one who served in the affair, "were shot indiscriminately, women as well as men, and even though they offered no resistance;" but he adds, by way of apology, that "the women were killed unintentionally, because the boors could not distinguish them from men among the bushes."[1] The murderous work continued till the Kaffirs were forced to retire; but four years elapsed before the district seized from them could be safe without the presence of armed militia. Then the fort erected thereon was named Graham's Town, in honour—if it was any honour—of Colonel Graham, the officer who had commanded in the work.

In such ways the English brought upon themselves the deadly hatred of the Kaffirs. Equal mischief sprung from their ways of making friends among the black races. A leader of one of their tribes, named Gaika, being at feud with other chiefs, was in 1817 made an ally by the governor, Lord Charles Somerset; and it was agreed between them that Gaika and his people should have exclusive right of trade with the English, and should be aided in war against his rivals, on condition of their helping to punish those rivals for their misdeeds. One curious provision in this treaty was that, whenever cattle were stolen from the colony, the colonists should seize an equivalent number from the nearest and most convenient kraal, or village, of the Kaffirs, and that Gaika should make good the loss, if it fell upon his own tribe, by seizure from some of his neighbours. Certainly the Cape colonists were more apt in learning the crafts

[1] Pringle, "Narrative of a Residence in South Africa," p. 291.

of barbarism from the natives than in teaching them
the arts of civilization. Hardly could a more effective
plan have been devised for encouraging ill-will and
perpetuating the trade of cattle-stealing, which was
now the favourite excuse for raids upon the Kaffirs,
as it had been before in the case of the Hottentots.

In accordance with this treaty, Gaika, who had
been defeated in a battle with his enemies, was in
1818 aided with a force of 3352 soldiers and armed
colonists, who went against a league of several Kaffir
tribes. These Kaffirs expostulated against the intrusion, alleging that they had done no harm to the
European towns, and wished to be at peace with them,
and claiming that they should be allowed to settle
their own quarrels amongst themselves. The answer
of the English was a march through the territories
of the associated tribes, whose members, not daring to
engage in open fight, were slaughtered in their villages, or forced to take refuge in the woods while
those villages were destroyed. The gains of this
inglorious exploit were 30,000 stolen cattle, of which
9000 were given to Gaika, the rest being distributed
among the colonists. The associated tribes, goaded
by famine, sought to revenge themselves by raids on
the English borders, whereby much injury was done.
Of their number 9000 attacked Graham's Town, but
its garrison of 350, and a corps of Hottentots, used
their muskets with such deadly effect that the Kaffirs
were soon put to flight, 1400 of them being killed in
the fight, and many others dying on the way back
to their kraals. Thither they were pursued, to be
further cruelly punished for their honest resistance of
English tyranny. About 10,000 natives were driven

from their homes, and a new province was added to Cape Colony.

It is well that we should understand the disgraceful way in which the English quarrel with the Kaffirs was begun and continued; but it is not necessary here to detail all the painful incidents of the strife, perhaps the most disgraceful in all the annals of English colonial policy, too often dishonourable in itself and unfortunate in its issues. The slender excuse for the treatment to which the Kaffirs were subjected is that England had to govern a colony, chiefly composed of foreigners, whose disaffection to the new rule set over them was only to be checked by humouring the evil passions to which they had long given free vent.

To make willing vassals of the Dutch boors was a hard task. In 1815 an insurrection broke out among them, which was with difficulty quelled, and then many of the old settlers only submitted to English government with a sullen discontent that was very injurious to the well-being of the colony. Quiet was not easily maintained, and a healthy honourable temper could in no way be produced. Every effort to do good was a fresh cause of opposition. So it was especially in 1828, when a wise law for protecting the Hottentots, by which slavery was practically done away with, was passed.

In 1834 and 1835 another cruel war was waged against the Kaffirs, among whom Gaika, the former favourite of the colonists, was now included. "Their loss during our operations against them," wrote the governor, Sir Benjamin D'Urban, to Lord Glenelg, then Colonial Secretary, "has amounted to 4000 of their warriors, and, among them, many captains. Ours, fortunately, has not in the whole amounted to 100, and of them only two officers. There have been taken from these, also, besides the conquest and alienation of their country, about 60,000 head of cattle, almost all their goats; their habitations everywhere destroyed, and their gardens and corn-fields laid waste. They have been therefore chastised, not extremely, but perhaps sufficiently."[1] "The enemy," wrote Colonel Smith, concerning one part of the "not extreme" chastisement, "although his traces were numerous, fled so rapidly that few were killed, and only three shots fired at the troops. The whole of the country has been most thoroughly traversed. Upwards of 1200 huts, new and old, have been burnt; immense stores of corn, in every direction, destroyed. Cattle of all sorts, horses and goats, have fallen into our hands. It is most gratifying to know that the savages, being the unprovoked aggressors, have brought down all the misery with which they are now visited upon the heads of themselves and their families, and that the great day of retribution, and the punishment of the unprovoked atrocities committed by these murderous savages on our colonists, had arrived."[2]

Lord Glenelg's condemnation of these proceedings, and of the satisfaction with which they were regarded by their authors, was honourable. "I must own that I am affected by these statements in a manner the most remote from that which the writer contemplated. In the civilized warfare of Europe this desolation of an enemy's country, not in aid of any

[1] Parliamentary Papers, May 1836, p. 89.   [2] Ibid., p. 69.

military operations, nor for the security of the invading force, but simply and confessedly as an act of vengeance, has rarely occurred, and the occurrence of it has been invariably followed by universal reprobation. I doubt, indeed, whether the history of modern Europe affords an example even of a single case in which, without some better pretext than that of mere retribution, any invaded people were ever subjected to the calamities which Colonel Smith here describes —the loss of their food, the spoiling of their cattle, the burning of their dwellings, the expulsion of their wives and families from their homes, the confiscation of their property, and the forfeiture of their native country. I am, of course, aware that the laws of civilized nations cannot be rigidly applied in our contests with barbarous men; for those laws presuppose a reciprocity which cannot subsist between parties of whom the one is ignorant of the usages, maxims, and religion of the other. But the great principles of morality are of immutable and universal obligation, and from them are deduced the laws of war. Of these laws the first and cardinal is, that the belligerent must inflict no injury on his enemy which is not indispensably requisite to ensure the rights of him by whom it is inflicted, or to promote the attainment of the legitimate ends of the warfare. Whether we contend with a civilized or a barbarous enemy, the gratuitous aggravation of the horrors of war, on the plea of vengeance or retribution, or on any similar grounds, is alike indefensible. Now I must confess my inability to discover what danger could be averted, or what useful object could be attained, by the desolation of the Kaffir country."[1]

[1] Parliamentary Papers, May 1836, p. 70.

By Lord Glenelg's instructions, the land seized and the property stolen from the Kaffirs were restored in 1836, and thus a slight recompense was made for the wanton injuries inflicted upon them. Lord Glenelg also introduced a new system of dealing with the Kaffirs, which, if they had not been already so deeply injured by English rule, might have been altogether beneficial, and which, as it was, led to very good results. Treaties were entered into with most of their chiefs, by which trade was encouraged, and their territories were reserved to them without interference, on the condition of their respecting the rights which the Europeans had hitherto acquired by conquest. Thereby peace was kept, and the colony improved rapidly during ten years.

In spite of misrule, its progress had been considerable ever since the establishment of British dominion. In 1773 there were less than 24,000 white, black, and coloured residents in the Cape Colony. In 1807 they amounted to 56,051; in 1817 to 74,099; in 1823 to 85,656; in 1833 to 129,713; and in 1836 to 150,110. In 1846 they numbered 285,279, having nearly doubled in ten years. In the ensuing twenty years the population was again doubled. In 1865 there were 566,158 inhabitants in the colony, of whom 204,859 were Europeans.

This rapid growth of population was not due solely to the establishment of better relations with the Kaffir tribes, and the improved trade that resulted therefrom. It was also partly caused by the abolition of slavery. In 1834 freedom was given to 29,120 slaves, who, as free men, became better servants and made the farms more profitable. The kinder treatment to which they were subjected, moreover, not only enabled the resident black population to multiply rapidly, but caused a further increase of its numbers by the settlement in the colonial territory of Kaffirs and Hottentots, who, now that the tyranny of slavery was at an end, gladly sought employment and civilization under the English planters and traders.

In 1846 there was another dismal Kaffir war. It began through the imprudence of Sir Peregrine Maitland, a benevolent but unwise governor, who arrived in 1844. His arbitrary behaviour towards the natives in abolishing some of the treaties made with them, aroused their opposition. Cattle-stealing was increased, and disputes about boundaries were revived. Kaffir "insolence," as it was called, showed itself in various ways; and this, being resented by the colonial authorities and the war-party among the colonists which had lately been kept under, led to a renewal of hostilities. In April 1846 the Kaffir territory was invaded by a small force, and this movement being to a great extent unsuccessful, the blacks were led to retaliate. The old vindictive strife, disgraceful to England, began again, and it was continued with intermissions till 1852. Its details need not here be given. One little incident will suffice to illustrate the temper in which it was carried on by English officers and gentlemen. Sir Harry Smith, who had promised the Duke of Wellington that, with 4000 troops, he would utterly subdue the Kaffirs in two or three weeks, was sent out as governor in 1847. On landing at Port Elizabeth, he was welcomed by all classes, the war-party hoping that he would further its objects, the more peaceable section, including a vast number of native settlers, trusting that he would further the ends of justice in honourable ways. Among the crowd who came to greet him was Macomo, formerly a great independent chieftain, now a willing subject of the English Crown. "Sir Harry recognised him, half drew his sword from his scabbard, shook it at him, and stamped his foot on the ground. Shortly after he sent for the chief, who, upon being introduced, extended his hand; in return for which his excellency gave him his foot, collared him, laid him prostrate, put his foot upon his neck, and then brandished his sword over his head. Macomo, on rising, looked the governor quietly in the face, and said, 'I always thought you a great man till this day.'"[1]

By policy of that sort the British possessions in South Africa were increased, the largest increase being Sir Harry Smith's addition of the great Orange River district to British territory, but injury was done to the progress of civilization, which no territorial gains or multiplying of subject races can compensate. In 1853 the internal troubles had become so serious that many descendants of the old Dutch settlers, still rebellious against English rule, were allowed to join with the discontented natives of the Orange River territory, and there to found a republic quite independent of Great Britain. Thereby the dimensions of Cape Colony were considerably reduced, but its strength and value were greatly augmented. Its limits, however, were again greatly extended by the

[1] Martin, vol. iv. p. 104.

addition to it of British Kaffraria, whose inhabitants, so long hostile to our Government, have now become peaceable subjects.

The most noteworthy fact in the recent political history of the colony is the re-shaping of its constitution in 1852. In lieu of the old military government, responsible only to the English Crown, the management of affairs is now vested in a civil governor, aided by a Legislative Council of sixteen members, and a House of Assembly, comprising forty-six representatives elected by the towns and country districts.

Cape Colony and British Kaffraria now comprise an area of 200,610 square miles, nearly as large as Spain and Portugal. Cape Town, the metropolis, is a well-built and thriving city; and Graham's Town, Port Elizabeth, and other towns, are vicing with it in importance. In them trade prospers, and agricultural and pastoral pursuits make steady progress in the interior districts, which, if their scenery is less attractive than that of some other of our colonies, are healthy and fertile. The value of the imports, which in 1836 was £541,038, had risen to £1,277,101 in 1850, and to £1,942,281 in 1866. The exports, worth £362,280 in 1836, amounted in 1850 to £637,252, and in 1866 to £2,599,169. That last sum represented, among other articles, 35,231,607 pounds of sheep's wool, 1,018,296 sheep-skins, 678,364 goat-skins, and 21,220 cowhides, with 40,969 pounds of ivory, 15,144 pounds of ostrich feathers, and 93,164 gallons of wine. Gold, which has recently been found in so many other parts of the world, was discovered in Cape Colony in 1868, and, later still, a promise has been given of a considerable supply of diamonds.

But without these glittering prizes the colony is rich enough in solid advantages. "In addition," we are told, "to a vast extent of upland soil, park-like downs, and sheltered vales, and a climate well adapted to the English constitution, and so fine and dry as to necessitate no winter provender or shelter for sheep or cattle, it affords suitable temperature for an endless variety of culture, by means of proximity to the ocean on either shore, and by the diversified elevation of its lofty mountains and immense plateaux. Here wheat, bringing nearly the best price in the London market, may be grown to an incalculable extent. There two crops of maize or millet may be annually reaped. The vine flourishes over large tracts, and where the grape ripens the olive and mulberry will thrive. Animal food of the best quality abounds; and the fishery on L'Agulhas bank is scarcely inferior to that of Newfoundland. The sugar-cane, tea and coffee plants, flax and cotton, may be eventually added to the present staple colonial products."[1]

[1] Martin, vol. iv. p. 158.

CHAPTER XIV.

NATAL.

THE KAFFIRS—FIRST ENGLISH VISITS TO THE EASTERN COAST OF SOUTH AFRICA—THE SETTLEMENT OF PORT NATAL—ITS EARLY TROUBLES AND LATER PROGRESS—THE PRESENT CONDITION AND RESOURCES OF THE COLONY. [1688-1869.]

THE various tribes of South African Kaffirs are supposed to be of the same stock as the Kaffirs of Persia, and to have emigrated four or five thousand years ago from the neighbourhood of the Tigris or Euphrates, passing northwards through Egypt, and carrying with them the language, habits, and religious practices of their forefathers. In all these respects their affinity with the Asiatic race is still traceable. They differ essentially from the Hottentots and other yet more degraded inhabitants of Africa. "The physical conformation of the body is fine. The men ordinarily stand about five feet ten inches to six feet high, slenderly built, but compact and wiry. Not unfrequently the head is well developed, displaying considerable mental power; and amongst the men the numerous ways in which they are called to engage in intellectual gladiatorship impart an intelligence and expressiveness to the whole contour which are far removed from the low savage or the sordid barbarian."[1] Many of their customs and institutions are savage and bar-

[1] Holden, "The Past and Future of the Kaffir Races," p. 174.

barous enough; but even their vices often show traces of a perverted worth never possessed by their neighbours. These are the people with whose southern tribes the Dutch and English residents in Cape Colony have been in contact and conflict during upwards of a century, and with whose northern tribes, especially the Zulus, we have lately been brought into relationship by our colonization of Natal.

Port Natal—so called because he entered its harbour on Christmas Day—was discovered by Vasco de Gama in 1498. But for more than three centuries the eastern shores of South Africa were rarely visited by Europeans, unless they were shipwrecked on the coast or forced to pay it a brief visit in search of provisions for their onward voyages to the East Indies.

The first English intercourse was in 1683, when a trading vessel was lost near Delagoa Bay, about a hundred leagues north of Natal. "The natives," says the old chronicler, "showed the shipwrecked men more civility and humanity than some nations that I know who pretend much religion and politeness; for they accommodated their guests with whatever they wanted of the product of their country at very easy rates, and assisted what they could to save part of the damaged cargo, receiving very moderate reward for their labour and pains. For a few glass beads, knives, scissors, needles, thread, and small looking-glasses, they hired themselves to carry many things to a neighbouring country, and provided others, who also served as guides towards the Cape of Good Hope, and provided eatables for their masters all the while they were under their conduct. And, having carried them about two hundred miles on their way by land, they provided new guides and porters for them, as the others had done, for seven or eight hundred miles farther, which they travelled in forty days, and so delivered their charge to others, till they arrived at the Cape. And, some of the English falling sick on the way, they carried them in hammocks till they either recovered or died; and out of eighty men there were only three or four that died; but how long they journeyed before they got to the Cape I have forgotten. This account I have from one of the travellers. He told me that the natural fertility of those countries he travelled through made the inhabitants lazy, indolent, indocile, and simple. Their rivers are abundantly stored with good fish and water-fowl, besides sea-cows and crocodiles; their woods with large trees, wild cattle and deer, elephants, rhinoceroses, lions, tigers, wolves, and foxes; also many sorts of fowl and birds, with ostriches."[1]

It was probably by the report of the travellers, who certainly had no reason to charge their kind friends with being "lazy and indocile," that a few years afterwards, in 1689, the Dutch colonists at the Cape sent a vessel to explore the eastern coast. "One may travel two or three hundred miles through the country," said one of the party, "without any cause of fear from men, provided you go naked, and without any iron or copper; for these things give inducement to murder those who have them. Neither need one be in any apprehension about meat and drink, as they have in every village a kraal, or house

[1] Chase, "Natal Papers," vol. I. p. 2.

of entertainment for travellers, where they are not only lodged, but fed also."[1]

So well pleased were the Dutch with this district and its people, that, in 1704, they sent an agent to purchase the Bay of Natal and its neighbourhood for "some merchandise, consisting of copper, arm and neck rings," valued at 20,000 guilders. But, fortunately for the Zulu Kaffirs, the Dutch, fully occupied at the Cape, made no use of their purchase. For a hundred years the natives had undisturbed possession of their homes, and then they were troubled, not by Europeans, but by another race of Kaffirs, who, coming down from the inland mountain region, spread desolation over the district north and south of Natal Harbour.

No European colony in this district was seriously thought of till 1823, when Lieutenant Fairwell, R.N., visited it; and, being welcomed by Utshaka, the victorious Kaffir chieftain, sought and obtained permission of Lord Charles Somerset, governor of Cape Colony, to plant in it a settlement of Englishmen. This he promptly did. Accompanied by Mr Flynn, Captain King, a few other Europeans, and some Hottentots, he proceeded to Natal, when Utshaka gave him a grant of about 3000 square miles of land and several herds of cattle. "We had an opportunity of further gaining his friendship," wrote Lieutenant Fairwell to the governor, "by curing him of a dangerous wound he received since we have been here; and I trust I shall, by frequent communications and a studious endeavour to avoid giving offence, increase his and his subjects' confidence in us."[2]

[1] Holden, p. 128.   [2] Chase, vol. I. p. 17.

Lieutenant Fairwell began his work nobly; but it was jealously regarded by the Cape colonists. Having built a little vessel at Natal, he sent it with a cargo of ivory to Algoa Bay, where it was refused admittance, and forced to rot on the beach, on the plea that it was not provided with any official register as a British trading-ship.[1] Thus thwarted, the brave pioneer of Natal colonization managed to open a route by land, and thus sent his wares for sale in Graham's Town. He was not allowed, however, to pursue his enterprise for long. In 1828 Utshaka, a fierce despot who had discernment enough to desire the benefits likely to result from intercourse with Europeans, was assassinated by his younger brother Udingaan; and this new tyrant, apparently enraged at the conduct of some Dutch settlers on the borderland between his territory and Cape Colony, soon caused or sanctioned the destruction of the little colony at Natal. Perhaps also he was alarmed at its rapid progress, and at the friendship shown by the English to the older inhabitants of the district, who, having fled into the woods when it was invaded by Utshaka, now came back in considerable numbers to share in its prosperity. Fairwell and some of his followers were murdered while crossing the mountains in 1829. An attack was then made upon Natal, and many of its residents being put to death, the rest were compelled to abandon the settlement.

It was revived in 1835. In the previous year the authorities at Cape Colony, at length alive to the value of the enterprise, obtained the permission of the British Government to enter upon it with spirit.

[1] Parliamentary Papers, 1835, part ii. p. 97.

Captain Allen Gardiner, whose miserable death at Terra del Fuego is well known, proceeded on a mission to the tyrant; and, after some difficulty, partly removed by the promise of a red cloak, obtained from him not only a renewal of the grant of land made to Fairwell, but about 4000 more square miles. The town of D'Urban, in Natal Harbour, was laid out, and to it came some Englishmen and a larger number of Dutch, who, having left Cape Colony in disgust at the liberation of their slaves in 1834, came in search of fresh means of aggrandizement in the new settlement. Their coming had a memorable issue. Quarrels soon broke out, as before, between them and the Kaffirs; and in 1838 a battle was fought in which the Europeans were defeated with great slaughter. It seemed as if Natal was to be once more abandoned. A small military force, however, was sent up from Graham's Town to protect it. This protection, otherwise inactive, enabled the settlers to make arrangements for fighting their own battles. They boldly attacked Udingaan in 1840, and overcame him, thereby so weakening his repute among his own people that he was soon afterwards assassinated. The Dutch residents, now having supremacy in Natal, announced their intention of making it independent of English authority, and the centre of a republican settlement. An English force was sent to quell this rebellion; and its result was the formal annexation of the settlement to Cape Colony in 1844. In the following year a Lieutenant-Governor and Executive Council were appointed. In 1848 the settlement was allowed to have its own Legislative Council; and in 1856 it was converted into a separate and distinct colony, and its inhabitants were allowed to choose their own House of Assembly.

Since then it has grown rapidly. Its white population, which in 1846 numbered about 6000, is now about thrice as numerous. The white, coloured, and black inhabitants, comprised within an area of 16,145 square miles, were in 1866 estimated at 193,103. In that year the imports of the young colony were worth £263,305; and its exports, consisting chiefly of wool, sugar, cotton, and coffee, were valued at £203,402. Much of the trade, however, only passed through Natal on its way to and from the Orange River Republic, on the other side of the Drakenberg Mountains.

The wealth-producing powers of the colony itself, though much developed during the past few years, are yet only in their infancy. Few possessions of Great Britain have more attractive features or fairer prospects. Every part of the district is described as fertile and healthy. "The country rises from the sea-coast in a series of terraces to an elevation of several thousand feet, and presents a rare variety of scenery, soil, and climate. Along the Indian Ocean is a belt of land about fifteen miles in breadth, the greater part of which rises and falls in a succession of round swelling hills and small valleys, carpeted with long grass, over which are scattered clumps of trees, chiefly of mimosa and euphorbia. In some places the uniformity of the scenery is relieved by forests and dense jungle; in others, by vast masses of lofty and abrupt hills and deep ravines. This lovely region favours the vegetation both of the tropics and of southern Europe. Sugar, coffee, indigo, and almost every other tropical plant flourish, along with the mulberry, olive, and vine. Nor is it unfavourable to some of the productions of a cooler climate; for oats, beans, and potatoes, especially the first two, thrive well. Having crossed this belt, we ascend into a country where the hills take a longer sweep, something like the downs of Sussex. They are still covered with long grass, but the wood has disappeared, except in small patches in the hollows and on the banks of the streams. The character of the vegetation has changed, and we no longer see that of the tropics. Good crops of wheat, oats, potatoes, and other productions of a temperate climate, are produced, and the district is admirably suited for horses and horned cattle. Many fruits also flourish in this part, among which are the orange, pomegranate, peach, and apricot. Proceeding still farther, and ascending another terrace, we find the hills more massive, with a still longer and bolder sweep, covered with grass, but generally bare of wood. They are frequently flat-topped, and sometimes expand into table-land. At intervals, on the crests of the hills, we meet with stony ridges, composed of large boulders, stretching across the country like huge dykes. In the distance farther inland we see rugged hills cut by deep ravines, and beyond them the mountain range, rising abruptly like a wall 8000 feet above the level of the sea, and nearly 4000 above the country at its base; with here and there buttresses thrown out like towers and battlements—in summer casting a dark rugged outline against the deep blue sky, and in winter radiant in a mantle of snow. Sweeping round to the north-west, the range sinks into lower hills, presenting a softer outline, with passes winding over them. The long coarse grass of the lower country is here exchanged for a shorter and finer kind, and everything about him tells the traveller that he has now reached a land admirably adapted both for horned cattle and for sheep. He finds, too, that the country produces abundant crops of wheat, oat, and other cereals of England; while he is refreshed by the taste of excellent peaches, apricots, apples, pears, and other fruits of a temperate climate. Scattered at intervals over the whole face of the country are vast clusters of hills. These localities seem to have been subject to violent convulsions of nature. The hills, or rather mountains, rear their rugged or scarped sides in every fantastic form, overhanging deep and gloomy glens, the channels of rushing rivers or foaming torrents."[1]

[1] "Encyclopædia Britannica," vol. xv. p. 802.

CHAPTER XV.

BRITISH INDIA.

THE PROGRESS OF BRITISH TRADE AND CONQUEST IN INDIA—ITS PRESENT CONDITION. [1600-1869.]

BRITISH India is hardly, according to the usual sense of the word, a colony; and the memorable story of its gradual acquisition forms a separate and eventful portion of the annals of our empire. Only some of the most salient features in that story, therefore, need be briefly touched upon in this volume.

The great peninsula was unvisited by Englishmen, with the exception of a few daring travellers by land and sea, until a century after Vasco de Gama's discovery in 1498 of a passage to it by way of the Cape of Good Hope. In 1599 the English East India Company was formed; and in 1601 its first trading fleet went out to sow the seeds of commerce and conquest, not on the mainland, but in some of the rich islands south-west of it. The first British factory on the peninsula was established in 1612, by Captain Best, at Surat; and after that commerce throve mightily, and conquest slowly advanced during a hundred and fifty years. The Dutch the Portuguese, and the French, were rivals of the English in the prosperous trade, and most of the early fighting was with them. In furtherance of their strife, however, the Europeans

sought allies among the natives of the country.
Thus each acquired a sort of jurisdiction far beyond
the narrow limits of their forts and factories; and at
length the English, having driven out their rivals,
found themselves associated with numerous local
potentates who acknowledged their supremacy, and
at variance with others who had aided the cause of
the now defeated European rivals. In that way the
conquest of India was brought about in the middle
of the eighteenth century. The daring and dishonourable exploits of Clive and Warren Hastings are well
known. The territorial rule of the East India Company began with Clive's war in the Carnatic, and his
great victory at Plassey in 1757. It was partly won
by aid of some native soldiers, now for the first time
employed under English officers, and destined, during
just a century, to be the main instruments of English power in overcoming one native prince after
another, and in acquiring great districts in quick
succession, until the whole peninsula was brought
into subjection, and kept in order by means of the
famous Sepoy army. At the end of the century, the
Sepoys, overpetted in some respects and needlessly
offended in others, turned against their employers.
The great Indian Mutiny of 1857 was the result; and,
overcome by bravery and martial wisdom rarely
equalled in the whole world's history, it led to the
transference of the vast Indian empire from the rule
of the East India Company to the direct dominion
of the British Crown.

The territories thus transferred comprise an area
of more than 1,000,000 square miles, eight times as
large as that of Great Britain and Ireland, and con-

tain a population five times as numerous. The inhabitants more than suffice for the cultivation of the land and the development of its resources; and the only openings in it for European residents are as agents of Government, teachers, and traders. Much has yet to be done in education of the people as to better ways of agriculture, and more useful methods of interchanging their commodities, and great progress has been made in these respects during recent years. The revenue, which was £27,000,000 in 1851, and £36,000,000 in 1859, exceeded £44,000,000 in 1864, and £48,000,000 in 1868. The imports of merchandise, worth £4,261,106 in 1834, rose in value to £11,558,788 in 1850, and to £36,093,938 in 1868. The exports of the same years were £7,993,420, £18,164,149, and £53,062,165. The incoming trade had been multiplied nearly nine times, and the outgoing trade nearly seven times, in the course of four-and-thirty years. The raw cotton alone sent from India to the United Kingdom in 1864 was worth nearly £38,000,000; and the cotton goods sent back exceeded in value £12,000,000. Besides cotton, this great territory, possessing nearly every variety of soil and temperature, furnishes rice, wheat, sugar, coffee, tea, silk, wool, flax, indigo, and other dyes, with spices, oils, and a hundred other commodities.

Bombay, the great trading capital of India, contains, with its suburbs, hardly fewer than a million inhabitants; and the population of Calcutta, the centre of government, and scarcely inferior as a resort of trade, exceeds a million. The English residents in the whole dependency, however, including 84,083 military men, numbered only 125,945 in 1861.

CHAPTER XVI.

OUR ASIATIC COLONIES.

CEYLON — ITS EARLY CIVILIZATION — ITS SUBJECTION TO THE PORTUGUESE, THE DUTCH, AND THE ENGLISH — ITS PRESENT CONDITION — THE STRAITS SETTLEMENTS: PENANG, MALACCA, AND SINGAPORE — HONG KONG — BORNEO AND LABUAN — THE ACHIEVEMENTS OF SIR JAMES BROOKE. [1795-1869.]

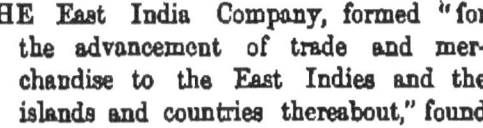HE East India Company, formed "for the advancement of trade and merchandise to the East Indies and the islands and countries thereabout," found so much profit in its intercourse with the mainland of Hindostan, that, during two centuries in which other European nations were establishing in them forts, factories, and colonies, it gave little thought to the outlying portions of the East Indies. Not till near the close of the eighteenth century was their value understood or effort made to appropriate some of them as dependencies of England. And even then this was done rather in jealousy of the rival nations than in the interests of trade.

So especially it was with Ceylon. This beautiful island, with an area of nearly 25,000 square miles, and therefore not much smaller than Ireland, was famous for its wealth and civilization in the days of Alexander the Great. Anuradpoora, its ancient capital, founded in the year 437 B.C., covered sixteen square miles, and was adorned with splendid architectural works, the remains of which yet exist. Huge tanks and sluices, so stoutly built of granite and other hard stone that some of them are still, after the lapse of more than two thousand years, but little injured, served to irrigate the land, and helped it to maintain the five or six million inhabitants whom it is supposed to have contained in its ancient days of splendour. It was still populous and thriving, though much decayed, when the Portuguese began, in 1518, to build a fort and plant a settlement at Colombo. Much misery resulted to the inhabitants from that settlement. War between the natives and the aggressors lasted nearly all through the century and a half of Portuguese occupation; and the Dutch, who expelled and succeeded their rivals in 1656, brought no better fortune to the Singhalese during their tenure of Colombo, which also lasted for nearly a century and a half. In 1795 they were twice expelled by the English, and Ceylon became a British possession. At first in the hands of the East India Company, it was made a Crown colony in 1802.

The first incidents of British rule were inauspicious. An unwise invasion of Kandy, then the centre of native authority, in 1803, issued in the ignominious defeat and slaughter of nearly all the invaders. Other troubles followed, which ended in the conquest of the whole island in 1815. Measures, for the most part prudent and generous, were then taken for the improvement of the colony; and latterly its progress, unmarked by any memorable incidents, has been very rapid. In 1814, Ceylon contained about 852,940 inhabitants. In 1832 the number was estimated at 1,009,008; in 1852, at 1,707,194; and in 1866, at 2,008,027. The revenue of the island, only about £200,000 in 1827, was £962,874 in 1866. The imports were valued at £329,933 in 1828; at £1,181,149 in 1853; and at £3,517,184 in 1866. The exports amounted to £215,372 in 1829; to £979,874 in 1853; and to £3,070,248 in 1866. The principal commodities then exported were 899,480 hundredweight of coffee, 869,484 pounds of cinnamon, 25,143 hundredweight of tobacco, and 83,801 hundredweight of cocoa-nut oil.

This great increase of trade is chiefly due to British enterprise; but hardly more than 15,000 of the inhabitants are Europeans. The rapid growth of population is native, or derived from Oriental colonization. The natives are of four races, varying much in civilization and powers of development. The Veddas, or aborigines, frequent the forests stretching from the south to the north-west, and all the more inaccessible parts of the island, where, hardly superior to monkeys, they form nearly the lowest and most degraded of all the members of the human family. The Singhalese, found chiefly around Kandy and in the region south of it, handsome in body, show traces of an effete civilization, and regard the white men with a hatred for which some excuse may be found in the hard treatment they have received from Europeans. "Jealousy, slander, litigation, and revenge," says Sir James Emerson Tennant, "prevail among them to an unlooked for excess. Licentiousness is so universal that it has ceased to be opprobrious, and hatred so ungovernable that murders are by no means rare. Falsehood, the unerring index of innate debasement, is of ubiquitous prevalence. Theft is equally prevalent; and deceit in every conceivable shape, in forgery and fraud, in corruption and defamation, is so notorious amongst the uneducated mass, that the feeling of confidence is almost unknown; and in the most intimate arrangements of domestic life the bond of brotherhood or friendship, of parent and of child, inspires no effectual reliance in the mutual good faith and honour of the interested parties." Superior to these are the Malabars or Hindoos, who appear to have long ago settled in Ceylon, and who most abound in the northern and eastern parts of the island; and the Moors, a mixed race, containing African blood, and perhaps partly formed out of the slavery established by the Portuguese and Dutch, who are hardworking traders and artizans in all parts of Ceylon. These last two races prove the best servants of the English merchants and planters.

Ceylon is particularly rich in all vegetable productions, from coffee, cinnamon, and rice, to the huge teak and palm, with ebony and other cabinet woods. Agriculture yields employment to most of the inhabitants. Yet, as Sir Emerson Tennant has said, "in Ceylon agriculture, in all its branches, must be regarded as an art almost unknown. Notwithstanding all the advantages in variety of soil, graduations of temperature and adaptability of climate, the cultivation of rice may be said to be the only successful tillage of the natives. With the favourable circumstances alluded to, and the expanse of surface to be applied, it is impossible to foresee the extent to which the productions of nearly every other country might be domesticated and extended throughout this island. In the highlands and mountain regions, and particularly in the wooded valleys and open plains, which are found at an elevation of from 3000 to 7000 feet, there is an encouraging field for the introduction of most of the grains and vegetable productions of Europe." Much has been done since those words were written; but vast tracts of country still wait to be reclaimed from the aggressions of tigers and elephants upon the scenes of by-gone civilization in Ceylon.

Almost the same may be said of the districts east of Ceylon, on the other side of the Bay of Bengal, now known as the Straits Settlements, including Singapore, Penang, and Malacca. The Malayan peninsula, a long strip of land containing about 1000 square miles, belonged to the Portuguese from 1571 till 1640. It was then held by the Dutch for a century and a half. It was afterwards twice captured by the English and twice restored to its former owners, before finally becoming British property in 1825. In it tin abounds; and rice, sugar, coffee, cotton, indigo, chocolate, and various spices are prolific. On its western side, the little island of Penang, about as large as the Isle of Wight, is a fertile garden of spices; and Singapore, an island about twice as large, adjoining the southern extremity of the mainland, is rich in timber of every sort. The smaller island was acquired by the East India Company in 1786; the other was taken by Sir Stamford Raffles in 1818 from a horde of about a hundred and fifty Malayan pirates. All the three dependencies were united under one government, as the Straits Settlements, in 1867. Their aggregate population exceeds 250,000, amongst whom Chinese immigrants are numerous and most active; and they derive great profit from trade between all the East Indian Islands and Europe, for which the situation of Singapore—"the little shop," as the name implies—is especially adapted. The goods passing in and out each year are valued at more than £10,000,000, and give employment to ships with a total tonnage of nearly 2,000,000, although the resources of the colonies themselves, save in the production of opium, are yet but scantily made use of.

Much of the trade by which Singapore is enriched is derived from China, and passes through the little island of Hong Kong, the smallest of all the colonies of Great Britain. "The island consists of a broken ridge of mountainous hills at an average height of about 1000 feet; but from this ridge and its spurs various conical mountains rise to the height of 1500 or 2000 feet above the sea, and are very precipitous. The greater part of the coast shelves abruptly from the ocean, particularly on the north face. There are a few narrow valleys and deep ravines through which the sea occasionally bursts, or which serve as conduits for the mountain torrents; but on the north side of the island, especially where the town of Victoria is built, the rocky ridge approaches close to the harbour; and it was only by hewing through this ridge that a street or road could be made to connect the straggling lines of buildings which extend along the water's edge for nearly four miles. Here and there, on the tops of some isolated hills, or along the precipitous slopes of the mountains, scattered houses have been constructed; but rugged, broken, and abrupt precipices, with deep rocky ravines, must effectually prevent any contracted population from being able to provide efficiently for its own protection, cleanliness, and comfort. Hong Kong cannot be said to possess any vegetation; a few goats with difficulty find pasturage."[1] A rugged beauty characterizes the island-rock; but its geological formation, and the pernicious climate to which it is exposed, render it one of the most unhealthy spots in the world.

This inhospitable little island, with an area of about 30 square miles, for centuries the haunt of Chinese pirates and smugglers, was ceded to Great Britain by China in 1842 as a free port for trade, and a naval station for the protection of British interests in Chinese waters. To it was added the small peninsula of Kowloon in 1861. Its population, about 12,000 in 1842, was 29,507 in 1849, and 117,471 in 1867; but of these only 1644 were Europeans, and 30,537 of the natives, unable or unwilling to find homes on the barren shore, lived in boats in the rivers. The revenue of the colony rose from £31,078 in 1847 to £160,226 in 1866. But it derived its importance from the jealousy of the Chinese in excluding foreign trade from other ports; and now that a better policy has been established, commerce is passing from the unhealthy rock in the south to more attractive and more commodious places on the northern coast.

South of Hong Kong, and west of Singapore, is Borneo, the largest island in the world, with the

[1] Martin, vol. vi. p. 63.

exception of Australia, famous as a resort for pirates
through many centuries, and for the philanthropic
efforts towards its redemption made in recent times
by Rajah Brooke. The English and other nations
had more than once sought to effect a settlement and
open trade on its shores; but on each occasion they
were forced to retire by the murderous conduct of
native marauders. At length, in 1839, Mr James
Brooke, then thirty-six years of age, resolved to attempt the establishment of a better state of things.
"I go," he said, "to awaken the slumbering spirit of
philanthropy with regard to these islands. Fortune
and life I freely give; and, if I fail in the attempt, I
shall not have lived wholly in vain." Proceeding to
Saráwak, on the western coast of Borneo, he con-
ciliated the inhabitants, and was soon chosen by them
as rajah. This office he accepted in 1841, on condition that slavery and piracy should be abolished in
the region assigned to him, and that he should use
any means he found necessary for their entire suppression; that Englishmen should have right of trade
in any part of the great island, and that the smaller
island of Labuan should be ceded to Great Britain.
To these proposals the nominal King of Borneo
agreed; and for his services Mr Brooke was rewarded
by the English Crown with knighthood, and endowed
with the functions of Governor of Labuan and Con-
sul-general in Borneo. He also sought to have his
dominions in Saráwak recognised by the British
Government, and to receive national aid in the work
on which he had already expended £12,000 of his
own. This, however, was denied, and he was forced
to carry on the work in his own way. The people

over whom he had to rule, and ruled successfully for more than twenty years, occupy an intermediate position between the Malayans who have in modern times acquired a footing and a nominal dominion over the whole island, and the aboriginal and only half-human Malanaus, or Paketans, who occupy the interior. They are of two classes: the Hill Dyaks, who occupy the greater portion of Sariwak as well as other parts of Borneo, and are poor, industrious, and peaceable; and the Sea Dyaks, scattered over the coast and on the banks of large rivers, who are of much fiercer disposition. It was these whom Rajah Brooke sought especially to reclaim. "They have never been more than nominally subject to the Malays," we are told; "and Sir James Brooke is the first master whom they have really obeyed. Every year a cloud of murderous pirates issued from their rivers and swept the adjacent coasts. No man was safe by reason of his poverty or insignificance, for human heads were the booty sought by these rovers, and not wealth alone. Villages were attacked in the dead of night, and every adult cut off. The women and grown girls were frequently slaughtered with the men, and children alone were preserved, to be the slaves of the conqueror. Never was warfare so terrible as this. Head-hunting became a mania which spread like a horrible disease over the whole land. Murder lurked in the jungle and on the river. The aged warrior could not rest in his grave till his relations had taken a head in his name: the maiden disdained the weak-hearted suitor whose hand was not yet stained with some cowardly murder."[1]

[1] Boyle, "Adventures among the Dyaks of Borneo."

This spirit ruled among the Sea Dyaks when Sir
James Brooke went to rule over and to reform
them. From his nephew and successor, Mr Charles
Brooke, he received important help in the good work
he was able to do. "He first gained over a portion
of these Dyaks to the cause of order," says the
nephew, "and then used them, as instruments in the
same cause, to restrain their countrymen. The result
has been that the coast of Saráwak is as safe to the
traders as the coast of England, and that an unarmed
man can travel the country without let or hindrance."[1] That end, if quite gained yet, was not
gained without difficulty. The chief trouble came
from the custom of head-hunting. Every now and
then a raid would be made upon Saráwak from some
inland part, and half a dozen or more of the natives
would be decapitated. As often, parties of four or
five of Rajah Brooke's subjects would make an excursion inland, in hopes of returning with a few
stolen heads as trophies of their prowess. "As soon
as ever one of these parties started, or even listened
to birds of omen preparatory to moving," says Mr
Brooke, "a party was immediately dispatched by
Government to cut them off, and to fine them heavily
on their return; or, in the event of their bringing heads,
to demand the delivery of them up, and the payment
of a fine into the bargain. This was the steady and
unflinching work of years; but, before many months
were over, my stock of heads became numerous and
the fines considerable." All who offered resistance
were declared enemies of the Government, and burnt
out of their houses, alien tribes being employed to

[1] Brooke, "Ten Years in Saráwak."

do the work. Occasionally larger expeditions were organized, under the leadership of the Rajah himself or his nephew, who went inland or on water, with two or three hundred followers, to punish the more remote or more troublesome tribes, when English guns easily succeeded against native swords and spears. Thus some sort of order and civilized behaviour has been established. " It is a singularly easy government to carry on," we are assured; "tribes, one with another, being so well balanced that, in the event of danger arising from one party, the other may be trusted to counteract evil influences."[1]

Whether this bold enterprise of Sir James Brooke's will secure all the benefits expected by him time only can show. But from it benefits have already resulted. Borneo has been opened to European trade, and Labuan has become an English colony. This little island, with an area of 45 square miles, had in 1865 a population of 2785, employed in trade with Borneo or in rendering available the timber that abounds on the surface of the island, and the coal which is no less abundant beneath the surface. The local revenue of Labuan, which was £59 in 1848, had risen to £2535 in 1854, and to £7370 in 1865. Most of its trade is in exchanging European produce for the hides, spices, and other commodities of Borneo.

[1] Brooke.

CHAPTER XVII

EARLY AUSTRALASIAN DISCOVERIES.

PORTUGUESE AND DUTCH DISCOVERIES OF AUSTRALIA—TASMAN—
ENGLISH VOYAGERS—DAMPIER IN AUSTRALIA—CAPTAIN COOK
IN NEW ZEALAND AND AUSTRALIA—FRENCH EXPEDITIONS.
[1601-1788.]

AUSTRALIA, a vast island more than three-quarters of the size of Europe, and only the largest of a numerous group which with it, in pre-historic times and before it was the sport of volcanic action, seems to have formed one vast southern continent, was first visited among Europeans by some Portuguese voyagers early in the sixteenth century. The nearer regions of the East Indies, however, then proved more attractive; and no distinct effort to explore it appears to have been made till after 1601, when it was again seen by another Portuguese, named Godinho de Heredia, and then the effort was not made by Portuguese but by Dutchmen. Chiefly by them it was often reached, and its most accessible parts, as well as the adjoining islands, were gradually explored during the eighteenth century. Tasman's expeditions, sent out under the direction of Anthony Van Dieman in 1642 and 1644, being the most famous and fruitful of all. Tasman first discovered the island which, now known by his name, was formerly called Van Dieman's Land, in honour of his employer. Then he traversed the northern shore of Australia or New Holland. Others of his race carried on the work of exploration; but still the voyages of discovery failed to issue in colonization; and after the close of the eighteenth century the Dutch resigned the quest, as the Portuguese had done before them.

The English, who had not before been altogether idle, then succeeded to the enterprise. William Dampier, who began his seaman's life as a buccaneer in the West Indies, was the first of our nation to engage in it. In 1688 he visited the north-western part of Australia, of which he gave an unfavourable report. " It was only low and sandy ground, the points only excepted, which are rocky, as some isles in the bay. This part had no fresh water, except what was dug, but divers sorts of trees, and among the rest the dragon-tree, which produces the gum called dragon's-blood. We saw neither fruit-trees, nor so much as the track of any living being of the bigness of a large mastiff dog; some few land-birds, but none larger than a blackbird, and scarcely any water-fowl. The inhabitants are the most miserable wretches in the universe, having no houses, nor garments, except a piece of the bark of a tree, tied like a girdle round the waist; no sheep, poultry, or fruits. They feed upon a few fish, cockles, mussels, and periwinkles. They are without religion or government. They are tall, straight-bodied, and thin, with small, long limbs. They have great round foreheads and great brows. Their eyelids are always half closed to keep the flies out of their eyes, they being so troublesome here that no fanning will keep them from coming to one's face. So that, from their infancy being thus annoyed with these insects, they do never open their eyes as other people do; and, therefore, they cannot see far, unless they hold up their heads. They are long visaged, and of an unpleasing aspect, having no graceful feature in their faces. The colour of their skin, both of their faces and the rest of their body, is coal black, like that of the negroes of Guinea. They live in companies, twenty or thirty men, women, and children together. Their only food is a sort of small fish, which they get by making weirs of stones across little coves or branches of the sea, every tide bringing in the small fish, and there leaving them for a prey to these people, who constantly attend to search for them at low water."[1]

Dampier went to Australian waters again, and made some further explorations, in 1699, though his chief visit was paid to the same western districts to which he had gone before. Except for the pleasure of discovering the barrenest spot on the face of the globe, he said, his achievements in New Holland would not have charmed him much.[2] He then sailed north, explored New Guinea, and discovered New Britain.

His dismal account of these regions helped to deter other voyagers from following in his track. Nothing memorable was done till 1769, when Captain Cook, proceeding from Otaheite in his famous voyage round the world, reached the south-eastern side of New Zealand, and established some intimacy with its bold natives. His friendly advances being at first rejected, he killed four and captured two of them, thus beginning

[1] Howitt, "History of Discovery in Australia, Tasmania, and New Zealand," vol. 1. pp. 66, 67.
[2] Howitt, vol. 1. p. 72.

a strife still fruitful in misfortune both to Englishmen and to Maories. Through his captives, however, whom he treated kindly, he and some of his party afterwards were able to land, and had the first English experience of New Zealand life. "They entered some of their huts and saw them at their meals. Their huts were very slight, and generally placed ten or fifteen together. They found them generally dining on fish, and eating to it the bruised and roasted roots of fern. This was in October. In the more advanced season they understood that they had plenty of excellent vegetables; but they saw no animals except dogs. They found both men and women painted with red ochre and oil, but the women much the most so; and, like the South Sea Islanders, they saluted by touching noses. They wore petticoats of native cloth, made from the New Zealand flax, and a sort of cloak or mantle of a much coarser kind. They found them more modest in manner and more cleanly in their homes than the Otaheitians. They bartered their cloth and war-weapons for European cloth; but nails they set no value on, having as yet evidently no knowledge of iron and its uses. What astonished the English greatly was to find boys whipping tops exactly like those of Europe. They found some houses larger and more strongly built than those on the shore. They measured one canoe, made out of the lobes of three trees, which was $68\frac{1}{2}$ feet long, 5 wide, and 3 high. These, as well as their houses, were much adorned with carvings, in which they seemed to prefer spiral lines and distorted faces."[1]

With other New Zealanders, as he sailed along the

[1] Howitt, vol. i. pp. 81, 82.

south-east coast, Captain Cook attempted to have friendly dealings; but his attempts generally ended in quarrel and bloodshed, both then and in the whole of his voyage right round the New Zealand group. Meaning well, he and his party acted with rashness and severity, which have had deplorable results in later times, whereas more forbearance might have been attended with the best consequences. "Without measuring the past by the present standard," says one who had access to native traditions, "the savage New Zealanders on several occasions acted as civilized men, and the Christians like savages. Lieutenant Gore fired from the ship's deck at a New Zealander in a canoe, who had defrauded him of a piece of calico. In the excitement of paddling to escape, the injury done by the musket was not noticed by the natives in the canoe, although detected by Lieutenant Gore from the ship's deck, as Maru-tu-ahua, the man shot, scarcely altered his position. When the canoe reached the shore, the natives found their comrade sitting dead on the stolen calico, which was stained with his life's blood, the ball having entered his back. Several chiefs investigated into the affair, and declared that Maru-tu-ahua deserved his fate; that he stole and was killed for so doing, and that his life blood should not be revenged on the strangers. Seeing, however, Maru-tu-ahua had paid for the calico with his life, it was not taken away from him, but was wrapped round his body as a winding-sheet. Singular to relate, Captain Cook landed soon after the murder, and traded as if nothing had occurred. Would Cook's ship's crew have acted thus if one of them had been slain?"[1]

[1] Thomson, "The Story of New Zealand," vol. L p. 231.

CAPTAIN COOK IN AUSTRALIA. 203

From New Zealand Captain Cook sailed northwards to the Australian coast, first touching at Cape Howe, in Victoria, but not finding a convenient landing-place till they were in Botany Bay. "While the master was sounding the entrance," says the historian, "the ship lay off, and observed some natives who were upon the shore watching them. As the vessel neared, they retired to the top of a little eminence. Soon after, the pinnace, which was employed in sounding, came close to them, and the natives did all they could to induce the master to land. But they were all armed with 'long pikes and wooden scimitars,' as the master said, and therefore he returned to the ship. The natives who had not followed the boat, seeing the ship approach, used many threatening gestures, and brandished their weapons. They were all painted for battle, as the custom is amongst them. The paint generally consists of white pipeclay, smeared all over the face and along the arms, across the ribs, and, in fact, in every sort of pattern, making them look exactly like skeletons. The weapon like a scimitar, which was evidently a boomerang, they brandished most of all; and they seemed, says Cook, to talk to each other with great earnestness. Notwithstanding all this, Cook continued to sail up the bay, and early in the afternoon anchored under the south shore, about two miles within the entrance. As he came in he saw on either side of the bay a few huts, of the usual wretched character of the Australian dwelling, and several natives sitting near them. Under the south head he saw four small canoes, with one man in each. They were striking fish with a long spear,

They ventured very near the surf in their fragile
barks; and were so engaged in their employment
that they did not see the ship go by them, though
it passed within a quarter of a mile. Opposite to
where the ship anchored there were seven or eight
huts. While they were hauling out the boat, an old
woman and three children were seen to come out of
the forest with firewood. Several children in the
huts came out to meet her at the same time. She
looked very attentively at the ship, but did not seem
very anxious about it. She then kindled a fire;
whereupon the four fishermen rowed on to the land,
hauled up their boats, and commenced to dress the
fish for their meal. The ship did not excite their
astonishment in the least. This apathy is one of the
most distinctive features in the character of the
Australian savage. Preparations having been completed, the crew prepared to land. They proposed
doing so where the huts were; and hoped that, as
they cared so little about the ship, the natives
would remain and communicate with them. In
this they were disappointed. As soon as the boat
approached the rocks, two of the men came down to
dispute the landing, and the rest ran away. Each of
the two champions was armed with a lance about
ten feet long, and a woomra, or throwing-stick.
They brandished their weapons in a very daring
way, though they were only two to forty, and
called continually, in a strange harsh language, what
was evidently a warning to the explorers not to
land. Cook, admiring their courage, ordered his
men to lie upon the oars, while he tried to pacify
them. He threw them beads and ornaments, which

they seized eagerly, and seemed well pleased with
them. But all inducements to allow the boat's crew
to land were thrown away. Cook tried to intimate
to them that nothing but water was wanted.
But it was no use; they seemed resolved to defend
their country from invasion. One was a mere lad,
the other about middle age; and yet there they stood
before their huts, confronting forty men, rather than
yield their ground. A musket was fired between
them. At the report, one dropped his bundle of
spears; but he recollected himself in a moment, and
stood again on the defensive. A charge of small
shot was now fired at the legs of the elder. Upon
this he retreated to the huts, and Cook and his men
immediately landed. But the battle was not over.
Scarcely had they set their feet upon the sand when
the savage returned. He was armed with a shield
this time, hoping thus to protect his bleeding legs.
Both savages threw spears where the men stood
thickest, but they easily avoided them. Another
charge of small shot was given; and this completed
the victory. Native legs could stand it no longer,
so they were immediately put to another use. After
the retreat of the blacks, Cook went to the huts,
and found there three or four children huddled
together, and evidently in the greatest state of fear.
This was the cause of the heroic resistance of the
two natives." [1]

Captain Cook made some further explorations in
Botany Bay; but here, as elsewhere in the course of
his northward voyage, he was regarded with sullen

[1] Woods, "History of the Discovery and Exploration of Australia,"
vol. i. pp. 39-41.

aversion by the natives. They rejected his presents; and when they did not obstinately oppose him, avoided all intercourse with him. He sailed all along the eastern shore of Australia, for the first time clearly defining its appearance and configuration; and, having passed Cape York, landed at the curious rock known as Booby Island, from one of whose lofty summits he took his last look at Australia.

In 1773 he returned to New Zealand, and also visited Tasmania, and to both of these islands he went again in 1777; but he added little, on either of these occasions, to the information he had acquired in his first and most famous voyage.

That voyage excited much interest in Europe, and led to many other expeditions to the Australasian regions. De Surville, a French navigator, went to New Zealand in 1769, and treated its natives with gross treachery and cruelty; and Marion du Fresne, another Frenchman, though perhaps with less intention of doing evil, engaged in yet more disastrous strife with the aborigines of both New Zealand and Tasmania, whom he visited in 1772. In 1785 La Pérouse was sent by the French Government on an intended voyage round the world, which was to surpass all previous exploits of that sort in the value of its contributions to geographical science and natural history. He proceeded as far as Botany Bay, where he anchored in January 1788; but there he disappeared, and the voyages undertaken in search of him or his remains almost vie in interest with those by which, in our own time, and in very different scenes, it was sought to discover the fate of Sir John Franklin. But the work of Australasian discovery was chiefly to be carried on by Captain Cook's own countrymen.

CHAPTER XVIII.

THE FIRST AUSTRALIAN COLONY.

THE CONVICT SETTLEMENT IN NEW SOUTH WALES—ITS FIRST TROUBLES—THE EVIL HABITS OF THE COLONISTS—THE BEGINNING OF BETTER WAYS—GOVERNOR MACQUARIE—AUSTRALIAN DISCOVERERS: FLINDERS AND BASS—INLAND EXPEDITIONS—THE PROGRESS OF NEW SOUTH WALES. [1767-1821.]

IN 1723, not very long after Dampier's visit to the distant country then known as New Holland, it was proposed by Colonel Purry that an English colony should be there planted; and the proposal was revived almost as soon as the result of Captain Cook's researches was announced. But England, then busy with the defence of Canada, and with her efforts to bring back the inhabitants of the United States to subjection, was not ready to take in hand the formation of a settlement in so remote a region. The American war, however, in the end, gave encouragement to the new enterprise. One use to which the now independent colonies had been put, was the sending thither a number of criminals, nearly two thousand in every year, for whom no room was to be found in the crowded gaols at home; and when the old ways of transportation were cut off, new ways had to be discovered. Then Cook's discoveries were thought of. In 1784 an Act of Parliament was passed, empowering King George III. and his Council to appoint some place beyond the seas to which offenders might be conveyed; and in 1786 it was decided that they should be sent to the eastern coast of New Holland and the neighbouring islands. Thus the colonization of Australia was begun.

With Captain Arthur Phillip, R.N., as commander of the expedition, and governor of the projected settlement, a small fleet left England on the 13th of May 1787. On board were 565 male and 192 female prisoners, with 209 officers and soldiers, and 65 women and children. It entered Botany Bay in January 1788; but Captain Phillip, not deeming the harbour safe enough, sailed northward for a little distance, and thus reached Port Jackson, with Sydney Cove close to it. Here he halted with his party of convicts, and their guards and servants, on the 26th of January. A few rude buildings were put together; and early in March the unwilling colonists were landed, and employed in the construction of a more permanent home in New South Wales, as it was called.

The work was not easy, as the colonists had no liking for it. They took every opportunity of escaping, and were caught with difficulty, if caught at all. Numbers perished in the woods of hunger, or by the hands of the natives. Others, without running away, were too idle to be of use, and severe measures had to be resorted to, by which the whole progress of the settlement was hindered. The town of Sydney was slowly built; but the crops planted on the rugged soil were not properly tended, and the cattle brought out from England were recklessly killed or lost. A ship, intended to proceed to China for supplies, was wrecked, and another, coming with ample store of provisions from England, was lost on the way out. By these misfortunes the colony was brought almost to starvation. Many died. Fresh cargoes of convicts arrived at intervals; but the food that came with them did not suffice for the wants of the older colonists as well as those for whom it was intended. The first five years passed painfully, and the settlement of New South Wales was only saved from destruction by the exemplary zeal and forbearance of the governor. By him the flagging spirits of the colonists were quickened; disaffection was stayed in a community especially fitted to become mutinous, and his constant self-sacrifice endeared him to all alike, and promoted union among all. He even sought to civilize the stubborn natives; and, when this was found impracticable, succeeded in preventing his people from acting towards them with the cruelty and injustice too often shown by colonists in their dealings with inferior races.

Captain Phillip returned to England in 1792. By that time the early troubles of the colony had been in great measure overcome. The fields were in cultivation; herds had been naturalized, and supplies of provisions came from Europe with tolerable regularity. These supplies from Europe, however—not merely articles of general commerce to be exchanged for Australian produce, but stores of food and clothing for which no return was made—were necessary to the colony, both then and for long after. It was a convict settlement, not expected to be self-supporting, although it was hoped that the prisoners would be gradually induced to contribute more and more to their own maintenance. And it continued to be little more than a convict settlement, to a great extent unproductive, until 1821.

Its history up to that time, during a period of thirty-four years in all, was marked by many painful details. Its governors, after Captain Phillip, were military and naval men, employed chiefly in seeing that the unwilling colonists performed their task-work, and in attempting to maintain something like prison discipline in a prison thirty times as large as the island of Great Britain. All that prison was not then habitable by white men. A vast proportion of it was wholly unexplored. The settlement of New South Wales comprised only a very small portion of the colony now bearing that name, and was comprised within the immediate neighbourhood of Sydney and Botany Bay. But the great districts north, west, and south afforded easy means for the escape of convicts from the garrison in charge of them; and while many thus escaped, generally to die, or be for ever lost sight of, the task of restraining them was a constant source of trouble, and added greatly to the difficulties in the way of good government among the convicts who remained. It gave them a certain power over their masters, since, to keep them from running away, they were allowed much licence which ought to have been avoided. Their governors must not be blamed too severely for their failures in doing work that it was hardly possible to do well. But their failures were often egregious. Arrogant and despotic in some of their actions, they were culpably lenient in others. The murderers, forgers, and convicts, guilty of a hundred different offences, who

formed the bulk of the colonists, and who, if they
began to settle down into peaceable ways, were every
year contaminated by fresh tides of criminals, formed
a lawless and disreputable community. Vice was
nearly everywhere rampant. Men exiled from England for their vices were often entrusted with functions
for which virtue was pre-eminently needed. Convicts
became judges and clergymen. The leaders of
society were often men whose violation of social
laws had been so gross that they would not be
tolerated in the mother-country; and, as a consequence, nearly every sort of dishonesty was the
rule, and none but the honest were punished.
Licentiousness and drunkenness, parents of every
sort of evil, were almost universal. "Not only," we
are told, "was undisguised concubinage thought no
shame, but the sale of wives was not an unfrequent
practice. A present owner of broad acres and large
herds in New South Wales is the offspring of an
union strangely brought about by the purchase of a
wife from her husband for four gallons of rum. Rum
supplied the place of coin. Lands, houses, and property of every description, real and personal, were
bought and paid for in rum. It is recorded of one
of the officers of the 102d Regiment, that, a hundred
acres of land having been distributed in half-acre
allotments as free grants amongst some soldiers of
the regiment, he planted a hogshead of rum upon the
ground, and bought the whole hundred acres with the
contents of the hogshead. A moiety of this land, a
few years ago, realized £20,000 at a sale in Sydney."[1]

[1] Therry, "Reminiscences of Thirty Years' Residence in New
South Wales and Victoria" (1863), pp. 71, 72.

ITS EARLY GOVERNORS. 213

That these evils should have prevailed during the first period of New South Wales colonization is not to be wondered at so much as that they should so soon have begun to be corrected. The era of reformation commenced in 1808, when Captain Bligh, the most incompetent of the early governors, was expelled by the best of the colonists, the special cause of this rough act of justice being his gross treatment of the worthiest colonist of all, John Macarthur, to whom is due the merit of first discerning the value of Australia as a wool-producing country. By him sheep were first imported in 1797; and in 1803 he improved the breed by purchases from the flocks of King George III. at Kew. His zeal and that of his wife for the improvement of New South Wales in other ways besides sheep-rearing brought on him much persecution; but he and his friends were supported by the authorities in England, and a better governor, General Macquarie, was sent in 1810 to rule the colony for eleven years. Governor Macquarie established some sort of order among his convicts. He rewarded all who were worth rewarding, and employed each in the crafts in which they had been trained in England, thus raising up an army of artizans, engineers, and other useful labourers. By him Sydney was nearly rebuilt; hospitals, churches, and other public buildings were erected, roads and bridges were constructed, and the whole colony was extended and enriched. " He found a garrison and a gaol, and left the broad and deep foundations of an empire."[1]

Other men joined in that work. In 1821 the

[1] Therry, p. 79.

population of New South Wales was 29,783, of
whom the great proportion were convicts, either still
undergoing punishment, or "emancipists," as they
were called, being now in the main free men. But
some of these were persons of high character and
great ability; and in the colony there were also some
free settlers, John Macarthur being the chief, of
remarkable worth. By them the resources of the
colony were being rapidly unfolded, and farm settlements were already planted at a considerable distance from Sydney.

From Sydney, too, had gone forth, during these
four-and-thirty years, numerous expeditions for the
investigation of more distant portions of Australia
and the neighbouring islands, all destined soon to
become fruitful colonies. Captain Phillip, the first
governor, had sent out naval exploring parties both
by land and water; and if his successors in the
government were less energetic, there were not wanting private adventurers to carry on the work. The
foremost of these adventurers, the great heroes of
Australasian discovery, were Flinders and Bass.

Flinders was a young midshipman, Bass was a
navy surgeon, when in 1795 they resolved to use all
the leisure they could get from their duties on board
the *Reliance* in examining the vast coasts and waters
which had only hitherto been vaguely described by
Dampier, Cook, and other voyagers. They bought a
little boat, eight feet long, which they named the
Tom Thumb, and which, with the help of a boy, they
were able to manage for themselves. They managed
her so well, in 1795 and 1796, in surveying the coast
and country near to Sydney, that the fame of their

achievements led to their being entrusted with larger
boats, and permitted to engage in more extensive
voyages. Sometimes together and sometimes apart,
they persevered in their bold exploits, as often as their
professional duties and other circumstances allowed.

In 1797 Bass, in charge of a whale-boat, sailed
southwards from Port Jackson to Cape Howe, and
then, passing westwards, discovered Wilson's Promontory and Western Port, with many creeks and
islands lying between the Australian coast and Van
Dieman's Land, which, instead of being a part of the
continent, as had hitherto been supposed, was thus
proved to be an island divided from it by the waters
called Bass's Straits, in honour of the explorer.
Forced by want of provisions to turn back in February 1798, he found that Flinders had, during the
same time, been also exploring in nearly the same
quarter, and discovering several islands north of Van
Dieman's land. In September 1798 the two friends
were allowed to continue their researches in a larger
vessel. They sailed right through the straits and all
round Tasmania, and examined all its principal bays.
Then the friends were parted. Soon after his return
to Sydney, Bass started for England, on a visit to his
wife and mother, but the vessel in which he sailed
appears to have been wrecked on the way home. He
was never heard of afterwards.

Flinders lived to achieve greater successes. He
made many voyages of great service along coasts
already roughly marked out, but which he was the
first to define with precision. Other voyages were
attended by more memorable discoveries. In 1801
and 1802, as commander of the *Investigator*, he sailed

along the southern coast of Australia, past Kangaroo
Island, to the Great Australian Bight. Then turning
back he surveyed more carefully the bays and coasts
of what are now the provinces of South Australia and
Victoria, loitering long in the splendid harbour on
which Melbourne was soon to be built. He next,
after refitting at Sydney, proceeded in a different
direction. Sailing northwards, he investigated the
coast with the same care which he had shown in his
previous work, until he entered the Gulf of Carpentaria. A hundred and five days were spent by him
in examining this great bay and discovering its islands;
and at the end of that time he was forced, by the
sickness of many of his crew, to make his way back
to Sydney. In July 1803 he started upon another
expedition; but the loss of one of the two vessels
entrusted to him forced him to return. In September
he sailed out again, intending to visit England, report
his discoveries, and seek assistance for yet more
extensive enterprises. He was not, however, to
engage in them. Calling at Mauritius, he was taken
prisoner by its French governor, and there detained
for six years and a half. His charts were seized, and
many of his most important discoveries falsely claimed
for the French explorer, Captain Baudin. Enabled
at length to reach England, he found that his greatest
exploits had been taken from him, and that he himself was forgotten. That justice might be done to
him, he lost no time in setting his journals in ordei
for publication. He died on the very day in which
this work was completed, in 1814.

In the interval use had been made of his researches
by the planting of several small settlements in various

parts of New South Wales; but there were no further explorations for several years, and then the exploration was on land instead of by sea. In 1813 a party of adventurers crossed the Blue Mountains, thus taking the first step towards an understanding of the interior of the continent; and in 1814 the town of Bathurst was founded by Governor Macquarie, who employed his convicts in constructing a road between the new settlement and Sydney. Thence other expeditions set out, and by them were discovered the Macquarie, the Lachlan, and other rivers. Oxley was the first great traveller by land; and his painstaking excursions from Bathurst to the country round about, and far inland, helped to make clear the nature of the inner districts of the New South Wales province.

Thus before the close of the year 1821, when the colony entered on a new period of growth, much progress had been made in the discovery of the great eastern half of Australia, though the western coasts and districts had been hardly visited, and of the central parts nothing at all was known. Sydney, on Port Jackson, and Parametta, a little way inland, were the only settlements then worthy to be called towns; and hardly more than fifty square miles of land were under cultivation, though an area about ten times as large was used for pasturage. That, however, was four times as much as it had been in 1810. In 1788 there were in the colony only 7 horses, 7 horned cattle, and 29 sheep, the first imports from Europe. In 1810 the numbers respectively had risen to 1114, to 11,276, and to 34,550; in 1820 they were 4014, 68,149, and 119,777. In 1807 only 245 pounds of wool had been exported from New South Wales; in 1816 the quantity was 73,171 pounds; and in 1821, 175,433 pounds.

The little colony in the far-off island continent was already in the highway of progress, and justified the poet's prophecy :—

> "Methinks I see Australian landscapes still ;
> But softer beauty sits on every hill.
> I see bright meadows decked in livelier green,
> The yellow corn-field and the blossomed bean.
> A hundred flocks o'er smiling pastures roam,
> And hark ! the music of the harvest home.
> Methinks I hear the hammer's busy sound,
> The cheerful hum of human voices sound ;
> The laughter and the song that lightens toil,
> Sung in the language of my native isle.
> The vision leads me on by many a stream,
> And spreading cities crowd upon my dream.
> Where turrets darkly frown, and lofty spires
> Point to the stars, and sparkle in their fires.
> Here Sydney gazes from the mountain-side,
> Narcissus-like, upon the glassy tide.
> O'er rising towns Notasian commerce reigns,
> And temples crown Tasmania's lovely plains."[1]

[1] T. K. Harvey.

CHAPTER XIX.

OLD NEW SOUTH WALES.

PROGRESS OF NEW SOUTH WALES AS A FREE COLONY—SERVICES OF REFORMED CONVICTS—JOHN MACARTHUR AND THE WOOL-TRADE—SYDNEY IN 1829—CRUEL TREATMENT OF THE CONVICTS—GROWTH OF FREE INSTITUTIONS—SIR RICHARD BOURKE—DEVELOPMENT OF THE COLONY—EXPLORATIONS IN THE INTERIOR—THE ABORIGINES OF AUSTRALIA. [1821-1839.]

NEW South Wales was little more than a convict settlement till 1821, and, up to that time, its limits did not extend very far beyond the outskirts of Sydney. Farms dotted the country round; a settlement had been begun inland, at Bathurst; and other settlements had been begun along the coast, from Port Macquarie, in the north, to Port Phillip, now Melbourne, in the south. But the 20,000 convicts, and the 9000 soldiers and free men and women, most of whom gained their living by attending to the necessities of the convicts, were chiefly to be found in the neighbourhood of Port Jackson. Governor Macquarie, who had ruled the settlement wisely, as an overseer of a very extensive prison, had done his best to turn his lawless subjects into good colonists, but had discouraged the coming of voluntary emigrants among them. By his successor, Sir Thomas Brisbane, and the home authorities who guided him, a different policy was adopted; and from his time the population of Australia began to be rapidly augmented by settlers of all classes, who sought, with wonderful success, to share the advantages afforded by this new and almost boundless field for enterprise.

In 1821 the convicts formed more than two-thirds of the whole population of 29,783. In 1828 they were hardly more than half, the whole number having then risen to 36,589. In 1833 they were only about a third of the 71,070 persons then in the colony. In 1839, when there were 114,386 inhabitants, they were only a fourth; and, after that, further transportation being nearly abolished in that year, they gradually disappeared altogether, save that, as "emancipists," or liberated convicts, they continued to leaven the whole mass.

During those eighteen years New South Wales was thus in a state of transition. Its rapid growth of population, and the energy of the new-comers, naturally superior to the earlier and involuntary importations, caused a very great increase of its limits, and a corresponding increase of its wealth. The vices planted in the beginning were not easily eradicated, but virtues flourished beside them, and the old haunt of infamy was gradually turned into a fruitful garden of honest enterprise. The evil propensities of the criminals with whom the colony was stocked by the mother-country, no longer allowed supremacy in the towns and outlying settlements, led their possessors to seek a precarious living, and sometimes large fortunes, as bush-rangers, until the progress of civilized habits, and the strengthening of the agencies of justice, put an end to even this dangerous class, and law prevailed everywhere, or at least with as wide and vigorous a sway as in any other resort of Englishmen.

The rapidity with which this reformation was effected, indeed, was a marvel to all, and reflects high honour upon the colonists of the last generation; and especial honour is due to many of the former convicts, who, while some of their comrades found exercise for their old habits as bush-rangers, won back the good names they had forfeited, and attained eminence as honourable men and wise philanthropists. "They form," it was said in 1844 by a local historian, "no uninteresting part of the population. Feeling that they had a bad character to lose and a good one to gain, they have in many instances set themselves about the work of reformation. Some of them are reckoned among our most honourable tradesmen and merchants; among the most liberal supporters, too, of the benevolent institutions which adorn our land. Some of these institutions have been all but entirely founded, and are now mainly supported, by their means. In many cases they have, by their industry and perseverance, acquired considerable wealth; and in most instances the wealth thus obtained has been generously and honourably devoted to the public benefit, the real and substantial advancement of this land of their expatriation. Nor do we know a more pleasing trait in human character than that which is thus displayed. Once degraded, they have paid to a violated law the satisfaction it imperatively demanded. But when the debt was paid, another obligation was felt to remain behind. Society had lost that beneficial influence which each member is called upon to exercise, and to atone for this was now their honourable desire. In the fair and honest pursuit of commerce, by untiring industry, they acquired those means which enabled them to gratify their wish; and no sooner was wealth poured into their lap than they gave it back, spreading it through numerous channels, through each of which, as it flowed, it left blessings that even succeeding ages may enjoy."[1] If "there is more joy in heaven over one sinner that repenteth than over ninety and nine just persons that need no repentance," hearty praise is due on earth to those reformed criminals who aided in the good work by which Australia, at one time thought to be only a vast play-ground for evil passions, has been turned into one of the most luxuriant fields of honest and honourable enterprise. "Why we are to erect penitentiaries and prisons at the distance of half the diameter of the globe, and to incur the enormous expense of feeding and transporting its inhabitants," it was said in 1803, "it is extremely difficult to discover. It is foolishly believed that the colony of Botany Bay unites our moral and commercial interests, and that we shall receive hereafter an ample equivalent in the bales of goods for all the vices we export."[2] The foolish belief has been verified beyond the most sanguine anticipations of its holders.

This, however, could hardly have been but for the tide of free emigration, which, slowly ebbing before, set in with a continued and ever increasing vehemence in 1821. Wise colonists like John Macarthur,

[1] Braim, "History of New South Wales," vol. II. pp. 315, 316.
[2] *Edinburgh Review.*

the first sheep-farmer and wool-merchant of Australia, who has been already alluded to, set a fashion which thousands every year have followed to their own and others' great advantage. In 1803 this "Father of the colony," as he was justly called, brought to England the first small sample of Australian wool, and earned the mockery of many who heard his prophecy, that "the quantity and quality would so increase and improve, as at no distant time to render England altogether independent, not only of Spain, but of all the nations of the continent, for its supply." He persevered in his "wool-gathering theories," as they were termed, brought sheep from India and the Cape, and afterwards from Spain and England—being enabled to do the latter, in violation of a law against the import of these animals, by a special Treasury warrant, and found that the soil and climate of Australia made bad fleeces good, and good ones better. He obtained a grant of 5000 acres of land on which to try his experiment; and when in 1821 that was well stocked, 5000 other acres were assigned to him. In 1807 Australia exported 245 pounds of wool. In 1834, when he died, the exports amounted to 2,246,933 pounds, of which no small portion came from his own well-ordered sheep-runs; and in 1839 they had risen to 7,213,584 pounds, valued at £442,504.

That rapid development of the wool-trade in New South Wales caused the chief energies of the colony to be applied in sheep-farming and the associated callings. There was some exportation of cedar and other woods, and a considerable trade in whale-oil and seal-skins obtained in the neighbouring fisheries.

But all these employments were chiefly carried on within a short distance from Sydney; and at this time it and its outskirts comprised nearly half of the entire white population of Australia.

Of the bright and painful aspects of the capital in 1829, when it contained about 15,000 inhabitants, we have a vivid description. "In the evening of the day of our arrival," says a traveller, "I was very favourably impressed. The streets were wide, well laid out, and clean. Two regiments, their headquarters stationed in Sydney, were then on duty in the colony, and this considerable force, with a large commissariat establishment, imparted quite a military appearance to the place. The houses were for the most part built in the English style, the shops well stocked, and the people one met with in the streets presented the comfortable appearance of a prosperous community. The cages with parrots and cockatoos that hung from every shop-door formed the first feature that reminded me that I was no longer in England. George Street, the principal street in the town, was brilliant with jewellers' shops; and I soon ascertained that Sydney had been remarkable, even at an earlier period, for the same phenomenon, the receivers of stolen plate and articles of *bijouterie* in England having chosen Sydney as a safe depôt for the disposal of such articles. Ground was not so valuable as it soon afterwards became, and commodious verandahed cottages, around which English roses clustered, with large gardens, were scattered through the town. Nothing met the stranger's eye to convey the notion that he was in the capital of a penal colony. The first impression of Sydney, on a summer evening's visit was pleasant, and full of agreeable promise. When, however, day dawned, the delusion of the evening was dispelled. Early in the morning the gates of the convict prison were thrown open, and several hundred convicts were marched out in regimental file, and distributed amongst the several public works in and about the town. As they passed along, the chains clanking at their heels, the patchwork dress of coarse grey and yellow cloth, marked with the Government brand, in which they were paraded, the downcast countenances and the whole appearance of the men exhibited a truly painful picture. Nor was it much improved throughout the day, as one met bands of them, in detachments of twenty, yoked to waggons laden with gravel and stone, which they wheeled through the streets. In this and in other respects they performed all the functions of labour usually discharged by beasts of burden at home. These were painful spectacles, but to the pain was soon added a thrill of horror by a scene I witnessed a day or two subsequently. The Sydney hospital, well situated, was in a line with the prisoners' barracks, and at a short distance from them. In an enclosed yard of these barracks, shut out from the public road, flogging was administered. A band of from ten to twenty were daily at one period marched into this yard to be flogged. As I passed along the road, about eleven o'clock in the morning, there issued out of the prisoners' barracks a party consisting of four men, who bore on their shoulders (two supporting the head and two at the feet) a miserable convict, writhing in an agony of pain, his voice piercing the air with terrific screams.

Astonished at the sight, I inquired what this meant, and was told 'it was only a prisoner who had been flogged, and who was on his way to the hospital!' It often took a sufferer a week or ten days, after one of these lacerations, before he was sufficiently recovered to resume his labour; and I soon learned that what I had seen was at that period an ordinary occurrence."[1]

That excessive severity, by which the worst convicts were made far worse—"When I landed here," said one of them, "I had the heart of a man in me, but you have plucked it out, and planted the heart of a brute instead"—was often reflected in the treatment adopted by the early governors towards the free settlers in the colony. General Macquarie had sought to make the whole district a home for convicts. The two governors who succeeded him, Sir Thomas Brisbane, from 1822 to 1825, and Sir Ralph Darling, from 1826 to 1831, introducing many beneficial measures, and desiring to increase the number of colonists, could not abstain from practising upon them some of the tyranny which they learnt as prison-overseers. The colonists, however, growing more influential every year, were strong enough to resist such conduct; and if unfortunate party-feeling sprang therefrom, it also issued in much good to New South Wales. In 1823 the functions of the governor, who had hitherto ruled the colony by a sort of martial law, were curtailed by the institution of a supreme court of justice for hearing all civil, criminal, and other pleas. And in the same year a Legislative Council of seven members was appointed to aid the governor in making

[1] Therry. pp. 39-43.

laws for the colony; and this Council was re-elected on an improved basis in 1829. Before that, the inhabitants had claimed a more independent power, both in legislation and in oversight of administrative arrangements, but representative privileges were not accorded to them till 1841. The chief cause of the delay was the wise use made of his powers by a new governor who was sent to New South Wales in 1831, and remained in office until 1838.

The new governor, the most statesman-like and liberal-minded ever sent to the colony, was Sir Richard Bourke. Readily discerning the great resources of the vast district assigned to him, he promptly set himself to aid their development, so as to benefit both the colonists and the mother-country. Previous governors had striven to keep the settlers as much as possible in the neighbourhood of Sydney. He had not been many months in New South Wales before he inaugurated a directly opposite policy. "The proprietors soon find," he wrote in a despatch to England, "from the increase of their flocks and herds, that it becomes necessary to send their stock beyond the boundary of location, and to form what are termed 'new stations;' otherwise the only alternative left to them would be either to restrain the increase of their stock or to find artificial food for it. The first of these courses would be a severe falling off in the supply of wool; and as to artificial food, from the uncertainty of the seasons and the light character of the soil, it would be quite impracticable. Besides, either course would seem to be a rejection of the bounties of Providence, that spreads, with a prodigal hand, its magnificent carpet of bright green sward over boundless plains, and clothes the depths of the valleys with abundant grass. Moreover, the restraint on dispersion would entail an expense in the management which could not profitably repay the Government." Therefore he resolved, instead of hindering them, to give free encouragement to "squatters," as they now began to be called. He had the country, far and wide, surveyed and parcelled into lots; and these lots he sold as often as there was demand for them, at whatever prices they could command at public auction. Instead of keeping the convicts at useless drudgery, he facilitated their employment in all sorts of ways beneficial to the colonists, and made them better workmen by treating them less cruelly. Thus he had fewer runaways to become bush-rangers; and the bushrangers already prowling about the country he zealously, though with no undue severity, hunted down and punished. He reformed the magistracy, and improved the machinery of justice. He gave freedom to the press. He established religious equality, and encouraged unsectarian education. No wise project for the advancement of the colony was offered to him in vain; and his own wise projects, admirably conceived, were no less admirably worked out. During his eight years of office, Australia advanced greatly in material ways, and its moral advancement was yet greater.

The material progress, however, can alone be told in figures. The revenue of New South Wales, which in 1824 had been £49,471, and was £121,065 in 1821, had risen in 1839 to £425,269; the public income from land having increased in the eight years from £3617 to

£172,273. The exports in 1831 were valued at £324,168, and the imports at £490,152; in 1839 the former were worth £948,776, the latter £2,236,371. The shipping which in 1831 entered the ports of the colony—Sydney being almost the only port—had an aggregate tonnage of about 34,000; in 1839 it had reached 135,474 tons. The population had nearly doubled in the eight years; and this population, instead of being kept nearly exclusively within a few days' reach of Sydney, had spread over a large extent of the immense colony. In 1839 the new race of squatters had attained the number of 77,287; and these squatters had among them 7088 horses, 371,699 horned cattle, and 1,334,593 sheep; and these squatters and their herds were in occupation of 17,730 square miles of picked land, lying along the coast, at intervals, from Fort Macquarie to Fort Phillip, and far inland.

Farther inland, as well as to many parts of the coast yet ill-defined, some memorable exploring visits were made during these years. The greatest of the early land adventurers, the rival of Flinders on the sea, was Captain Sturt. The Blue Mountains having been crossed in 1813, and Oxley having gone thence into the neighbouring districts of the interior in 1817 and 1818, Sturt was sent in 1827 to see whether there was in the remote interior, as was currently believed, a great inland sea, which could be favourable to further colonization. He found no sea, and gave good reasons against the existence of any large extent of water beyond the point which he reached; but during successive expeditions, lasting to 1831, he discovered the Darling, and tracked its course into the Murray, the greatest of the Australian rivers, about which very little had hitherto been known. Major Mitchell followed in his track, and explored new districts in 1832, 1835, and 1838; his most memorable discoveries being in the district called by him, for its beauty and fertility, Australia Felix, now part of Victoria.

These expeditions of Sturt, Mitchell, and others, marked by patient endurance rarely equalled, but not attended by many very striking episodes, were chiefly memorable as opening up new fields of enterprise to planters and squatters. They also helped to make clear the character of the aborigines, and to prove that all the natives of Australia, differing considerably amongst themselves, were alike in their physical and mental degradation. "On the sea coast," we are told, in an epitome of the researches of residents and travellers, " they live principally upon fish, turtle, and shell-fish. In the interior, they hunt the kangaroo, wallaby, and emu, with their boomerangs, spears, and waddies, besides which they procure an uncertain supply of opossums, flying squirrels, sloths, storks, cranes, ducks, parrots, cockatoos, eels, lizards, snakes, grubs, and ants. They have no fixed habitations, the climate generally allowing of their sleeping in the open air, in the crevices of rocks, or under the shelter of the bushes. Their temporary hovels consist of the bark of a tree, or a few bushes interwoven in a semicircular form. They seem to have no idea of the benefits arising from social life. Their largest clans extend not beyond the family circle. They are totally without religion, paying neither respect nor adoration to any object, real or imaginary. They have nothing to prompt them to a good action, nothing to deter them from a bad one. They are savage even in love; the very first act of courtship, on the part of the husband, being that of knocking down his intended bride with a club, and dragging her away from her friends, bleeding and senseless, to the woods. No evidences of tilling the ground, planting, sowing seed, and reaping the harvest have been seen by travellers amongst them, which distinguishes them essentially from the Maori race in New Zealand, the races inhabiting the Polynesian Islands, and the Malays. They do not trade or barter with each other or with strangers. Though each family or tribe has a generally recognised boundary within which they hunt, and beyond which they seldom stray, they neither exchange, buy, nor sell land among each other. Slavery, as understood in the negro sense of the term, does not exist. The married females, however, are, to all intents and purposes, the slaves of their husbands. Polygamy is recognised and adopted. Cannibalism exists among them. They show very little affection for their offspring; and their treatment of the aged is even worse than their neglect of the young. That they are capable of being civilized in a measure is shown by the organized troops of black mounted police throughout the south-eastern colonies, and the general employment of them by the colonists as shepherds and mountain herdsmen. In a few instances they have been taught to read and write. But at best they are uncertain retainers, and cannot be kept to constant labour, while they have a very faint conception of the relations between master and servant.

Like most other savages, they exhibit the extremes of indolence when their appetite is satiated, and of activity when hunger prompts them to hunt for food. Treachery and cunning among them are considered virtues. In their relations with the Europeans no faith can be placed in what they say. They have, on the other hand, their redeeming qualities. They will cheerfully share their meals with an unsuccessful neighbour, and will seldom refuse the white man a portion, from whom, however, they expect an equivalent. Like children, they are easily pleased; and, when their appetites are satisfied, they become a jocular and merry race, full of mimicry and laughter."[1]

[1] Westgarth, "Australia: its Rise, Progress, and Present Condition," pp. 113-116.

CHAPTER XX.

TASMANIA.

THE OFFSHOOTS OF NEW SOUTH WALES—THE EARLY HISTORY OF
TASMANIA, OR VAN DIEMAN'S LAND—ITS ESTABLISHMENT AS AN
INDEPENDENT COLONY—ITS CONVICTS AND BUSH-RANGERS—
EXTERMINATION OF THE ABORIGINES—ITS BEST GOVERNORS:
SIR GEORGE ARTHUR AND SIR JOHN FRANKLIN—ITS GREATEST
PROSPERITY—ITS DETERIORATION AND PRESENT STATE.
[1797-1869.]

WHEN, in 1786, it was resolved to establish an English colony in Australia, the limits of the new settlement were declared to extend "from the northern cape or extremity of the coast called Cape York, in the latitude of 10° 37′ S., to the South Cape, the southern extremity of the coast, in the latitude of 43° 39′ S.; and inland to the westward, as far as 135° E. longitude, including all the islands in the Pacific Ocean within the latitudes aforesaid." By that arrangement New South Wales was made to include about two-thirds of Australia, with Norfolk Island and other tributaries, and Van Dieman's Land, not then known to be a separate island. As the vast dimensions and capabilities of the territory came to be better understood, and as the settlers in its various parts became more numerous, this huge colony, half as large as Europe, was broken up into sections, each under separate governors, and with independent centres of jurisdiction. Van Dieman's Land was so parted off in 1824, South Australia in 1834, Victoria in 1851, and Queensland in 1859. New South Wales is thus the mother of four younger colonies, which now vie with her in wealth and importance.

Van Dieman's Land, now generally called Tasmania, in honour of its discoverer, the oldest rival of the mother-colony, is the least successful. More favoured by nature than any other of the Australasian group of settlements, unless we except New Zealand, it has had a less profitable career than any of them. Soon after Bass and Flinders showed, in 1797 and 1798, that it was a separate island, and one excellently adapted by its genial climate, its splendid harbours, and its well-watered coasts, for a residence of white men, it began to be used both by the Government of New South Wales and by the home authorities as a receptacle for convicts. Hobarton, on the Derwent, in the south-west, and George Town, on the Tamar, in the north, were both founded in 1804; but in both the convicts and the soldiers in charge of them came almost immediately into collision with the aborigines, and a fierce war of extermination was begun, to be carried on at intervals during the sixty years required for killing out all barbarous but comparatively harmless natives. Much suffering, also, was endured by the early settlers, ill-fitted for cultivation of the soil and for making good use of the resources of the island. Better times began about the year 1810. In 1813 merchant ships were allowed to visit the ports, and trade with their inhabitants. In 1816 the first export of grain was made; and in 1819 free immigrants, who had already come in small numbers, notwithstanding the obstacles thrown in their way, and had done nearly all the good that had been effected, were formally allowed to settle in the island. In 1824 its English population comprised 5938 convicts, 266 soldiers, and 6029 free residents.

In that year Van Dieman's Land was made an independent colony, with a Legislative Council of its own, and a Supreme Court of Judicature. Sir George Arthur, the first governor, who held his office till 1836, wisely used the powers entrusted to him. He reformed the magistracy of the island, divided it into well-ordered police districts, and, in various important ways, sought, to a great extent successfully, to bring about the well-being of its inhabitants.

The reforms were sorely needed. The troubles that prevailed in the chief settlements were surpassed by those caused in the less frequented districts, where a few enterprising farmers tried to make profit out of the fertile soil, and which they, and the traders connected with them, occasionally traversed in pursuit of their callings. These districts were infested by bush-rangers, who, as in New South Wales, were generally runaway convicts of the worst sort. Of their lawless conduct one illustration may be given. "In 1824," says the historian, " fourteen desperate convicts, of whom the leaders were Crawford, Brady, Dunne, and Cody, made their escape from the penal settlement at Port Macquarie in a whale-boat. They coasted the south-west shores of the island, and ultimately reached the shores of the Derwent river, where they landed, and were soon joined by numerous associates, provided with arms and other necessaries. Crawford, a clever

Scotchman, said to have been formerly a lieutenant
or mate in the Royal Navy, organized and disciplined
this gang of free-booters, who soon filled the respectable colonists with alarm. One of their earliest
attacks was directed against the mansion of Mr
Taylor, of Valley-field, on the Macquarie river. The
banditti mustered thirteen: the family consisted of
the venerable old gentleman, in his seventy-fourth
year, three sons, two daughters, a carpenter, and
another free servant. While the robbers were ad-
vancing they made prisoner of Mr Taylor's youngest
son, whom they placed in front, threatening his
immediate destruction if they were opposed. The
gallant veteran, despite the disparity of numbers and
the fearful position of his son, sallied forth, accompanied by two other sons and a servant, to give battle.
The fearful contest was kept up for a considerable
period, the ladies charging the fire-arms of their
father and brothers, and the whole party fighting for
life, and more than life, since the treatment these
defenceless females were likely to receive at the
hands of these wretches was more to be dreaded
than death itself. At length the bush-rangers were
compelled to retreat, leaving Crawford and two of
his gang on the field dangerously wounded. They
were handed over to justice, and perished on the
scaffold. The command of the gang then devolved
on Brady, whose name operated like a spell in giving
confidence to the bush-rangers, and whose rapid and
daring movements struck terror into every part of
the island. For nearly two years this Tasmanian
brigand, who made it his boast that he 'never wan-
tonly sacrificed human life, and never outraged female

delicacy,' set every effort for his capture at defiance; and his traits of generosity and reckless daring threw a *prestige* around even his worst actions, which, among the less depraved convicts, rendered his example more injurious because more alluring. The superior knowledge of the bush possessed by the brigands, together with the information acquired by their scouts scattered all over the country, and obtained from among the convict servants assigned in private houses, enabled them to out-general every military or police movement. The military at this period consisted of only two or three small detachments, and there was then no effective police. Large rewards were in vain offered for the capture, or for the heads of the robbers. The contributions levied upon the settlers enabled the leaders to purchase connivance; and the residents at out-stations feared to become marked men by aiding in the attempts at capturing the ringleaders. Some of the small settlers not only supplied the gangs with provisions and ammunition, but kept them acquainted with every plan projected for their apprehension."[1]

Brady's gang was only one, and one of the most gentlemanly, of the robber hordes that infested Van Dieman's Land; some of the most degraded being even suspected of adding cannibalism to their other crimes. For their suppression all the energies of Governor Arthur were taxed, and often with only a slight result. He had difficulties almost as great also in overcoming another class of enemies raised up by the misconduct of the early rulers of the island. The aborigines, akin to the natives of Aus-

[1] Martin, vol. viii. pp. 7, 8.

tralia, but more barbarous and vindictive, were turned into deadly foes; and during his term of government, as well as before and after, an ugly and unequal war was waged between them and the colonists, quite as painful and disastrous as that which has characterized the relations between Europeans and the Kaffirs of the Cape, and the Maories of New Zealand. Hideous tales are told of the atrocities of the blacks, and the less excusable ferocities of the whites, who saw no way of ridding themselves of their foes than by gradually exterminating them.

The effect upon the colonists was not good. Yet Sir George Arthur's care, and the zeal of his subordinates, enabled the settlement to make rapid progress both in agriculture and in commerce. Hobarton, in the south, became a flourishing capital; and Launceston, in the north, which soon became more important than the neighbouring George Town, was a hardly less influential centre of enterprise. Open enemies, whether bush-rangers or aborigines, were by degrees suppressed; the bad passions of many of the settlers were kept under; better or more prudent men found easy ways of money-making. In 1836, when Governor Arthur resigned his office, the island had a convict population of 17,611, and its free residents numbered 25,914, four times as many as in 1824; and in 1840, the convicts being about as numerous, there were 28,294 free inhabitants. The revenue of the colony, which was £32,126 in 1824, rose to £101,016 in 1834, and to £183,171 in 1840. The imports of those three years were valued respectively at £62,000, £476,617, and £988,357; the exports at £14,500, £203,522, and £867,007—the former having increased more than fifteen times, the latter nearly sixty times, in sixteen years. The year 1840 was the most prosperous in the whole history of Van Dieman's Land.

That prosperity was partly due to the wise conduct of the next governor, Sir John Franklin, most famous by reason of his subsequent ill-fated expedition in search of a north-west passage to India. His greatest service in Van Dieman's Land was in ameliorating the condition of the convicts, whereby a good influence was exerted upon the whole community. Bad influences, however, came from the excessive tide of convict emigration which set in in 1840, when, transportation to New South Wales being abolished, the other penal settlements in Australasia, were over-weighted with criminals. "The whole colony," said Earl Grey, when Colonial Secretary, "was thrown into confusion and disorder, owing to the large number of convicts who had no employment. This led to a state of things which was absolutely frightful. The demoralization which took place among the probation gangs was shocking to contemplate." In the five years subsequent to 1840 there were 19,878 convicts transported to Van Dieman's Land. "In 1840," said Captain Stokes, sent specially to inquire into and report upon the condition of this and other settlements, "everything wore a smiling prospect. The fields were heavy with harvests, the roads crowded with traffic, gay equipages filled the streets. The settler's cottage or villa was well supplied with comforts, and even with luxuries. Crime, in a population of which the majority were convicts, or their descendants, was less in proportion than in England. Trade was brisk, agriculture increasing. New settlers were arriving. Everything betokened progress. No one dreamt of retrogression or decay. In four years all this was reversed, and, though many other causes may have co-operated in producing this change, it seems acknowledged by most persons that the result is chiefly traceable to the disproportionate increase in the amount of transportation, which first checked free immigration; and, secondly, by glutting the labour-market, the free population was necessarily displaced, and those who had actually established themselves on the island as their second home were driven away from it."

In 1850 Van Dieman's Land received a new constitution. The frequent petitions of its inhabitants for full representative privileges were not at once granted; but, in lieu of the old machinery of government, a new Legislative Council was appointed, of whose twenty-four members one-third was to be chosen by the Crown, the other two-thirds by election of the free colonists. In 1855 somewhat fuller liberties were accorded. The Legislative Council, nominated by the Crown, was reduced to fifteen members; but thirty delegates of the inhabitants were formed into a House of Assembly. In 1853 the yet more frequent and more urgent petitions of the people were listened to; and further transportation of convicts was abandoned, so that now the whole population is free. Since then the population has almost constantly, though not very rapidly, increased. In 1848 it numbered 74.741. two-thirds free and one-third bond. In 1867 it amounted to 98,455. The revenue, in the latter year, exclusive of a loan, was £223,814; the imports were valued at £856,348, the exports at £790,494; both of the latter being lower than in 1840, though nearly twice as much as in 1844. Wool constitutes about half of the exports; much of the rest being wheat, butter, cheese, and other agricultural products sent to the neighbouring colonies. Of the whole area of the island, comprising 26,215 square miles, not much less than that of Ireland, hardly a sixtieth part, is under cultivation. About a fifth is occupied in sheep-farming. The rest, for the most part fertile and healthy, with rich stores of timber on the surface, and an abundant supply of coal, iron, copper, and other minerals underground, is yet unused.

"Nature," says a recent traveller, "is bountiful enough. In the world there is not a fairer climate. The gum-trees grow to 350 feet, attesting the richness of the soil; and the giant tree-ferns are never injured by heat, as in Australia, or by cold, as in New Zealand. Even more than Britain, Tasmania may be said to present in a small area an epitome of the globe; mountain and plain, forest and rolling prairie-land, rivers and grand capes, and the noblest harbour in the world. It is disheartening, in an English colony, to see half the houses shut up and deserted, and acre upon acre of old wheat-land abandoned to mimosa-scrub. Such is the indolence of the settlers, that vast tracts of land in the central plain, once fertile under irrigation, have been allowed to fall back into a desert state from sheer neglect of the dams and conduits. Though iron and coal are abundant, they are seldom, if ever, worked; and one house in every thirty-two in the whole island is licensed for the sale of spirits, of which the annual consumption exceeds five gallons a-head for every man, woman, and child in the population. The curse of the country is the indolence of its lotus-eating population, who, like all dwellers in climates cool but winterless, are content to dream away their lives in drowsiness, to which the habits of a hotter but less equable clime—Queensland, for example—are energy itself. In addition, however, to this natural cause of decline, Van Dieman's Land is not yet free from all traces of the convict blood, nor from the evil effects of reliance on forced labour. The old free settlers will tell you that the deadly shade of slave labour has not blighted Jamaica more thoroughly than that of convict labour has Van Dieman's Land."[1]

[1] Dilke, "Greater Britain," pp. 354, 357, 358.

CHAPTER XXI.

NEW SOUTH WALES AND THE PORT PHILLIP DISTRICT.

THE DISCOVERY OF PORT PHILLIP—CAPTAIN COLLINS' ATTEMPTED SETTLEMENT ON ITS COAST—LATER ENTERPRISES—HENTY, BATMAN, FAWKNER, AND MITCHELL—BUCKLEY'S ADVENTURES AMONG THE ABORIGINES—ESTABLISHMENT OF THE PORT PHILLIP SETTLEMENT—THE PROGRESS OF NEW SOUTH WALES—THE SQUATTERS AND THEIR WORK—MELBOURNE BETWEEN 1836 AND 1850—SYDNEY IN 1848. [1802-1851.]

O sooner had Bass's Straits been discovered than projects began to be formed for making use of the districts on either side. The experiment in Van Dieman's Land, on the south, has been described. The experiment in Port Phillip, now the colony of Victoria, on the north, was more successful, though the success has only recently become very notable.

The bay still known as Port Phillip was first entered by Lieutenant Murray, R.N., in the *Lady Nelson*, in February 1802, and within a few weeks the harbour was also visited by Flinders and by Baudin, the French explorer. It was thus discovered thrice over in the space of less than three months; and it was probably the fear that France would lay claim to a district that all three voyagers joined in praising, which led the authorities in New South Wales and the British Government to make speedy arrangements for its settlement. The arrangements were made too speedily to be prosperous. Two ship-loads of convicts

and military guards, about 500 in all, were sent out
from England under Captain Collins, with orders to
form a penal establishment in Port Phillip on the
model of that already flourishing at Sydney. They
arrived in October 1803, and were landed near Point
Nepean, at the mouth of the bay, where there was no
adequate supply of fresh water to be obtained without
sending the colonists far inland on excursions which
made escape easy to them. Captain Collins, dissatisfied with this position, did not care to seek a better
one in a different part of the bay. Early in the following year he abandoned it, with all the convicts
remaining in his charge, and, crossing Bass's Straits,
and passing round the west coast of Van Dieman's
Land, there founded Hobarton. His indolence
caused the colonization of Victoria to be delayed for
a generation, but saved it from the troubles that
might have befallen it as a convict settlement.

After that, Van Dieman's Land being able to
receive all the criminals for which there was not room
in Sydney and its neighbourhood, Port Phillip was
forgotten till 1824, when two bold colonists of New
South Wales, Hume and Hovell, crossed overland to
the bay and visited the site of Geelong. They thought,
however, that they had reached Western Port, and
their favourable account of what they had seen led
to the sending of an exploring party by sea to the
latter district in 1826, with the view of fixing the
locality for another convict settlement. But this
project, being badly conducted, also failed.

The first successful colonizing expeditions to this
part of Australia came from Van Dieman's Land, now
almost at the height of its prosperity. Thomas Henty,

an enterprising farmer of Launceston, visited Portland
Bay in 1833, and in the following year transferred to
its shores his family, a flock of sheep, and all the
materials necessary for pastoral and agricultural
pursuits. Much more was done in 1835. In June,
John Batman, another resident in Launceston, who had
been planning the exploit for eight years, went with
his family in a small vessel to Indented Head, near
Geelong; then went through the form of buying about
600,000 acres of land with £200 pounds' worth of
merchandise, and with amusing boldness assumed
the title of King of Port Phillip. He had hardly
done this, however, before his assumed prerogatives were disputed by another party, headed by
John Pascoe Fawkner, who entered Port Phillip in
August, and, passing on to its inmost corner, landed
on the bank of the Yarra Yarra, and there built a hut
which was to become the centre of the great city of
Melbourne. The quarrels of Batman and Fawkner
are only important in that they helped to direct
attention to this most valuable of all the scenes of
Australian enterprise.

The enterprise was also encouraged by the inland
discoveries of Sir Thomas Mitchell in 1834, 1835, and
1836. Starting from Sydney he wandered through
the beautiful regions watered by the Murray and the
Darling, and then, proceeding farther south, explored
the yet more beautiful expanse of mountains, valleys,
and table-lands, to which he gave the name of Australia Felix. He visited Portland Bay, where, to his
astonishment, he found Henty's little settlement, and
thence journeying eastward, had a distant view of the
Yarra Yarra and the other districts of Port Phillip, in

which Batman and Fawkner were roughly laying the foundations of a prosperous settlement, which seems still to have only begun its career of wealth and greatness. His description of what he had seen in all this noble territory stirred up an enthusiasm in the already peopled districts of New South Wales, and in the mother country, which, leading at once to notable results, has never since been lessened.

Thus was founded the district of Port Phillip, as it was termed during the fifteen years in which it flourished as a province of New South Wales.

In memorable contrast with its busy history during the last thirty years or more, is the history of its single white inhabitant throughout the previous term of thirty years. Of the many convicts who escaped from Captain Collins's shortlived settlement in 1803, one, and apparently the only one who was not lost in the bush or did not return to captivity, was William Buckley, then a strong man about twenty-four years old, and six feet five inches in height. With three others he made his escape and traversed the whole circuit of Port Phillip. Soon after that he lost sight of his comrades, and for more than thirty years he had no intercourse with any Englishman. At first he wandered about alone on the sea-shore, or lived in a hut of his own building. Then a tribe of natives came in his way, and by them he was treated with high honour. "These, as well as other Australian natives," we are told, "had a superstitious belief that white people are persons of their own race who have come to life again after death. If such resuscitated persons are deemed to be their own friends, the tribe will treat them well.

Buckley came upon the scene opportunely in this respect. A chief of the tribe with which he afterwards lived had died about the time he was spending his first summer of wild independence near the Port Phillip Heads, and had been buried near his rude domicile. A piece of a native spear had been left to mark the grave. Buckley had seen and appropriated this fragment, and, as he carried it in his hand when first seen by the tribe, they joyfully hailed him as no other than their deceased chief come again to life. In accordance with this happy prepossession, Buckley found he was always well cared for. He often saw himself indeed to be the subject of very ardent and earnest discussion, and on the occasion of the frequent tribal battles, he was carefully secluded among the females so as to be out of harm's way."[1] Once, or more than once, weary of his life among the natives, he went back to his hut, though there a native woman installed herself as his wife, and helped him to collect the shell-fish, herbs, and fruits on which he subsisted. Having gradually acquired the language of the aborigines, he gained fresh influence over them, which he was able to use to his own and their advantage, whenever he chose to mix with them. Thus he lived till he was fifty-five, now and then seeing a ship's sail passing along the coast, but failing to make any signal which might enable him to return to his own countrymen, if indeed he greatly cared to do so. The one and thirty years passed so easily that he imagined they were only about twenty, when he heard that a party of white men had come to settle in the neighbourhood, and

[1] Westgarth, "The Colony of Victoria," pp. 47, 48.

that a plan was being hatched by the natives for murdering them. To warn them of the danger, he sought them out, and, very soon after the appearance of Batman's party at Indented Head, showed himself among them. Great was their astonishment at seeing a man, evidently no Australian, though more than thirty years of nakedness had half-browned his skin, who vainly tried to address them in their own language. Hardly even could he understand their speech to him, until one, cutting a slice from a loaf, offered him "bread." That word acted like a spell. He found himself able to converse in broken terms, and soon he regained his native language. Batman then found him very useful in his dealings with the natives, until his disgust at the treachery shown towards his protectors during so long a time caused him to hold aloof from the negotiations. For a few years he lived in the new town of Melbourne, whence he afterwards went to Hobarton, and there he died in 1857.

Poor Buckley had little reason to be satisfied with the new tide of enterprise that invaded the districts over which he had wandered so long. "One great cause of his distress," we are told, "was the mutual ill-will and misunderstanding that were daily extending between the colonists and the natives. The former, pouring in one after another with their flocks, rushed away with hot haste into the interior, anxious to receive a share of the fine pastures lying still unoccupied, and ready at nature's hand for immediate use. It was Buckley's earnest wish that the poor natives, whose territories were thus summarily disposed over their heads, should be approached with consideration on the subject, and with a patient effort to gain their consent and good-will, and he thought that he might himself have been successful in dealing with them. But as all such preliminaries seemed mere waste of time to our eager and competing colonists, there was a lamentable result between them and the natives in constant mutual distrust, frequent hostilities, and repeated atrocities on either side. Many of the natives were shot down as though little better than so much game; and they, in their turn, stole sheep and murdered shepherds as often as their fewer means and opportunities gave them the power."[1] But that ugly work has attended nearly all intercourse between Englishmen and the inferior races whom they have had to dispossess in their career of colonial aggrandizement; and perhaps it was less extensive and disgraceful in the Port Phillip District than in many other parts of the world.

The new settlement grew apace. On the 25th of May 1836 it contained an English population of 177, and in April 1837 the number of colonists had risen to 450. In the previous month Sir Richard Bourke, the governor of New South Wales, had visited the colony, and superintended the laying out of the towns of Melbourne and Geelong. The land therein was sold by auction. One half acre in Melbourne realized £80, more than double the usual price. Two years afterwards it was re-sold for £5000, and about twelve years later it was sold again for £40,000.

In 1835, on the first report of the new settlement

[1] Westgarth, p. 55.

it was formally claimed as a province of New South
Wales. In 1836 Captain Lonsdale was sent to act as
chief magistrate and representative of the Sydney
Government. In 1839 he was succeeded by Mr
Charles Joseph Latrobe, who, first as superintendent
and afterwards as governor, directed the affairs of
Port Phillip during fifteen years, Captain Lonsdale
being his able secretary. The limits of his jurisdiction at first comprised about half of the present
territory, excluding Gipps' Land and most of the
Murray and Wimmera Districts. In 1842 these
regions were added to it; and the Port Phillip District, also called the Southern District of New South
Wales, was enlarged to the dimensions of the more
modern Victoria, comprising an area of 86,831 square
miles. Then, too, it was admitted to a share in the
new constitution given to New South Wales. The
Legislative Council was now made to consist of
fifty-four members, eighteen of whom were nominated by the Crown, the rest being elected by all the
colonists entitled to the franchise, fixed at a £20
annual rental. Six out of the thirty-six representatives were chosen in the Port Phillip District.

The progress of New South Wales up to 1839 has
already been described. The good Sir Richard Bourke,
after a brief interregnum, was succeeded as governor
by Sir George Gipps in 1838. The change was not
fortunate, though the new governor, a high-minded
but rather tyrannical ruler, was not to a great extent
responsible for the troubles that arose during his
term of office. While the Port Phillip District was
rising in importance, the older and central portion
of New South Wales suffered some serious reverses.

New immigrants arrived in large numbers, and trade was active, but this show of prosperity was fictitious. Perhaps, indeed, both trade and immigration extended for a time too rapidly. At any rate, during the first few years following the conferment of the new constitution, in 1842, there was a speedy falling back of the old tide of wealth. "It was notorious," said a speaker in the Legislative Council, "that in 1843 and 1844 nine-tenths of the houses, lands, and mansions of the proprietors were mortgaged up to their full value. As to the squatting interest, it was known that gentlemen with 10,000 sheep could not get credit for a bag of sugar or a chest of tea. The merchants were without custom, traders without business, and mechanics and artizans were pining for want in the streets." The Government was not very wise in its efforts to improve this state of things; but unreasonable complaints were made against it by the opposition party that grew up in the Legislative Council and throughout the colony. Faction prevailed, which, if it issued in good, also brought fresh difficulties to the settlement. This time of trouble, however, was perhaps only a necessary sequel to the change by which New South Wales passed finally from its first condition as a great receptacle for convicts into the hands of free and self-governing colonists.

The tide of fortune soon set in again, and now the prosperity of the colony resulted more than ever from the squatters, and their zeal in sheep-farming and preparing wool for the European market. "A 'squatter' is a term first applied to the early emigrants in America, who settled or squatted down upon a small piece of land in the forest there, cleared

it of the native timber, and grew wheat or other
grain and vegetables upon it, sufficient for the maintenance of his own family. The surplus he disposed
of at any market convenient to the spot on which he
squatted. The American squatters, as a class, are
generally persons of mean repute and small means,
who have taken unauthorized possession of those
patches of land. The squatters of New South Wales
form a very different class of persons. They are
amongst the wealthiest of the land, occupying, by
the tenure of Crown leases or annual licences, thousands and tens of thousands of acres. Young
men of good family and connection in England,
retired officers of the army and navy, graduates of
Oxford and Cambridge, are all amongst them. To
these must be added most of the settlers, a class of
persons who lease large tracts of land in their own
right, obtained by purchase or free grant from the
Crown, but which, by reason of the land soon
becoming insufficient for the support of their rapidly
increasing herds and flocks, oblige them to take up
stations, as it is termed, in unoccupied parts of the
country; so that the principal settlers are also the
principal squatters—settlers as to their own lands,
squatters as to the Crown lands they occupy."[1]

The method of squatting and the nature of its services in the development of New South Wales will
best be shown by quoting here part of a squatter's
own narrative of his career. "In the month of June,
1832," he says, "being then twenty years of age, I
left Glasgow for Sydney. I was induced to do so
from reading a book upon Australia. My father,

[1] Therry, pp. 240, 241.

who was an extensive farmer near Glasgow, having asked me, while at home during the holidays, to assist at some work upon the farm, I became rather discontented, and told him I had read such favourable accounts of New South Wales that I wished he would allow me to go there. He said he would pay my passage out and give me £50 to bring me home, as he knew I would not remain long there. On my arrival in Sydney I delivered several letters of introduction, but found them of no use. A list of passengers who had come out in the ship having been published in the Sydney papers, and my name appearing with the description of 'farmer from Scotland,' I had several inquiries from stockholders to ascertain what I was going to do. Among others was Mr Cadell, and he recommended me very strongly to see the Colonial Secretary, Alexander M'Leay, Esq., who was then in want of a manager. Being admitted to a personal interview with that worthy and kind-hearted man, I entered into an engagement with him to take charge of his station, about 150 miles from Sydney, with about 2000 sheep, at a salary of £40 a year, with one per cent. upon the clip of wool the first year, and an additional one per cent. each succeeding year. In eight or ten days I left Sydney for his station, situated between Goulburn and Yass. On arriving at the station the person in charge handed over to me the sheep, with some stores, and about a dozen assigned convict servants, and he left on the same day. I now found myself, without any colonial experience, placed alone in a position of great responsibility. In the first place, I made myself acquainted with the nature of the country, the sheep, and the servants I had to deal with. I gave additional allowances to those servants who proved themselves honest and careful. The result of this system, together with a careful and economical management, was a rapid and steady increase in the flocks. In 1836 a severe disease broke out among the sheep, which spread rapidly, and in some instances almost exterminated the flocks of many of the settlers. My loss did not exceed one fifth of the entire stock during the three or four years that this disease prevailed. I had observed that, even when in perfect health, the sheep were fond of licking rock-salt, and that they evidently improved upon it. I therefore resolved on forming a station on the Murrumbidgee, where I had heard of the existence of salt-bush plains, and there I took up a tract of country with thirty miles of frontage to the river for Mr M'Leay, and about two miles of frontage for myself. I had to pay £10 a year, and Mr M'Leay about £30 for his stations. These proved excellent and healthy runs, but, being farther out than any squatter, I found at first some difficulty with the natives, who were inclined to attack the shepherds and drive off sheep. By treating them with kindness, however, I succeeded in making them useful in sheep-washing and such-like work. I had also then, being 400 miles from Sydney, great difficulty in getting up provisions—a difficulty which was increased when, a few years afterwards, I pushed out 100 miles farther, and took up additional stations on the Lachlan river. During the last few years, whilst I was in charge of Mr M'Leay's stations, I had been also engaged in purchasing sheep for my-

self. Upon my ceasing to act for him, he made
me a present of 1000 picked ewes, which, with the
sheep I had already purchased for myself, gave me a
considerable stock to go on upon. Soon after, about
the years 1842-1844, so great was the depreciation
of all kinds of colonial produce, that, although my
flocks were healthy and increasing in number, I
found, in common with all other settlers, the
greatest difficulty in obtaining the necessary money
to meet my current obligations, such as wages, supplies for the stations, and the like; and it was
only by exercising the strictest economy and by having saved a small amount, which now proved very
valuable, that I escaped being obliged to part with my
sheep for almost nothing—the fate of many at a time
when produce of all kinds was unsaleable, and an
advance of money could only be obtained upon ruinous
terms. But in the year 1845 a considerable rise took
place in the price of stock, from the fact of their
value, when boiled down for tallow, having been
ascertained by Mr Henry O'Brien, of Yass Plains;
and about the same time an annual assessment was
laid upon sheep and cattle, for the purpose of increasing the colonial revenues. As our profits increased,
the Government increased our taxation. The present
stock upon my stations"—in 1863—"consists of about
100,000 sheep, from 7000 to 8000 head of cattle, and
from 700 to 800 head of horses. This is the amount
independent of the annual reductions by the sale of
a considerable portion to the butcher for meat, and
of supplies to new squatters, and support of the men
employed on the stations."[1]

[1] Therry, pp. 259-265. "After twenty-eight years of meritorious

That squatter's history illustrates the career of thousands of enterprising colonists in Australia. Starting from Sydney, they gradually extended their sheep farms inland and far down to the south, till, crossing the Murrumbidgee, and entering Australia Felix, they met like adventurers who had gone north, east, and west from Melbourne, and by their enterprise raised the Port Phillip District to importance. In 1846 the central provinces of New South Wales contained 154,534 inhabitants, and there were 32,879 in Port Phillip, while the colonial sailors in all the ports numbered 2196, making the entire population 189,609, considerably more than twice as great as it had been ten years before. In March 1851 the total number of inhabitants had risen to 247,262; 189,951 in New South Wales proper, and 77,345 in Port Phillip. About ten million sheep were then collected in the various squatters' stations, and the wool produced from them and imported to Europe was worth about £1,500,000.

In that year wool ceased to be the one great staple of Australian commerce. The gold discoveries afforded a new and more glittering field for enterprise, by which the whole continent was to be enriched, and the fortunate District of Port Phillip was to be especially aided in its rapid career of prosperity. But already the young settlement had made wonderful advances, and was threatening to outrun the parent colony in the race of wealth. Starting with its population of 177 in 1836, it had 11,738

---

toil," says Mr Therry of this squatter, "he returned to England with a permanent well assured income (which I believe I much understate) of between £20,000 and £30,000 a year."

inhabitants in 1841; 32,875 in 1846, and, as has been just said, 77,345 in 1851. Of these 22,143 were in the town of Melbourne, about 8000 in Geelong, and the remaining 36,000, or more, were distributed in Belfast, Portland, and other smaller towns and villages along and near the coast, both east and west, and among the settlements and squatting stations spread over the fertile regions stretching up to the northern limits of the province.

The development of Melbourne within this short space of time, at the close of which it was still in its infancy, illustrates the progress of the whole District of Port Phillip. "In January 1838," we are told, "it consisted of a nucleus of huts, embowered in the forest foliage, and had much the appearance of an Indian village. Two wooden houses served the purpose of inns for the settlers who frequented the place. A small square wooden building, with an old ship's bell suspended from a tree, was used as a church or chapel by the various religious denominations. Two or three so-called shops formed emporiums for the sale of every description of useful articles. The flesh of the kangaroo and varieties of wild fowl were abundantly used, for fresh mutton was still scarce, and beef seldom seen. A manuscript newspaper, established by Fawkner, one of the enterprising men to whom England is indebted for the formation of this settlement, was the organ of public opinion in the new colony."[1] Brick houses soon took the place of wood, and in the course of a few years handsome buildings of stone were erected for public uses. Wide roads were marked out, and market-places

[1] Martin, vol. ii. p. 508.

were appointed. "The streets," it was said in 1850, "are planned at right angles, the larger ones being a hundred feet broad, the smaller about thirty. The principal street is, strangely enough, named Collins, after the brave officer who, when directed in 1803 to form a settlement at Port Phillip, declared it to be 'all barren,' and abandoned it as a hopeless undertaking. Elizabeth Street is situated in a hollow between two considerable acclivities to the eastward and westward, called the Eastern and Western Hills. The streets and by-ways of Melbourne, previous to 1842, were frequently rendered impassable from the operation of the weather and the ceaseless traffic of ponderous bullock-drays. Thick gum-tree stumps and deep ruts, forming vast reservoirs of mud, were varied by the intersecting gullies of temporary water-courses; and many an anxious wife and mother scanned the deep abyss of the urban excavations in search of a drunken husband or a wayward child. A visitor, writing in 1842, declares himself to have been startled, soon after his arrival in the colony, by a paragraph in the newspaper, headed 'Another child drowned in the streets of Melbourne.' In the following year, however, the stumps were removed by order of the town council, and the occasion of frequent accidents was thus removed."[1]

With the Melbourne of twenty years ago may be compared the Sydney of the same period. The capital of New South Wales was sixty years old, and contained about 40,000 inhabitants, with nearly 10,000 more in its suburbs, in 1848. "Its haven," it was

[1] Martin, vol. II. p. 599.

then said, "which is about fifteen miles long, and in some places three miles broad, is completely landlocked. Along the water-side, except that portion occupied by the demesne contiguous to Government House, there are wharves, stores, ship-yards, mills, manufactories, distilleries, breweries, etc. Behind these, in irregular succession, rise numerous public and private buildings. The streets are laid out generally at right angles. Thirty-four of them have each a carriage-way of not less than thirty-six feet, several from forty to sixty feet, and a footway of not less than twelve feet. Their length varies from one to three miles. They are well paved or macadamized, regularly cleaned, watered, and lit with gas. George Street and Pitt Street have continuous ranges of handsome stone or brick edifices, with shops that would do no discredit to Regent Street or Oxford Street in London."[1]

Sydney and its outlying districts had shaken off the contamination of their early state as a convict settlement, and the vast colony of New South Wales was now a thriving haunt of enterprising freemen, in which the resources already brought into use promised for it almost boundless expansion, although a new and yet more brilliant means of its advancement was yet to be discovered.

[1] Martin, vol. ii. p. 454.

CHAPTER XXII.

SOUTH AUSTRALIA.

THE DISCOVERY AND COLONIZATION OF SOUTH AUSTRALIA—THE WAKEFIELD SCHEME AND ITS FAILURE—EARLY TROUBLES OF THE COLONY—THEIR SPEEDY REMOVAL—THE COPPER MINES—THE EFFECT OF THE GOLD DISCOVERIES IN VICTORIA—LATER PROGRESS OF THE COLONY; COPPER, WOOL, WHEAT, AND WINE—ITS PRESENT CONDITION. [1822-1869.]

"THE south coast of Australia is barren, and in every respect useless and unfavourable for colonization." So said Captain King, one of the most enterprising followers of Captain Flinders in the work of exploration along the southern shores of the great island continent in 1822. Soon after that, however, in 1827 and the following years, Captain Sturt made his famous inland expeditions and discoveries, in the course of which he tracked the Murray through a large part of its winding, and visited the country between Lake Victoria and St Vincent's Gulf, now the splendid harbour of Adelaide. His report was very different to Captain King's. "Cursory as my glance was," he said, "I could not but think I was leaving behind me the fullest reward of our toil in a country that would ultimately render our discoveries valuable. My eye never fell on a region of more promising aspect or of more favourable position than that which occupies the country between the lake and the ranges of St Vincent's Gulf, and, continuing northerly, stretches away without any visible boundary."

That favourable description induced the Governor of New South Wales, in 1831, to send Captain Barker on a visit to the country around Lake Victoria, with a view of deciding as to its fitness for an English settlement. Captain Barker was attacked and killed by the natives; but his subordinate, Mr Kent, went back, to speak of the country in terms yet more favourable than those used by Captain Sturt. Rich soil, fine pasturage, and ample supplies of fresh water, always a great attraction in Australia, united, he said, in making the district one "in whose valleys the exile might hope to build for himself and for his family a peaceful and prosperous retreat."

Prompt measures were taken for enabling, not exiles, but willing adventurers, to find peace and prosperity in the newly explored district. The movement, however, did not begin in New South Wales, which had already founded the convict colony of Van Dieman's Land, and was now starting the free settlement of Port Phillip. The project for establishing South Australia was started in England by a group of philanthropists and speculators, anxious to try a new experiment in colonization, which was known as the Wakefield scheme, its chief advocate being Mr Edward Gibbon Wakefield. In the older Australian colonies, and in nearly all the other dependencies of Great Britain, immigration had been encouraged by offers of land at very low prices, and as the enterprise of the first settlers made property more valuable, the land was still disposed of for whatever price it could fetch at public auction. Mr Wakefield urged a different policy. "He held that, by placing a high value on the unreclaimed lands of a new country, and forwarding a labouring population out of the sale of those lands, the emigrants would of necessity work at low wages, as the purchase of the dear lands would be above their means, thereby securing the capitalist investing in the land a large interest for his money, and forming at once a community of labourers and artizans who would minister to the benefits of the landholders. Besides these large landholders, a class of small farmers was to be induced to emigrate, by disposing of the land in small sections to be cleared and cultivated by their families."[1] This foolish plan found so much favour that a committee for its adoption was formed in 1831, and the committee grew into a South Australian Colonization Association, founded in 1834, which in the same year obtained a charter for the enforcement of its views in the region visited by Captain Sturt.

In that way was originated the colony of South Australia, comprising an almost square block of about 300,000 square miles, cut out of the south-western part of the original New South Wales. A large capital was subscribed; and in 1836 Captain (afterwards Sir John) Hindmarsh went out with the first party of intending landowners, or their agents, and an organized body of "surveyors, architects, engineers, clerks, teachers, lawyers, and clergymen." These first ingredients for a ready-made colony landed at the mouth of the Glenelg, in St Vincent's Gulf, in December, and proceeded seven miles up the river to lay the foundations of Adelaide, appointed as the

[1] Westgarth, "Australia," p. 215.

capital of the settlement. Other instalments quickly followed, and the population amounted to 6000 in 1838, and to 10,000 in 1839.

The experiment failed dismally. Captain Hindmarsh did not satisfy his employers, and he was succeeded by Colonel Gawler in 1838. "When Colonel Gawler arrived in the colony," says a panegyrist of the project, "he found the government machinery in a great state of derangement. The country surveys were not well advanced. Persons who had gone out with land-orders and means for rendering their agricultural operations profitable, had fallen into land speculations after the sale of town allotments, or had engaged in building operations at a high cost in the capital, and brought themselves to a stand still. Labourers, who ought to have been dispersed over the country, were congregated in the town, demanding and receiving, as long as the money lasted, high wages for works that could not be remunerative to those who constructed them. The true objects of colonization had been lost sight of in the whirl of speculative excitement; and when the funds, brought into the colony for legitimate employment, had been nearly all sent away for the purchase of provisions, and hundreds of tons of flour had been imported at from £80 to £100 per ton, which should have been produced on the spot for £15 or £20, the prospect of a general collapse appeared to be inevitable."[1] It was not averted by the measures resorted to by the new governor. Finding his colony bankrupt and its inhabitants on the verge of ruin, if

[1] Forster, "South Australia: Its Progress and Prosperity," p. 61.

not of starvation, while fresh immigrants, tempted
by the nominally high wages and the fabulous price
of land produced by stock-jobbing manœuvres, were
arriving, he was led by a mistaken feeling of
generosity to embark in a reckless expenditure, and
to attempt remedies which only increased the disease.
Great public works were constructed by him in order
that the impoverished residents might get wages;
but, his exchequer was empty, and he had to pay
his labourers and contractors by drafts upon the
imperial treasury. The drafts, being wholly unauthorized, were dishonoured; and the colony was
only saved from utter destruction by a loan from the
English Government. Colonel Gawler, who, with a
revenue of £20,000 a year, had incurred expenses to
seven times that amount, was recalled; and his successor, Captain (now Sir George) Grey, who arrived
in May 1841, was instructed, at whatever cost of
temporary trouble, to pursue a different policy, and
one likely to bring about a better state of affairs.
This he did with praiseworthy prudence and energy.
The projectors of the colony, too, had already, to a
great extent, learnt the folly of their original schemes,
and where they still proposed to act unwisely they
were prevented by the Government. The colony
ceased to be a private speculation, and became a
Crown dependency. Many of the mischief-makers
who had come to it in the first two or three years,
now quitted it in disgust, or, ruined by their own
misdeeds, sank into insignificance, and their places
were taken by fresh adventurers, with whom came
crowds of new immigrants, aware of the evil circumstances with which they had to contend, and of the

real resources of the country by which it was easy for wise men to prosper.

South Australia did very soon begin to prosper. The population rose from 14,610 in 1840 to 22,390 in 1845, the acres of land in cultivation from 2503 to 26,218, and the value of colonial exports from £15,650 to £131,800. But in the same period the public expenditure had sunk from £169,966 to £36,182, the number of public-houses from 107 to 85, and the number of criminals from 47 to 22.

In 1845 Captain Grey left South Australia to be governor of New Zealand. During his four years' rule he had rescued the colony from bankruptcy, and placed it in the high road of prosperity, although much of that road was still to be rugged. Under his encouragement, and by the enterprise of the newer colonists, much of the fertile and beautiful land around Adelaide had been brought under cultivation, and far larger tracts had been appropriated by sheep-farmers. In 1845 large quantities of wheat and other grain were exported, though more than half the exports were in wool, amounting to 1,331,888 pounds, which were valued at £72,236. In the following years the wool trade continued to increase rapidly, as well as the commerce in corn and various other articles of food.

But another commodity was destined to become the main source of South Australian wealth. In 1842 copper was found at Kapunda, fifty miles north-east of Adelaide, and in the following year the first ton of ore raised there yielded £23. Even before that lead had been discovered, and the mines continued to be worked successfully; though soon the costlier metal became a far more important article of trade. The second year's yield of the Kapunda mine produced £4009, and the third £10,351.

That was only the small beginning of copper-mining in the colony. In 1845 ore was found by a shepherd at Burra Burra, about forty miles north of Kapunda. The report of his discovery caused the immediate purchase of 20,000 acres of land in that locality by two rival parties of adventurers. "These two parties," we are told, "were called respectively the 'nobs' and the 'snobs,' the former representing the aristocracy of the colony, the latter the merchants and trades-people. The nobs were unwilling to combine with the snobs in a joint-stock company for carrying on the mine, and therefore, although they united to purchase the ground—as neither party could, unaided, raise the hard cash—as soon as the survey was completed the land was divided by drawing a line through the centre from east to west. Lots were then drawn, and the snobs became the fortunate proprietors of this northern portion of the survey."[1] This proved an almost boundless source of wealth. The ore was so near the surface that it could almost be taken up by hand, and when that most accessible treasure was all appropriated, the working of the lower veins was found to be singularly easy. One lucky proprietor who had risked £500 at starting, was three years afterwards in the receipt of £11,000 a year. During the first six years 80,000 tons of ore were raised at Burra Burra, and the profits, divided between the few shareholders, amounted to £438,552, while a larger sum went to enrich the

[1] Austin, "The Mines of South Australia."

labourers, merchants, and others, who had come to aid in the work, and by whom during the period a busy town had been raised on the old sheep-walk.

Other mines, about thirty in number, were also found and worked within the distance of a hundred miles from Adelaide; and in 1849, only seven years after their first discovery, the copper raised from all exceeded 16,000 tons, and was worth £310,172. In 1850 the total exports from South Australia were valued at £545,839, and the population of the colony was 63,700, being treble that of 1845.

In 1851, however, a wonderful change arose, and South Australia had to pass through a second time of trouble. Its copper, its wool, and its wheat had promised to make it before long the richest of all the Australian colonies, richer even than its nearest rival, Port Phillip, which then had only wool and wheat for its staple articles of commerce. But the promise was marred by the discovery of gold in that rival, the circumstances and issue of which will have presently to be detailed. The immediate issue to Port Phillip was very disastrous. "For a time," said its Chamber of Commerce in 1852, "it seemed that the props of our material prosperity were about to fall. The streets of Adelaide were deserted, houses were abandoned by their tenants, rents fell, and property became unmarketable. The shops of our retailers presented their tempting wares in vain. There was a general arrest put on all business; and this at a time when the stock of merchandise in the market was unprecedentedly heavy, and when the bill engagements of the mercantile community were larger

probably than they had ever been before."[1] A great
many of the busiest labourers in South Australia
being miners, they immediately hurried off to use their
special skill in seeking for a mineral so much more
valuable than copper. Within twelve months about
16,000 persons, chiefly men, and the most industrious inhabitants, nearly a fourth of the whole population, passed over to the neighbouring colony; and
those who remained suffered heavily by their absence.

That depression, however, was only temporary;
and though the gold discoveries destroyed the hope
which had been entertained that South Australia
would attain supremacy among the trans-Indian
colonies, it really profited immensely by them.
Scanty supplies of gold were also found within its
limits, and many of the old settlers now came back,
recruited by many fresh arrivals, to seek for the
glittering treasure. Therein they were not very
successful, but their enterprise restored and gave
fresh life to the flagging trade of the colony. Great
benefit resulted also from a clever expedient resorted
to by the colonists and their new governor, Sir Henry
Young. Judging that the next best thing to finding
gold in their own territory was the bringing into it
of the gold found elsewhere, they resolved to accept
uncoined gold as currency. Offering for it a price
higher than the diggers and their agents could be
sure to obtain if they sent it all the way to Europe,
though less by about a shilling in the pound than it
was worth according to the English standard, they
induced the importation of vast quantities of it.
Between February 1852, when the plan was adopted,

[1] Forster, p. 62.

and the following December, the gold thus brought into Adelaide and converted into stamped ingots, was worth £1,395,208, and the supply was not diminished in the ensuing months. Much of this gold was hoarded and eventually taken to other markets, there to be sold at its full value, and thus to realize a considerable profit to the dealers; but much of it, as much as there was room for, circulated freely in the colony, and gave a great stimulus to trade.

For the wheat and other produce of South Australia, also, there was a greatly increased demand in consequence of the rapid increase of population in the gold districts. Thus the colony reaped a large share of the wealth of the Australian El Dorado. "The population returned to resume their ordinary employments," says the historian; "the large amount of money put into circulation restored property to its former value; and the colony commenced a new era of prosperity. It was pleasant to contemplate the marked improvement which had taken place in the circumstances of the community. The wives and families of returned diggers, many of whom had been left behind with very slender means when their husbands and parents set off for Victoria, were now enabled to exhibit themselves in personal decorations which gave conclusive evidence of their increased resources. An extensive patronage was bestowed upon the drapers and jewellers of Adelaide, but not such as to interfere materially with the reproductive employment of the newly-acquired wealth. Farms which had been taken with right of purchase were speedily secured in fee-simple; houses and stores were erected in town and country; industrial operations were entered upon with renewed life and vigour, and that which was at first looked upon as a dire calamity turned out to be an extensive and unmitigated blessing."[1]

Since then the career of South Australia has generally been one of rapid development. Sir Henry Young, who, after a short interval, succeeded George Grey, and was governor from 1848 to 1854, did much useful service to the colony, and after him it had a really able ruler, between 1853 and 1862, in Sir Richard M'Donald. " During his term of office responsible government was inaugurated, and the political changes were introduced which materially altered the position of Her Majesty's representative. Sir Richard readily adapted himself to the new state of affairs, and settled down as a constitutional governor, directed by the wishes of his ministerial advisers. He was full of physical and mental energy, in the prime of life, almost a giant in stature, and with a well-cultivated mind. He visited all parts of the colony, and made himself personally acquainted with the wants and capabilities of nearly every district; and being capable of enduring great fatigue, he made lengthened journeys into the distant bush, so as to earn for himself almost the character of an explorer."[2] Both by him and by his predecessor great care was taken in opening up roads to districts previously neglected and in improving the communications between stations already occupied, whereby they were made more serviceable to one another, and to the colony at large. Railways and telegraphic lines began to be established between the

[1] Forster, pp. 66, 67.   [2] Forster, pp. 77, 78.

principal towns. Those towns were aided by
many new institutions. The navigation of the two
great rivers, the Murray and the Darling, was improved, and the coast was provided with lighthouses.
The colony received a new constitution, by which the
old Legislative Council was reorganized, and a new
House of Assembly, elected by universal suffrage,
was added to it in 1856; and the inhabitants, thus
endowed with full rights of self-government, made,
in the main, good use of their powers.

By these means the colony has been enabled to
advance steadily in all ways of social, commercial,
and agricultural improvement. The mineral wealth of
the country has been greatly developed. Besides the
older mines, the chief being that at Burra Burra, many
new ones have lately been opened. The Wallaroo
field, or Yorke's Peninsula, discovered by Captain
Hughes in 1860, and the Moonta mine, in the same
strip of land, opened in the following year, are both
richer and more extensive than Burra Burra. "The
place," it is said of this district, "is not, to the eye of
a novice, a very likely one for mines. It is a vast
expanse of flat, scrubby country, interspersed with
open plains, covered with a dry and scanty herbage.
Underneath is an unbroken crust of limestone, extending over the entire area of the peninsula, and the
whole seems as if it had, at a very recent geological
period, emerged from the sea. Not a rock is to be
seen anywhere, nor a hill, to break the even surface
of the ground, nor a gully, nor a water-course of any
description, for miles and miles. The scrubs are full
of burrowing animals, and large holes are met with
at every two or three hundred yards. These are said

to be wombat holes, but they are more frequently occupied by the wallaby, a sort of miniature kangaroo, upon which the natives feed extensively. In the operation of scratching their holes, the animals throw up minute specimens of the rocks beneath, and amongst these particles was one day thrown up a small green stone, about the size of a pea, which on examination proved to be green carbonate of copper. The natural reflection that there was more where this came from, induced Captain Hughes to have a shaft sunk upon the spot, and, sure enough, at the depth of a few feet, he came upon a magnificent lode of ore, which has since been opened up through a large extent of country, and is yielding immense quantities of copper."[1] In nearly every part of the district within a hundred miles north, south, east, and west of Adelaide, copper has been found, or is likely to be found; and there seems no limit, when the metallurgic arts are properly established in the colony, to the amount of its mineral wealth. In 1866 the exports of this metal were valued at £584,509, though that was a poor year for the trade. In 1864 it yielded £677,096.

Yet more lucrative is the wool trade. In 1864 were exported 16,092,095 pounds, worth £775,656; in 1866, 20,908,085 pounds, worth £1,064,487. More than 60,000 square miles, about a sixth of the whole colony, are now occupied as runs for nearly 5,000,000 sheep of fine merino breed, each worth about a £1. This trade, however, profitable as it is, is hardly equal to the results of squatting enterprise in New South Wales and Victoria; while South Australia

[1] Forster, pp. 361, 362.

surpasses both the other colonies in the value of its agricultural resources. To them and to its other neighbours it still serves as a granary. In 1864, a year of exceptional good fortune, besides all the native consumption, the exports of corn and flour were valued at £1,408,332; in 1866, a year of depression, they were valued at £629,196.

Other branches of the farmer's calling have yet to be developed, the most notable among them being vine-growing, which has lately begun to be an important occupation. The land so employed in 1864 comprised 5779 acres, and the yield was 606,365 gallons of wine. The trade is now about twice as great. "The wine produced," we are told, "is of a light but excellent description, well suited to the requirements of a warm climate, and free from the noxious adulterations so frequently discovered in imported wines. It may be made by any person who has the industry to stick a few vine-cuttings into the ground, and the common intelligence to press the juice from the grapes when they have grown and ripened. A gentleman was hunting stray cattle in the bush on a hot day and became very thirsty, not having been able to fall in with water. Coming, towards evening, across a splitter's hut, he called and asked for a drink. The man regretted that he had no water in the house, but asked him if he would take a draught of his wine. The wine was brought, and the gentleman said it was the best he had ever tasted in his life. Being a vine-grower himself, he asked the man to explain to him the subtle process by which he had been enabled to produce so splendid an article. He was invited into the hut, and directed to a large cask without a lid, standing behind the door, which the man assured him was the only utensil employed in the manufacture. 'Sir,' he said, 'all we did was to put the grapes into that 'ere cask, and never trouble ourselves about them no more; and when we pulled out the spigot, out comes the wine you have just been drinking of!' The tub had been filled with grapes, from which the juice had escaped as they became heated and broken, and the process of fermentation had thrown the scum to the top, forming a hard air-tight crust, which had hermetically sealed the vessel, and prevented the liquor from becoming sour."[1]

All residents in South Australia are not so fortunate as that splitter, but the colony's good soil and climate make life easy to all who know how to employ it; and the number of these has been rapidly augmenting. Having risen, as we have seen, from 22,390 in 1845 to 63,700 in 1850, the population amounted to 96,982 in 1855; to 121,960 in 1860; and to 148,143 in 1864. It is now nearly 180,000. Adelaide, the well-built capital, contains about 25,000 inhabitants; and besides Port Adelaide, which serves as a distant suburb to it, there are at least six other thriving towns—Kapunda, Gawler, Glenelg, Brighton, Norwood, and Kennington—and threescore or more smaller cities, each of which promises to attain importance. "A remarkable development of patient and painstaking industry," says a competent authority, a resident in Melbourne, "is perceptible over the whole colony. Its resources may not bear comparison with those of some of its still richer neigh-

[1] Forster, pp. 109, 110.

bours; but, whatever those resources may be, they are certainly in course of development in a very intelligent manner. It is England in miniature, England without its poverty, without its monstrous anomalies of individual extravagances thrown into unnecessary and indecent relief by abounding destitution. It is England, with a finer climate, with a virgin soil, with freedom from antiquated abuses, with more liberal institutions, with a happier people."

CHAPTER XXIII.

VICTORIA.

THE ESTABLISHMENT OF PORT PHILLIP AS AN INDEPENDENT COLONY, UNDER THE NAME OF VICTORIA—THE AUSTRALIAN GOLD DISCOVERIES—THE BALLARAT GOLD-FIELDS—THE CONSEQUENCES OF THE DISCOVERY—THE PROGRESS OF VICTORIA—MELBOURNE IN 1856—THE BALLARAT OUTBREAK—POLITICAL CHANGES IN VICTORIA. [1851-1869.]

THE Port Phillip Settlement was not five years old when its inhabitants began to call for separation from New South Wales, and for establishment as a distinct colony, with equal privileges to those conferred upon Van Dieman's Land in the south, and South Australia in the west. A partial answer to their demand was made by the political reform of 1842, which gave a larger area and local institutions to the district, and allowed it to send six delegates of its own to the Legislative Council in Sydney. But the people of Melbourne and its neighbourhood found that Sydney was so far off from their own centres of enterprise that their leading men refused to go thither for political work, and they soon began to call more loudly than ever for parliamentary rights which could be exercised by and among themselves. For several years there was a hard fought battle of secession, waged not only in Australia but also in England. In the end the separatists succeeded. The division was authorized by the Australian Colonies Act of 1850; and on the 1st of July 1851 the District of Port Phillip, now named Victoria by express wish of the good Queen herself, became an independent colony. That political change was contemporary with a discovery destined to effect a mighty revolution in the social and commercial condition both of New South Wales and of Victoria. Stray hints of the existence of gold in Australia had been given long before it was put to any use. As early as 1836 a Sydney convict produced a lump of the precious metal, which he declared that he had found in the interior; but as he failed to point out the precise spot from which he had obtained it, it was assumed that he had stolen a watch and melted it down, and he was punished with a hundred and fifty lashes. A Scotch shepherd also brought several pieces of gold into Sydney, but he kept its source secret, and was accordingly only suspected of some dishonesty. In 1839 Count Strzelecki, an eminent naturalist and discoverer, found some gold in the Australian Alps, and gave reasons for supposing that it abounded in that district. But, he said, "I was warned of the responsibility I should incur if I gave publicity to the discovery, since, as the Governor argued, by proclaiming the colonies to be gold regions, the maintenance of discipline among 45,000 convicts, which New South Wales, Tasmania, and Norfolk Island contained, would become almost impossible, and, unless the penal code should be amended at home, transportation would become a premium upon crime, and cease to be a punishment. These reasons of State-policy had great weight with me, and I willingly deferred to the reasons of the Governor-General, notwithstanding that they were opposed to my private interests." Therefore the secret was kept for a dozen years, and this in spite of other discoveries and suppositions. Dr Clarke, a clergyman and geological student in Sydney, picked up some quartz freckled with gold, and was convinced of the extensive distribution of the metal in 1841, but did not take the trouble to carry out his speculation; and in 1844 Sir Roderick Murchison urged, on purely scientific grounds, the probable existence of gold-fields among the mountains south of Sydney, but no use was made of his hypothesis. At length, in February 1851, Mr E. H. Hargreaves, a practical miner, who had lately come from California, and who was struck by the resemblance of some Australian districts to the great American gold-country, began to make experiments. In May he announced their successful issue, and immediately there was a rush of adventurers to Summerhill, in Bathurst, the site pointed out by him. Unlike Count Strzelecki, to whom the honour of the first discovery is due, he was rewarded, not only by his share in the first proceeds of the gold-field, but by a grant of £10,000 from the Sydney Government.

In that way the El Dorado of New South Wales was opened up, soon to be surpassed by the El Dorado of Victoria. In that colony, too, there had been occasional findings of golden lumps in previous years; but no heed was taken of them until the discovery of the Bathurst gold-fields. Then some Melbourne citizens offered a reward of £200 to any one who would find an available gold-field within the limits of Victoria, and "prospecting" became an active pursuit. It succeeded; and all previous discoveries were eclipsed by those made at Ballarat on the 8th of September in the same year, 1851, and soon afterwards in other parts of the colony.

Thereupon ensued a turmoil, unparalleled even in the history of California. "Ere the first month expired," says the historian, "nearly 10,000 diggers, of all classes of society, who had rushed promiscuously to the attractive scene, were upon and around the famous Golden Point, the original nucleus of Ballarat mining. But hardly was this miscellaneous crowd settled at work ere it commenced shelving off to Mount Alexander, which rumour proclaimed to be a still richer gold-field. In October and November, Mount Alexander lived in a blaze of predominant fame; but it was in turn dimmed by the superior lustre of Bendigo, which made good its pre-eminence during several subsequent years. Bendigo was, indeed, a wonder of its day, and the extent and activity of the industrial field it presented at this early time have hardly since been exceeded in the colony. In the middle of 1852, the winter time of the antipodes, there were reported, no doubt with some exaggeration, to be 50,000 diggers along the Bendigo Creek. The great and sudden demand for food and other necessaries was met with difficulty, under the double drawback of the state of the roads and the state of the labour market. Prices rose in due proportion, until the price at length secured the supply. Two thousand carts and drays, and other vehicles, were said to be simultaneously toiling along the roads to the different gold-fields. Bendigo was one hundred miles distant from Melbourne, and £1 per ton per mile and upwards were the rates of carriage of the day. The local dealer must have his profit as well as the carrier; so that a ton of flour, which cost £25 at Melbourne, had risen to £200 before it reached the hungry consumer at Bendigo."[1] The profits made by the gold-diggers themselves, indeed, were generally far surpassed by the profits of those who catered for their wants. "When I visited England in 1848," we are told, "a steerage passenger and his wife were in the ship, the whole of whose property, when we landed at the London Docks, I believe could have been purchased for £10. This man was a lollipop maker. A few years after the gold discovery I met him in Sydney, when he told me he was going back to England in the next ship. Struck at seeing such an improved edition of my former shipmate, I remarked to him, 'You seem to have been doing well since we last met?' 'Oh, yes, sir,' he replied, 'remarkably well. I have been for the last three years near Melbourne.' 'Then,' I said, 'you seem to have had good luck at the diggings.' His answer was, 'I did not go near them.' 'What, then, did you do?' was my next natural question. 'Well, sir, I kept a public-house for the last three years. I took a good stand on the high road to the Ballarat diggings, and had little trouble in turning in £6000 a year; and I am now going home with £20,000, besides leaving behind me a freehold property of £1500 a year in Melbourne.'"[2]

There was plenty of money-making of that sort; and if some adventurers put to good use their easily acquired wealth, more squandered it in riotous ways,

[1] Westgarth, "Victoria," pp. 126, 127. [2] Therry, p. 371.

which helped to increase the confusion and disorganization of society that the gold-discoveries provoked. Men of all tempers and all grades of character rushed to the gold-fields first from the older districts of Victoria and the neighbouring colonies—not a few being escaped convicts and ticket-of-leave men from Tasmania—and afterwards from Europe, Asia, Africa, and America; and, many of them being reckless and lawless in their dispositions, the influence which they exerted upon the colony was often altogether baneful. An intoxication of success prevailed everywhere, save when, in the case of multitudes who failed in winning the wealth they sought, and in the case of others who became suddenly rich only to squander their money and become as suddenly poor, it quickly changed into an intoxication of despair. Ugly scenes were enacted in Melbourne, and all the adjoining districts up to Ballarat and Bendigo, which made quiet, steady-going colonists wish that this new source of wealth and encouragement to dissipation had never been discovered.

Yet, with all its drawbacks, the benefit that resulted to Victoria was truly wonderful. It is not to be measured by the store of glittering metal that was found at Ballarat, and afterwards in other parts as well; but the statistics of this are sufficiently remarkable. In 1851 the gold obtained in Victoria was worth about £600,000, whereas the yield in California was equal to £8,500,000. In 1852 California produced £9,300,000; Victoria £10,900,000. The following year was the richest of all. The yield of California was £11,500,000, that of Victoria was

£12,600,000. After that the Californian fields slightly decreased in value, though they have generally yielded between £8,000,000 and £9,000,000 a year. Victoria had an average of about £11,000,000 a year till 1847; but since then its supply has decreased more rapidly. In 1860 it had sunk to the level of California, being about £8,500,000. In 1864 it was £6,200,000, and in 1867 £5,700,000. In 1868, however, it ran to nearly £8,000,000; and the produce of this colony during the whole eighteen years between 1851 and 1868 has been about £150,000,000, enough to pay off a fifth of the whole national debt of Great Britain.

If this great supply of gold has enriched many thousands of diggers, it has enriched the colony at large still more. Victoria was enjoying a prosperity unrivalled among the dependencies of England in 1851; but its subsequent prosperity has been vastly greater. In 1851 its population was 77,345; in 1854 it had amounted to 236,776, being more than trebled in the three years. In 1857 it was 410,766; in 1861 it was 540,322; in 1865 it was more than 600,000; and in 1868 it exceeded 650,000.

Yet the resources of the country have given ample employment for all the new-comers, and the only need is for a larger number of inhabitants to put them to the best use. Manufactures of all sorts prosper in the towns, and agricultural pursuits offer easy facilities for advancement in the country districts, though in them Victoria is still far surpassed by South Australia; while in the more remote parts squatters carry on their profitable calling, and furnish what is, after gold, the staple export of the colony. Victoria exported 18,091,207 pounds of wool in 1850, 25,579,886 pounds in 1863, and 42,391,234 pounds in 1866, the value of the latter being £3,196,491.

Some account of Melbourne, in illustration of the early progress of the colony, has been already given. "A more striking contrast," says one writer, "could not well be furnished than the appearance Melbourne presented when I was there in the year 1845, and afterwards when I visited it in 1856. In 1845 Bourke Street contained but a few scattered cottages, and sheep were grazed on the thick grass then growing in the street. It was only known to be a street in that year by a sign indicating, 'This is Bourke Street.' In 1856 it was as crowded with fine buildings, and as thronged and alive with the hurrying to and fro of busy people, as Cheapside at the present day. In 1845, from my residence on the Eastern Hill, it was a pleasant walk through green paddocks to the Court House. Ten years afterwards the whole way from that house to the Court House was filled up with streets. Two branches of Sydney banks supplied the district in 1845 with banking accommodation that only occupied them with business a few hours each day. In 1856 eight banks could scarcely meet the pecuniary exigencies of the community. In the principal street, Collins Street, there was in 1845 but one jeweller, who displayed a scanty supply of second-hand watches and pinchbeck brooches in a shop similar to those in which pawnbrokers display their articles of used-up jewellery in the by-streets off the Strand. In 1856 might be seen in the same street jewellers' shops as numerous and brilliant as those that glitter in Regent Street. The harbour of

Hobson's Bay, on the morning on which I left it for Sydney, in 1846, contained two large ships, three brigs, and a few small colonial craft. In 1856 the same harbour was filled with about two hundred large London and Liverpool ships, and countless other vessels from America, New Zealand, and other parts. In 1845 there was little more than one clergyman of each religious denomination. In 1856 a numerous clergy of the various denominations officiated; the two principal, Church of England and Roman Catholic, presided over by bishops of their respective creeds. In short, in size, in wealth, in numbers, in varied social enjoyments, the humble town I had quitted in 1845 had been transformed in 1856 into a splendid city, and presented such a transition from poverty to splendour as no city in the ancient or modern world had heretofore exhibited in a corresponding period."[1] In 1856, however, Melbourne had not 90,000 inhabitants; now they are about 160,000—nearly as many people as there are in the entire colony of South Australia. Other thriving towns also exist in Victoria, which in rapidity of growth keep pace with Melbourne. Geelong, its earliest rival, has fallen behind-hand; but others, like Ballarat and Sandhurst, which owe their importance to the gold-discovery, are now centres of civilization, and markets for much besides gold.

Of the general history of the colony little needs to be said. By the constitution which it received with its independence, the management of affairs, under the governor, was vested in a Legislative Council of thirty members, ten being Crown nominees, and the

[1] Therry, pp. 855-857.

other twenty elected by all inhabitants who paid a £10 annual rental. Mr Latrobe, who had been made superintendent in 1839, continued in office as governor till 1854; but his quiet rule hardly gave satisfaction to the colonists. Still less were they satisfied with his successor, Sir Charles Hotham, who shared the blame thrown upon his predecessor for the Ballarat outbreak in the November of that year.

"The gold-fields by this time," says the historian, "comprised by far the most important interest in the colony, more than half of the population being connected with them. A growl of complaint from this miscellaneous mass of people had from the first scarcely ever ceased to be emitted; and this ominous noise had been gradually increasing in loudness and sharpness under an accumulating variety of evils. Some of these evils, so far at least as the authorities were concerned, were irremediable, such as the discomfort of digging life, and the precariousness of its results; both of these adverse features having been aggravated by the circumstance of a scanty rainfall in the year 1854, when the yield of gold was in consequence unusually small. Other evils seemed to admit of remedy, and the Colonial Government received plentiful blame at the hands of the diggings' community in regard to them. There was indeed much substantial ground for these complaints. A vast irregular society had been suddenly called up throughout the colony, and the Government, somewhat perplexed how to deal with it, had been fain to let the difficulty solve itself by doing nothing; that is to say, although they had appointed paid officers and paid magistrates, who went through a round of duties—and with especial strictness, that of collecting the gold mining licence fee of thirty shillings monthly, as well as the other Government dues—they had never taken any steps to make the gold-fields' population, socially and politically, a part of the colony. There was no arrangement for a mining franchise and a gold-fields' representation, and no social status, even by the simple and usual expedient of graduating the people to the Government by enrolling the more respectable of the great mining community as local justices of the peace. This state of things had lasted three years, and it was greatly aggravated by the vain efforts of the colonists to induce the hesitating Government to sell adequate quantities of the public lands. Many a digger longed for a few adjacent acres, on which he might rear a home and plant a garden or potato-field of his own; and for such a rare luxury he would willingly have exchanged the tin pannikin or pickle-bottle full of gold that lay concealed in a corner of his tent, and represented the last six months of his mining toils. Discontent centred itself in the question of the monthly licence fee, as this was a subject on which a demonstration could be most effectually made. The Government had tried some palliatives in the licence difficulty; and, by allowing a discount on prepayments for longer terms than a month, had hoped to supersede many of the collector's visits, and so diminish the occasions for hostile manifestations. These efforts had not been successful. The Ballarat riot took its more immediate rise from one of the "raids" upon the diggers for the obnoxious licence money. Upon the first serious threatenings of disturbance, however, a party of military were sent up from Melbourne, who, on arrival, were confronted by a stockade erected by the rioters on the famous Bakery Hill. At early dawn of the 3d of December, this place was stormed and taken, not without loss of life on both sides; and thus this very exceptional and unhappy colonial occurrence came to an end."[1]

The cause of offence also soon came to an end. In 1855 the political condition of the gold-diggers was entirely reconstituted. The monthly licence fee was abolished, and, in lieu, a small export duty on gold was appointed; while the diggers were enabled, on payment of £1 a year, to secure for themselves both mining privileges and the franchise. The gold-fields were divided into districts, each under the charge of a warder, who saw that the local courts did their duty, and was aided by a staff of unpaid justices. These arrangements gave satisfaction to the mining community, and helped to convert a discontented and lawless race of men into good citizens and friends of order.

These reforms were part of a change which occurred in the management of the whole colony. The people, both of Victoria and of the neighbouring settlements, were not satisfied with the political arrangements that had been made for them in 1851. They asked for public representative rights, and greater power of self-government; in fact, for a complete democratic system. "The Ballot, No Property Qualification, Equal Electoral Districts, and Manhood Suffrage," were the four "points of the charter" claimed by the Australian radicals, and they were advocated most vehemently in Victoria. The

[1] Westgarth, pp. 148-150.

British Government wisely allowed the colonists to
have their own way. A new constitution, transferring complete functions of self-government to two legislative chambers, both of them elected wholly by the colonists themselves, under a governor who became for all practical purposes only their chairman, was proclaimed on the 23d of November, 1855; and since then the details of political power, hardly fought over by the colonists themselves, have been gradually tending in the direction of uncurbed republicanism. The result has in the main been satisfactory to all who consider that government is only a machine for forwarding the best interests of all classes of the governed, and that any machine which thus works most efficiently is the one most to be commended. The colony of Victoria affords the interesting spectacle of a democracy, more complete even than that of the United States, yet notably loyal to the sovereign whose name it bears.

CHAPTER XXIV.

NEW SOUTH WALES AND QUEENSLAND.

THE LATER PROGRESS OF NEW SOUTH WALES—ITS GOLD-FIELDS AND THEIR FRUIT—SQUATTER-EXTENSIONS—THE RISE OF THE MORETON BAY DISTRICT, AND THE OPENING UP OF CENTRAL AUSTRALIA—THE FERTILITY OF THIS REGION—ESTABLISHMENT OF THE COLONY OF QUEENSLAND—ITS RAPID GROWTH—THE PRESENT CONDITION OF NEW SOUTH WALES—ITS COAL-FIELDS.
[1851-1869.]

THE limits of the colony of New South Wales, originally comprising about 1,500,000 square miles, and thus nearly half as large as Europe, were sucessfully curtailed by the partition of the three colonies of Van Dieman's Land, South Australia, and Victoria, which, though all three constituted less than a third of the entire area—Van Dieman's Land being about a sixtieth, South Australia about a quarter, and Victoria about a sixteenth—were in value very much more than a third. Of the 1,000,000 or more square miles left to New South Wales in 1851, only a very small section was under cultivation or parcelled out in townships; and if the squatters tended their sheep in far-off regions, and over vast extents of ground, the chief portion of the territory was put to no use at all. Of the population of 189,957, about a third was in Sydney and its suburbs, about a sixth in other towns, and less than half spread over the neighbouring country districts.

The mother-colony, however, was not too old to compete, and that successfully, with her offspring. She had by this time, indeed, fairly shaken off the pernicious influences of convict life that had marred her early career, and was now able to vie even with Victoria as a nation of vigorous and independent men, worthy to enjoy the powers of complete self-government wisely conferred upon them by Great Britain. These self-governing powers of New South Wales almost kept pace with those of Victoria. The old constitution was here, as in the south, abolished in 1855, and the colonists were left to choose their own legislative machinery, and alter it to their taste. Except that the Upper House of Parliament, instead of being elected by the people as in Victoria, continues to be composed of Crown nominees, the machinery is now almost as democratic as in the younger colony. The seventy-two members of the Lower House are elected by universal suffrage, aided by the ballot.

The later growth of the colony is mainly due to the discovery of gold in the district of Bathurst, which has already been referred to, although, as the Bathurst mines proved far less rich than those in the neighbourhood of Ballarat, New South Wales, while it had quite as much temporary derangement as Victoria, has profited far less. The entire yield of the mines near the Australian Alps between 1851 and 1868 was only worth about £30,000,000, against the £150,000,000 drawn from the region of the Australian Pyrenees.

"The immediate effect of the discovery in Sydney and throughout the colony," says a resident, "was a state of society in which there was the minimum of comfort combined with the maximum of expense."[1] "There was," says another, "a heterogeneous scramble for the coveted ore throughout the length and breadth of the land. Artizans of every description threw up their employments, leaving their masters and their wives and families to take care of themselves. Nor did the mania confine itself to the labouring classes, for these were soon followed by responsible tradesmen, farmers, captains of vessels, and not a few of the superior classes; some unable to withstand the mania and the force of the stream, or because they were really disposed to venture time and money on the chance, and others because they were, as employers of labour, left in the lurch, and had no alternative."[2] Some went to Bathurst; more to Ballarat, or Mount Alexander, or Bendigo. "Sydney looked like a deserted village. There the judicious purchaser stepped in, and bought whole streets of unoccupied houses for hundreds, which, in twelve months afterwards, he sold for more than as many thousands. In 1854 prices rose to quite a fever height, and in that year fabulous riches were realized. Shopkeepers, no longer selling their goods at a fair value, found the best customers in those to whom they charged the most exorbitant prices. When the drapers were dealing with the diggers, who knew nothing of the real value of the silks, satins, and laces with which they supplied the fair companions whom they treated, the custom was, on an article being shown to them, not to beat down the price, but to ask, 'Have you nothing dearer than that?' On such a hint, of

[1] Therry, p. 368. [2] Westgarth, "Australia," pp. 169, 170.

course, the seller acted, and, on exhibiting a showy article of inferior value, but on which was put a higher price, the article sold immediately."[1]

One benefit accruing from this disorganized state of society was that the wealth acquired by the great majority of the diggers, men unfit to put it to good uses, quickly passed, though often through demoralizing channels—the chief of all being gin-palaces—into better hands. Much of it soon left the colony; but more remained, to be employed in older and more productive ways. All trades in New South Wales were greatly stimulated by the gold discoveries, and, in the end, none more than the oldest and best—that of wool-producing. Squatters became more numerous, and their operations more extensive. After driving their sheep far south and far west, up to the boundaries of Victoria and South Australia, they advanced in northerly directions, and thus helped in the formation of another, and at present the youngest, of the Australian colonies.

The rich lands of the new colony, now bearing the name of Queensland, had long been vaguely known and slightly valued. Moreton Bay, in which the present capital of Brisbane is built, had been discovered by Captain Cook in 1770; and the River Brisbane, which runs into it from Darling Downs, had been explored in 1823 by Oxley, sent out by the New South Wales Government to choose a site for a new convict settlement. He chose Brisbane, which was so used until 1842, and many substantial buildings were there erected by the convicts. But the obstacles thrown in the way of free colonization for

[1] Therry, pp. 370, 371.

some time prevented their being advantageously employed, and until about twenty years ago the great resources of the district were almost entirely neglected. At length attention began to be called to them. "The whole country bounded by Moreton Bay," it was said in 1849, "is well adapted for grazing and agricultural farming. The indigenous timber is of great value. The mulberry tree grows very luxuriantly. The climate and soil appear well suited to the cultivation of the sugar-cane, cotton, arrowroot, tobacco, indigo, and other tropical products. They are also admirably adapted for the production of every species of European grain, as well as those peculiar to warmer climates; for, as vegetation goes on without interruption all the year round, the farmer has only to select, for the growth of any description of grain, the peculiar season that will ensure the exact temperature required to bring it to maturity. The barley harvest, that being the hardiest grain, comes immediately after the colonial winter, the wheat harvest at the commencement of summer, and the maize harvest so late as to give that intertropical grain the full benefit of the heat of summer. The English potato, and the Indian or sweet potato, are both cultivated successfully. Coal is found in the neighbourhood of the Brisbane, and the fisheries of the extensive bay and coast may be made very profitable."[1] If this coast region, and others adjoining it both north and south, were found to be excellently adapted for agricultural pursuits, the vast sweep of country stretching inland, embracing high mountains, fertile valleys, and rich table-lands, was no less fitted

[1] Martin, vol. II. pp. 483, 484.

to the needs of the squatter, and, after he had helped to make the best portions too valuable for his own more desultory use, for farming cultivation.

Much of the great Queensland district forms an Australia Felix only second to the Australia Felix in the south. The great explorer of this region was the unfortunate Dr Leichhardt. Sir Thomas Mitchell also visited it in 1845 and 1846, passing northwards from Sydney, and then in a north-western direction towards the Gulf of Carpentaria, visiting the Darling Downs and other parts already known, though still unused, and ending by discovering a beautiful plain, watered by many streams, besides the larger one to which he gave the name of Victoria. "The soil," he said, "consists of rich clay, and the hollows gave birth to water-courses, in most of which water was abundant. I found, at length, that I might travel in any direction, and find water at hand, without having to seek the river, except when I wished to ascertain its general course and observe its character. The grass consists of several new sorts, one of which springs green from the old stem. The plains were verdant. Indeed, the luxuriant pasturage surpassed in quality, as it did in extent, anything of the kind I had ever seen. New birds and new plants marked this out as an essentially different region from any I had previously explored. That the river is the most important of Australia, increasing as it does by successive tributaries, and not a mere product of distant ranges, admits of no dispute; and the downs and plains of Central Australia, through which it flows, seem sufficient to supply the whole world with animal food."[1]

[1] Martin, vol. ii. p. 894.

Reports like that induced adventurous squatters gradually to encroach upon the hitherto neglected solitudes to the far north-west of Sydney, and as other adventurers began to settle in considerable numbers in the neighbourhood of Morton Bay, the vast territory was in time fitted to become a colony distinct from New South Wales.

The change was made in December 1859, when the mother-colony, already deprived of a third of her territory, was mulcted of two-thirds of the territory remaining to her, and the colony of Queensland was parted off with an area 678,600 square miles, comprising all the country north of 28° 30' south latitude, and east of 141° east longitude. In 1851 it had about 8500 inhabitants, chiefly resident in Brisbane and its neighbourhood. In 1856 the population was double the former number; and in 1859, when the separation took place, it amounted to 25,146—Brisbane, the capital, having 7000 inhabitants, and Ipswich, a little island on a tributary of the Brisbane River, about 4500.

Since then the colony, which has a political constitution very similar to that of New South Wales, has grown rapidly. In 1861 it had a population of 34,885, and an export trade of £709,599, composed almost entirely of the wool, tallow, and skins obtained from about 4,000,000 sheep and 560,000 cattle. In 1863 the population had risen to 61,640, the stock of sheep and cattle had been increased by half, and the trade had been proportionately augmented. In that year there were two memorable additions to the list of colonial produce. Queensland began to export gold and cotton. Its gold mines, those at any rate which have as yet been discovered, are less important than those of the south, though the yield, which in 1863 was only worth £144,802, had risen to £593,516 in 1868. Its growth of cotton is still inconsiderable; but all that is produced equals the best that can be obtained from any other part of the world, and nothing but the sparseness of its population, and the ease of money-making in other ways, hinders the development of this branch of commerce so important to Great Britain.

"Since the establishment of Queensland in December 1859," said its governor, Sir George Bowen, at the close of 1865, "our European population has increased from 25,000 to nearly 90,000; that is, it has been augmented nearly fourfold; while our revenue and our trade, including imports and exports, have been more than trebled. The other chief elements of material prosperity have advanced in almost equal proportions. Cotton, sugar, and tobacco have been added to our lists of staple products. A line of new ports has been opened along our eastern seaboard from Keppel Bay to Cape York, a distance of a thousand miles; while pastoral occupation has spread over an additional area at least four times larger than the area of the United Kingdom. In 1859 our settlers had hardly advanced beyond the Darling Downs to the west, or beyond Rockhampton to the north. Now, in 1865, there are stations seven hundred miles to the west of Brisbane, and eight hundred miles to the north of Rockhampton."[1] And the progress has certainly not been less rapid during the last three years.

[1] "Reports of Colonial Governors (1865)," part ii. p. 23.

New South Wales has also continued to progress rapidly in recent years, although suffering much from the drain of emigrants, generally the most enterprising, to the yet more energetic colonies of Queensland on the north and Victoria on the south. Other settlers, however, have come to fill their place and more. Its population had increased from 189,951 in 1851 to 266,189 in 1856, and—in spite of the great reduction of its area by the formation of Queensland, leaving it only 323,437 square miles—to 358,278 in 1861, and to 431,412 in 1866; having nearly doubled in each period of five years. The growth of trade, though not proportionately rapid, has also been great. The loss of so many of its best squatting districts caused, in 1859 and the few following years, a considerable falling off in the supply of wool and tallow, and in 1866 the exports of these articles were hardly so great as they had been in 1856, when the wool was worth about £1,650,000, and the tallow about £125,000; but the increased value of the gold mines, the yield of which in 1866 was worth £2,924,891, had compensated for this.

Yet more important, though in itself less lucrative, has been the growth of the colony's coal-mining, which more than quadrupled in the ten years. Of this mineral, the one notable scarcity in Australia, New South Wales has almost the monopoly. There were raised in 1866 774,238 tons, valued at £324,049, of which about half was sold to the neighbouring colonies. "Such," says a recent traveller, "is the present rapidity of the growth and rise to power of Queensland, such the apparent poverty of New South Wales, that were the question merely one between the Sydney wheatgrowers and the cotton-planters of Brisbane and Rockhampton, the rich tropical settlers would be as certain of the foremost position in any future confederation as they were in America when the struggle lay only between the Carolinas and New England. As it is, just as America was first saved by the coal of Pennsylvania and Ohio, Australia will be saved by the coal of New South Wales. Queensland possesses some small stores of coal, but the vast preponderance of acreage of the great power of the future lies in New South Wales. On my return from a short voyage to the north, I visited the coal-field of New South Wales, at Newcastle, on the Hunter. The beds are of vast extent. They lie upon the banks of a navigable river, and so near to the surface, that the best qualities are raised, in a country of dear labour, at 8s. or 9s. a ton, and delivered on board ship for 12s. For manufacturing purposes the coal is perfect; for steam use it is, though somewhat 'dirty,' a serviceable fuel; and copper and iron are found in close proximity to the beds. The Newcastle and Port Jackson fields open a brilliant future to Sydney in these times, when coal is king in a far higher degree than was ever cotton. To her black beds the colony will owe not only manufactures, bringing wealth and population, but that leisure which is begotten of riches—leisure that brings culture, and love of harmony and truth."[1]

[1] Dilke, "Greater Britain." pp. 300, 301.

CHAPTER XXV.

WEST AUSTRALIA AND WASTE AUSTRALIA.

ORIGIN OF THE SWAN RIVER SETTLEMENT, OR WESTERN AUSTRALIA—EARLY MISFORTUNES OF THE COLONY—ITS PRESENT CONDITION—EXPLORATIONS IN THE INTERIOR OF THE AUSTRALIAN CONTINENT—THE FIRST DISCOVERERS—STURT, MURRAY, EYRE, LEICHHARDT—STURT AGAIN—STUART—BURKE AND WILLS—THE CHARACTER OF THE INTERIOR. [1827-1863.]

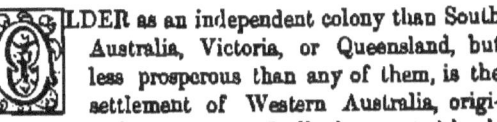

OLDER as an independent colony than South Australia, Victoria, or Queensland, but less prosperous than any of them, is the settlement of Western Australia, originally intended to consist of all the great island-continent which was not comprised in New South Wales.

Swan River, round whose shores still clusters most of the colony's feeble life, was first visited in 1697 by Vlaming, a Dutch navigator, who gave it its name in consequence of the number of black swans that he there found; but little was thought of the district till 1827, when Captain Stirling, of the *Success*, called attention to it, and urged the importance of its immediate occupation so as to prevent its being converted, as was thought likely, into a French settlement. Early in 1829 Captain Freemantle was sent in the *Challenger* to take formal possession of the country on behalf of the English Crown; and before the close of the year twenty-five ships had arrived at Swan River from England, bearing 850 emigrants, 57 horses, 106 pigs, 204 cows, and 1096 sheep. In 1830 there arrived 1125 other settlers, and more horses, pigs, cows, and sheep, and there were further, though not very considerable, importations of men and animals in the following years.

But the first colonists found themselves lodged on a barren coast, unfit for the agricultural and pastoral enterprise for which, had other things been favourable, they had no great aptitude, and they were seriously harassed by the multitudes of hostile savages, who resented this intrusion on their barbaric privileges. Great misery was the result, and it was not lessened by the civil, naval, and military officers in charge of the experiment, who divided among themselves about 300,000 acres of the best land that was to be obtained, shifting their dominions as often as one district after another was found or thought to be preferable. The emigrants had come out under promise of also receiving grants of land; but only the most useless parts were left for them. The result was deplorable. "The entire material of a settlement," they said, in an indignant protest forwarded to the British Government in 1831, "the official staff, settlers, property, and live stock, were hurried out to an unknown wilderness before one acre was surveyed, before one building had been erected, before even a guess had been formed as to the proper scene of their labours, before the slightest knowledge had been obtained of the soil, climate, products, or inhabitants. Nay, further, it was absolutely made a condition of the grants of land that the emigrant should bring his family, dependants, and property into the colony while in this state. The ghastly spectacle of the town-site of Clarence— its sole edifices crowded, buried, and neglected tombs —its only inhabitants corpses, the victims of disease, starvation, and despair—the sea-beach strewed with wrecks—the hills and borders of the rivers studded with deserted and half-finished buildings—bear witness to these consequences, and speak of brave men, delicate females, and helpless children perishing by hundreds on a desert coast from want of food, of shelter, and even of water, and surrounded by armed hordes of angry savages. It were impossible to estimate the vast amount of property of every sort buried for safety in the sands of the shore, and never again recovered, or the vast multitude of most valuable and high-bred stock of all descriptions, whose skeletons whitened the beach or filled the morasses they had been forced to enter in the desperate search for even fresh water."[1] The blame attaching to those who led them into this condition was, of course, shared by the emigrants who suffered themselves to be so led; but they paid the full penalty for their folly. "Some," we are told, "demanded to be led to their lands; others gave way to despair; servants attacked the spirit-casks; masters followed their example. The farmers were told they must wait— wait till lands were discovered, and then wait until they were surveyed. A quarter of a million sterling of property was destroyed; the means of the immigrants dissipated; their live-stock perished; many died; and numbers, as soon as practicable, fled from

[1] "Parliamentary Emigration Papers" for 1849, 50.

this scene of ruin, carrying with them the wreck of their fortunes."[1]

That was the dismal beginning of the Swan River Settlement, afterwards known as Western Australia, intended to turn into an English colony the 978,000 square miles of land assigned as its limits, being the whole of Australia west of the 139th degree of east longitude. Slowly and painfully, however, those who survived the first hardships, and the many new-comers who left England in ignorance of the lot awaiting them, or who boldly hoped that, amid the failures of others, they might find ways of succeeding, brought some sort of order and progress into the colony. The town of Perth was built on a well-chosen site by the side of the Swan River, and Freemantle was appointed as its port, at the entrance of the river into the Indian Ocean. The village of Albany, destined to become a town, was planted by St George's Sound, on the southern coast, and other settlements were formed along the shore and here and there inland. The country was gradually found to be less inhospitable than at first it seemed, and the colonists who were able to endure the difficulties of their strange life slowly secured for themselves a measure of prosperity by sheep-farming and agriculture. In 1834 the colony contained about 1600 English inhabitants and some 3500 sheep, and there were 918 acres of land under cultivation. In 1842 there were 3476 colonists and 60,380 sheep, yielding 84,640 pounds of wool, and the cultivated land comprised 3364 acres. In 1848 the people numbered 4622 and the sheep 141,123; the wool exported

[1] Martin, vol. II. p. 713.

amounted to 301,965 pounds, and 157,855 acres of land were under tillage.

In 1849, finding that very few new emigrants arrived, and that the progress of the colony was crippled by scarcity of labour, the West Australians petitioned that their numbers might be augmented by convicts; and the petition was readily acceded to, as the Tasmanians had refused, with a vehemence that could not be disregarded, to receive any more, and as New South Wales had long before been freed from them. By this means almost exclusively the population of West Australia has been increased during the last twenty years; but even this questionable advantage has been removed, at the earnest entreaty of the Victorians and other colonists of Australia, who resent the coming among them of runaway or liberated criminals from the west. Their distant neighbours take a different view. "The convicts available for public works," said the Governor of Western Australia in 1866, "have been distributed throughout the colony, in repairing and making roads and bridges, and generally on works for the benefit of the whole community. A natural feeling of apprehension exists that the approaching cessation of transportation will throw a heavy burden on the colonists in respect of the keeping in order of the public highways."[1]

In 1866 there were about 10,000 convicts or emancipists in the colony, out of an English population of 21,065. Among that number there were, in a single year, about 3500 convictions for offences. Dismal accounts are given by travellers of the contamination

[1] "Colonial Governors' Reports," 1867, part ii. p. 70.

produced among nearly all classes by the presence of so many criminals. "The contrast between the scenery and the people of West Australia," says one, "is great indeed. The aboriginal inhabitants of Albany were represented by a tribe of filthy natives —tall, half-starved, their heads bedaubed with red ochre, and their faces smeared with yellow clay; the colonists by a gang of fiend-faced convicts, working in chains upon the esplanade, and a group of scowling expirees hunting a monkey with bull-dogs on the pier; while the native women, half clothed in tattered kangaroo-skins, came slouching past with an aspect of defiant wretchedness. On the road between Albany and Hamilton, I saw a man at work in ponderous irons. The sun was striking down upon him in a way that none can fancy who have no experience of Western Australia or Bengal, and his labour was of the heaviest; now he had to prise up huge rocks with a crowbar, now to handle pick and shovel, now to use the rammer, under the eye of an armed warder who idled in the shade by the roadside. This was an 'escape man,' thus treated with a view to cause him to cease his continual endeavours to get away from Albany. Work is never done in West Australia unless under the compulsion of the lash, for a similar degradation of labour is produced by the use of convicts as by that of slaves. The convicts and their keepers form two-thirds of the whole population, and the district is a great English prison, not a colony, and exports but a little sandal-wood, and a little cotton."[1]

Some enterprise is shown by the colonists, how-

[1] Dilke, pp. 176, 177.

ever, not only in agricultural production and in sheep-farming, but also in working the copper mines, in which some parts are rich. Besides copper, iron, lead, zinc, and coal exist in more or less abundance, though they have hardly yet been used, and are not likely to be without more extensive colonization than the uninviting district has hitherto induced. Western Australia, still a Crown colony, without any form of popular government, affords a strange contrast to the free and vigorous nations that are growing up in the east. Its few inhabitants are spread over only a very small portion of the vast area, of which there are still more than forty square miles for each resident. The almost boundless regions of the interior have as yet been hardly visited by white men.

In the exploration of that interior, however, both in the parts belonging to West Australia, and the parts belonging to Queensland and South Australia, much has been done. To some of the exploring expeditions, slight reference has already been made. Here, however, it will be well to describe briefly all the most important of them. They constitute a story of heroic exploits in overland travel, only surpassed, in modern times, by the successive voyages undertaken in Arctic seas by the precursors of Sir John Franklin, and those who sought to rescue him, or at any rate to discover his fate.

The work was begun at Sydney, when it was the nucleus of all the later colonization and civilization of Australia. The coast and narrow strip of land about Sydney alone were known before 1813, when Blaxland, Lawson, and Wentworth crossed the Blue Mountains, and when Evans visited Bathurst and discovered the river Lachlan. But those modest achievements were quickly followed by others of greater magnitude, some of the most heroic being those which have been of least value in opening up new fields for English settlement.

In 1817 and 1818 Oxley traced the Lachlan and the Macquarie down a great part of their course. In 1824 Hovell and Hume tracked the road from Sydney to Port Phillip, now Victoria. In 1827 Allan Cunningham, the poet, discovered the Darling Downs; and in later years, as has been already noticed, all the eastern parts of Australia, north and south of Sydney, now included in Victoria and Queensland, were visited.

More adventurous than any of his predecessors was Captain Charles Sturt, who started on the first of three famous expeditions in 1828. Several rivers, large and small, had been found by inland travellers; but the coast explorers had not observed their outlets into the sea. Hence arose the theory that there was a great lake in the interior into which the rivers emptied themselves. Sturt was its chief supporter, and in the hope of proving it all his journeys were undertaken. In 1828 he discovered the Darling, and followed it almost to the point of its junction with the Murray. In 1830 he tracked the Murray to its mouth in Encounter Bay, though, wedded to the inland-lake theory, he refused to believe that that was its only or chief outlet. On this occasion, in an open whale-boat, with a crew of five, he rowed a thousand miles from his starting-point on the Murrumbidgee, a branch of the Murray, more than once having to fight his way through tribes of hostile natives, and during the thousand miles' return journey, he and his followers had little but flour for food. "Seventy-seven days after starting," we are told, "they reached the place were they had built their boat, having in the interim rowed at least two thousand miles. Here a terrible disappointment awaited them. They had expected all along that provisions would have been sent from Sydney to this point. The hope of this had buoyed them up amid all their fatigues. But the depôt was just as they had left it, and no one was there. The next rendezvous was two hundred miles away, and Sturt remembered with bitterness that he had told his companions that they need not come farther down unless some extraordinary delay took place. It was useless therefore to expect them, so the boat proceeded onward. For seventeen days longer they pulled against the stream. The daily journeys became gradually shorter and shorter. No murmur, however, escaped the crew, as they sat in the boat, pale and emaciated, and pulled against the current. At night, in their tents, before sleeping, when Sturt's presence no longer controlled them, their sufferings would find an utterance. 'I frequently,' says Sturt, 'heard them complain of great pain and severe exhaustion. "I must tell the captain," some of them would say, "that I can pull no more."' To-morrow came, and they pulled on. At last, one of them became deranged, and the others fairly gave up. This was still ninety miles from the depôt, but they absolutely could not take the boat any farther. Reluctantly they drew it on shore, and two of the strongest men were sent in advance, and the rest waited. For six days there was no sign of their return. The last day's provisions had been served out, and then they thought of nothing but saving their lives. The specimens were buried in cases made of the whale-boat, and they resolved next day to follow in the track of their comrades. That next day, however, brought them the long-expected relief. This was the last of their trials, and exactly six months after leaving they were all safe back again in Sydney."[1]

In such narratives of hazardous achievements and hair-breadth escapes the history of Australian discovery abounds. Not without danger were the expeditions of Sir Thomas Mitchell in 1831, 1835, and 1836, when, following up the discoveries of Sturt, he explored the beautiful country, now included in Victoria, to which he gave the name of Australia Felix. But there was greater danger in some of the minor enterprises of travellers in more distant parts of the island, as in the journeys undertaken by Lieutenants Grey—who, as Sir George Grey, was afterwards Governor of South Australia, of New Zealand, and of Cape Colony—and Lushington in Western Australia, and especially its north-western parts, between 1837 and 1840, by which were opened up some splendid regions, of which little use has yet been made.

Another bold Australian explorer, since famous for his connection, as governor of Jamaica, with the so-called insurrection of 1865, was Sir Edward, then Mr Eyre. Having made some researches around the new settlement at Adelaide in 1839, he set out next

[1] Woods, "History of Discovery and Exploration in Australia," vol. I. pp. 362, 363.

year on a more daring expedition. Attended by
only five men and two boys, and travelling due
north in search of the supposed inland sea, he went
much farther than any previous traveller had done,
and examined the neighbourhood of Lake Torrens.
Much farther into the unknown north he dared not
go. After being twice for many days without water,
and seeing around him nothing but monotonous
dangers, before him no passage to anything but
death, he abandoned the attempt to push on to the
northern shore of the island, and retraced his steps.
But then, not disheartened, he turned round and
traversed the dreary southern coast-land, past the
Australian Bight, from Port Lincoln to St George's
Sound, with one white and three black companions.
Here peril succeeded peril, and horror was heaped
on horror. On the 25th of March 1841, after
three months' journey, he had only reached the
head of the Bight. He was still six hundred and
fifty miles from St George's Sound, and he had only
three weeks' provisions in store. "The overseer,"
says the historian, "begged Mr Eyre to return, but
he would not. Yet he was suffering perhaps more
than the others; he was very ill from living upon
some unwholesome fish they had caught, and his
chances of life seemed very small if he persisted in
his undertaking. But go on he would. He consented to kill a horse for food; it was one which
was so ill that his life could not be saved in any
case, and the consequence of such unwholesome diet,
was that they were all ill again. Bad as it was, the
native boys thought they had not had enough of it,
so during the night they stole a large quantity. Mr

Eyre detected the act of dishonesty, and to punish
the two eldest of them, deducted a third portion of
their usual share of rations. They resented this by
leaving the party, and endeavouring to make their
way by themselves; but as they had been very
much disaffected ever since the rations were reduced,
Eyre was not surprised at their conduct. The last
sheep was now killed, as a preparation for another
journey. The overseer then went to examine the
country in advance. The news brought back was
not encouraging; the road lay along even more thick
and scrubby land than before. It seemed threatening rain, so the start was delayed. Anxiously they
watched each darkening cloud, praying earnestly for
some few drops of water; but the clouds cleared off,
and the night was clear and cold. Just as they were
turning in for the evening the native boys came
back; they could not exist upon their own resources,
and were sadly famished before they submitted to
the humiliation of returning. Eyre took them back,
believing them to be sincere, and little suspected the
treachery they meditated. Again, on the 26th and
27th, it seemed wild and stormy, and threatening rain,
but none fell. On the latter date they started, again
leaving behind them everything except the provisions, their arms, ammunition, and clothes. They
only advanced fifteen miles the first day. The next
stage was, however, eighteen, through a thick scrub,
and along the top of the limestone cliffs which had re-
appeared, but were now not more than three hundred
feet high. On the 29th they made nineteen miles;
but the day was so windy that they could scarcely
stagger along the tops of the cliffs. In the evening

the horses were all hobbled, and turned out to feed, and the stores were piled under an oilskin, while every one was obliged to make break-winds of boughs to protect them during the night. Mr Eyre on this eventful evening took the first watch, from six to eleven. The night was bitterly cold, and the wind was blowing hard from the south-west. The horses fed well, but rambled a good deal. At half-past ten Mr Eyre went to fetch them back. He found them at a short distance, and was picking his way, in the dark, among the bushes, when he was suddenly startled by a gunshot. It was from the camp, and of course he hurried there immediately. About one hundred yards from it he met Wylie, the King George's Sound native, running, and crying out, 'Oh, massa! oh, massa! come, look here!' He reached the camp, and there before him lay his overseer in the agonies of death, with a wound in his chest, from which the blood was flowing rapidly. A glance around explained the whole scene. The two younger natives were gone, whilst the scattered fragments of the baggage which had been piled under the oilskin told the reason why. The overseer was beyond human aid, for he expired immediately after Eyre's arrival. It was a horrible scene, and the feelings of the survivor were shocked as well by the crushing weight of the disaster as by its suddenness. Eyre describes it with a reality that none but a witness could do justice to. He says: 'The horrors of my situation glanced upon me. I was alone in the desert. The frightful, appalling truth glared upon me in such startling reality as almost to paralyze my mind. At the dead hour of night, with the fierce wind raging around me, in one of the most inhospitable wastes of Australia, I was left alone with one native boy. I could not rely upon his fidelity, for he was perhaps in league with the other two, who might be waiting to kill me. Three days had passed since we had found water, and it was very doubtful when we should find more. Six hundred miles of country had to be traversed before I could hope to obtain the slightest help or assistance, whilst I knew that not a drop of water nor an ounce of flour had been left by the murderers.' The guns were gone, and only a rifle and a pair of pistols left. The former was useless, as a ball was jammed in the barrel; and the latter had no cartridges to fit them. Obtaining possession of all the remaining arms, useless as they were, he went with the native to look for the horses. After a long search he found them, and when he brought them back to the camp he sat down to watch. He passed a bitter night. Every moment he tells us seemed to him an age, and he thought the morning would never come. The night was frosty. He had nothing on but a shirt and trousers, and to mental anguish was now added intense bodily pain. He tells us that suffering and distress nearly overwhelmed him, and life seemed scarcely worth the effort to prolong it."[1] But hope came in the morning. A small quantity of food was found, and one of the horses served for more, till, after slow travelling and frequent resting, Mr Eyre and his single companion reached a district in which kangaroos and fish were to be

[1] Woods, vol. ii. pp. 19-21.

procured. Two months of further travel brought them to their destination, where succour awaited them; and they were taken back to Adelaide, there to learn that they had long before been given up as dead.

That journey, one of the least profitable in the long list of Australian travels, was one of the most perilous. Dr Leichhardt's important expedition of 1844 and 1845, in a different quarter, was more useful and less dangerous. Starting from Sydney he went overland to Port Essington, and was thus the first to explore some of the finest parts of Queensland, and, after passing the borders of the Gulf of Carpentaria, discovered the less inviting regions of North Australia. In the course of fifteen months he conducted a party of ten men, save one who died on the way, over more than three thousand miles of ground, most of it never before trodden by Englishmen.

In the meanwhile Captain Sturt, who had chiefly encouraged all this enterprise, was not idle. Still in search of the great inland sea, he started on a third expedition in 1844, and wandered about in the interior, until, forced to abandon his old theory, he was induced to adopt a new one, and to believe that the centre of the island was a huge, impassable desert. A desert certainly he found, though he exaggerated its extent. During six rainless months he was detained in a region where, says Mr Stuart, the most notable of his sixteen comrades, "the heat of the sun was so intense that every screw in their boxes was drawn, and all horn handles and combs split into fine laminæ; the lead dropped from their pencils, their finger-nails became as brittle as glass, and their hair, and the wool on their sheep, ceased to grow."[1]

For more than a dozen years after his return to Adelaide in 1846, where he had nothing but fruitless discoveries and dismal adventures to report, Captain Sturt's new supposition of a vast inland desert was adopted by the colonists; or, if disputed, no attempt was made to disprove it. Throughout these dozen years there was plenty of fresh exploration, but it was chiefly along the coast or not far inland, the most important being a series of expeditions by which the northern districts were visited both from Sydney in the far east, and from Perth in the far west.

But in 1858 a spirit of bolder enterprise was revived. Its leader was Mr John M'Douall Stuart, who used his experience as a comrade of Sturt's to make no less than six expeditions into the interior between 1858 and 1862. In each of the six he was able to gather much fresh geographical information. The first expedition, in which he was attended only by one white man, and a native who soon ran away, was to Lake Torrens and its neighbourhood, and two other visits were paid to it by him in 1859. The result was his discovery that this district, always before a source of confusion to travellers, some of whom described it as a lake, others as a desert, is both. The winter rains, filling the surrounding channels, turn it into a shallow lake. The summer drought turns it into an arid desert. This, indeed, is the character of much of the interior of Australia, as was further proved to Mr Stuart by his fourth expe-

[1] Hardman, "Explorations in Australia: the Journals of John M'Douall Stuart."

dition, undertaken in 1860, when he proceeded to the very middle of the island, and reached the point named after him Central Mount Stuart.

In 1861 Mr Stuart left Adelaide again, intending in this journey to go right across the continent. He failed at first. An impenetrable forest of scrub blocked the route he had proposed to take, and he was forced to go home for fresh supplies. Next year he was more fortunate. Leaving Adelaide in December 1861, he made a clear passage from south to north, reaching the mouth of the River Adelaide, on the Indian Ocean, in July 1862, and there finding a district which he highly commended as the site for a new colony. "Judging from the experience I have had in travelling through the continent of Australia for the last twenty-two years," he said, "and also from the description that other explorers have given of the different portions they have examined in their journeys, I have no hesitation in saying that the country that I have discovered on and around the banks of the Adelaide River is more favourable than any other part of the continent for the formation of a new colony. The soil is generally of the richest nature ever formed for the benefit of mankind; black and alluvial, and capable of producing anything that could be desired, and watered by one of the finest rivers in Australia. This river was found by Lieutenant Helpman to be about four to seven fathoms deep at the mouth, and at one hundred and twenty miles up (the farthest point he reached) it was found to be about seven fathoms deep and nearly one hundred yards broad, with a clear passage all the way up. I struck it about this point, and

followed it down, encamping fifteen miles from its
mouth, and found the water perfectly fresh, and the
river broader and apparently very deep; the country
around most excellent, abundantly supplied with
fresh water, running in many flowing streams into
the Adelaide River, the grass in many places growing six feet high, and the herbage very close—a thing
seldom seen in a new country. The timber is chiefly
composed of stringy-bark, gum, myall, casurina, pine,
and many other descriptions of large timber, all of
which will be most useful to new colonists. There
is also a plentiful supply of stone in the low rises
suitable for building purposes, and any quantity of
bamboo can be obtained from the river from two to
fifty feet long. I measured one fifteen inches in circumference, and saw many larger. The river abounds
in fish and water-fowl of all descriptions. On my
arrival from the coast I kept more to the eastward of
my north course, with the intention of seeing farther
into the country. I crossed the sources of the running
streams before alluded to, and had great difficulty
in getting more to the west. They take their rise
from large bodies of springs coming from extensive
grassy plains, which proves there must be a very
considerable underground drainage, as there are no
hills of sufficient elevation to cause the supply of
water in the streams. I feel confident that, if a new
settlement is formed in this splendid country, in a
few years it will become one of the brightest gems in
the British crown. To South Australia, and some of
the more remote Australian colonies, the benefits to
be derived from the formation of such a colony would
be equally advantageous, creating an outlet for their

surplus beef and mutton, which would be eagerly consumed by the races in the Indian Islands, and payment made by the shipment of their useful products. Indeed I see one of the finest openings I am aware of for trading between these islands and a colony formed where I propose."[1]

Mr Stuart, however, was not the first Englishman who succeeded in traversing the Australian continent. While he was preparing for his journey from Adelaide, another expedition, disastrous in everything but the one object for which it was undertaken, was being fitted out at Melbourne. Its history forms the most affecting episode in all the annals of Australian discovery.

A party of seventeen, from whom three soon deserted, left Melbourne on the 20th of August 1860, under the leadership of Robert O'Hara Burke, and with William John Wills as second in command. They proceeded in an almost straight line to the north, turning aside to make small excursions on the road, and reached Cooper's Creek, a post just half-way between the northern and southern coasts of Australia, on the 11th of November. There they halted for more than a month, waiting for fresh supplies which had been ordered to follow from Melbourne; and at length, on the 11th of December, tired of waiting any longer, Burke resolved to leave the greater part of his company at Cooper's Creek, and to perform the rest of the journey with Wills and two men, named Gray and King, for his only companions. The travelling was dangerous, and numerous difficulties had to be overcome; but the brave men did

[1] Hardman.

overcome them, and on the 10th of February 1861 they reached the Gulf of Carpentaria.

Thus far they were fortunate, but no farther. The return journey was utterly wearisome. Gray died on the road, and his comrades were almost too weak to bury him. Tired almost to death, they slowly worked their way back to Cooper's Creek. They reached it on the 21st of April, and, to their dismay, found the station deserted. The men left in it had waited four months. On the very morning of the 21st, only a few hours before Burke, Wills, and King came up, they had gone homewards, believing that the others must have been lost. Had the three hastened on the road to the south they might have overtaken them. But they did not know that the chance of safety was so near. So they rested for a day at Cooper's Creek, and then crawled in an easterly direction. For eight weeks they wandered about, making friends of the few natives whom they met, and with their help picking up a scanty supply of food. But such dreary hopeless life could not last long. They grew weaker and sadder every day. "I feel weaker than ever," wrote Wills, in his note-book, on the 21st of June, when they had got back to Cooper's Creek, "and can scarcely crawl out of the mia-mia. Unless relief comes in some form or other I cannot possibly last more than a fortnight. Had we come to grief elsewhere, we could only have blamed ourselves; but here we are returned to Cooper's Creek, where we had every right to look for provisions and clothing, and yet we have to die of starvation." Provisions and clothing had not been left for them, as they should have been; but, strange to say, the man whom they had expected seven months before had come up in their absence, had looked about for them in a careless way, and finding no trace of their whereabouts, or even of their existence, had gone home again. Thus, for a second time, cruel misfortune stood in the way of their preservation. Believing themselves altogether deserted, they resolved on one last search for some stray blacks who might help them. Wills was too ill to move, however, and at his earnest request, and in the assurance that herein was their only hope, Burke and King left him on the 27th of June, with a little heap of the best food the woods could yield. "I think to live about four or five days," he wrote in the note-book that he thought might possibly some day reach his father. He died on the 29th. Burke seems to have lived only a day longer. He was not strong enough to walk on as he had intended. After two days of painful travelling, he too had to lie down and die. "I hope," he said to King, "you will remain with me here till I am quite dead. It's a comfort to know that some one is by. But leave me unburied as I lie." King had not long to wait. His companion died next morning. He, however, was strong enough to fight through the terrible battle with hunger and fatigue. He went back to the Creek, buried Wills's body in the sand, loitered in the neighbourhood for some days, was taken prisoner by a tribe of natives, who fed him and used him kindly, and at last he was found by a relief party sent from Melbourne in search of the missing heroes.

More than one relief party was so sent; and the latest explorations in the interior of Australia grew

out of the efforts—successful when it was too late to
do more than take back their bones for sumptuous
burial in Melbourne—to discover the fate of these
brave men and grievous sufferers. In connection
with this later work the names of Alfred William
Howitt, of John M'Kinlay, of William Landesborough, and of Frederick Walker, must be held in
honourable remembrance. But it is not necessary
here to detail their exploits. Burke and Wills were
not the earliest martyrs of Australian discovery; but
the story fitly ends with them.

After all, it is strange that we know so little concerning the great Australian interior. "What we
know of this vast continent," says the historian,
"does not go much beyond an acquaintance with
the coast. One has only to look at the map to be
convinced that we have as yet only obtained a very
small glance into the interior. A little to the west
of Central Mount Stuart an immense blank occurs;
and for twelve and a half degrees of latitude and
longitude there is scarcely a mark to tell us what is
contained therein. There are two small tracks on the
edges, but, with these exceptions, nothing whatever
is known of a tract of country nearly half a million
square miles in area. Mr A. Gregory described the
north side of it as a desert. His brother characterized the north-west side in the same manner.
Stuart, on the west side, was encountered by large
tracts of spinifex grass and stately gum-trees, apparently liable to occasional floods. Eyre, on the
south side, and the explorers on the west, have been
baffled by the same desert. It is, in fact, a sandy
table-land, elevated on the west side, about three

thousand feet above the level of the sea, and sloping down towards Lake Torrens, which is very little, if at all, raised above the surface of the ocean. From Lake Torrens and Lake Eyre it appears to rise again first in a range, and then in a series of terraces. This elevation terminates at last in the high, rugged Cordillera of the eastern coast. We may, therefore, regard the continent as tilted up on each side, and depressed in the centre to a kind of trough. The Gulf of Carpentaria would represent the northern portion, and the deep indented part of Spencer's Gulf the southern. Since, however, the northern coast is also tilted up, the trough or depression does not extend through the continent. It is a series of salt lakes, sand drifts, and stony deserts. A great portion of it is redeemed by the fact that it receives so much drainage from the east by the various channels of the Barcoo, and from the west by waters which burst out in the form of immense thermal springs. The extent and number of the latter is almost incredible, and the depth from which they come is manifested by the great heat of their waters. Nothing could more clearly show the character of the central depression, and the slow rate at which the table-land sinks down towards it, than the existence of these springs. Of the Sandy Desert, the greater portion is thickly covered with spinifex grass; but there are drifts of sand, with no vegetation whatever upon them, extending for several miles. This is probably drifted up into masses after the decomposition of the ferruginous sandstone. The siliceous fragments left behind form those shingle plains known as the Stony Desert; they exist over a far greater tract than that marked in the old maps of Australia as extending like an arm northwards from Lake Torrens. It would seem as if the decomposition of the rock here was owing in some measure to pressure, when the table-land on either side was uplifted. Thus we see that, after all the explorations have been made, we have adopted, with modification, the theory of the earlier colonists. It was thought in Oxley's time that the interior rivers must flow towards a central depression, and there form a kind of inland sea. Long after the abandonment of this theory we find it to be true, to a certain extent, and it is realized in Lake Eyre, the extent of which is as yet undetermined. The inland lake theory was abandoned, after Stuart's discoveries, in favour of a central desert. This, it appears, is also true in a modified sense. Let us hope that there are such germs of truth in all the predictions about the future of Australia, and that it may realize the aspirations of those who look upon it as the seed of a vast and flourishing empire."[1]

[1] Woods, vol. ii. pp. 509-513. Besides Mr Woods's very valuable "History of the Discovery and Exploration of Australia," there is a hardly less interesting "History of Discovery in Australia, Tasmania, and New Zealand," by Mr William Howitt. Among the many personal records of travel and adventure, Mr William Wills's account of his son's noble and melancholy history, entitled "A Successful Exploration through the Interior of Australia," is especially noteworthy.

CHAPTER XXVI.

PAKEHA NEW ZEALAND.

THE NEW ZEALAND ISLANDS AND THEIR INHABITANTS — FIRST INTERCOURSE WITH ENGLISHMEN—THE MASSACRE OF THE CREW AND PASSENGERS OF THE "BOYD" IN 1809—THE MISSIONARIES AND THEIR WORK — THE PAKEHA TRADERS — ARTICLES OF TRADE — TRAFFIC IN HUMAN HEADS — OTHER DEBASING EMPLOYMENTS OF THE PAKEHAS — PROGRESS OF ENGLISH INFLUENCES — SPREAD OF CIVILIZATION — THE CHARACTER OF THE MAORIS. [1809-1839.]

THE three islands of New Ulster, New Munster, and New Leinster, which, with a number of smaller islands, make up the colony of New Zealand, have an area of 106,200 square miles, being rather less than the dimensions of Great Britain and Ireland. The middle island occupies rather more than half of the whole; the northern island is a little smaller; the southern island, much less in size, is little more than a barren rock, about half as large as Yorkshire. The group differs widely—in climate, in scenery, and in the character of its inhabitants—from Australia and Tasmania. The aborigines of all three sections of Australasia may have been of the same stock; but in New Zealand, probably in the fifteenth century, they were exterminated or absorbed by a bolder Malayan race, which crossed over in canoes from the Polynesian region, and formed the Maori nation.

The adventures of Captain Cook and other early voyagers among the Maoris have already been referred to. Subsequent navigators carried on the irregular intercourse, and in some instances tolerably friendly relations were established between the natives and their visitors. Whaling and other ships from New South Wales halted frequently in the New Zealand ports; and now and then some of the natives went back in these ships to see for themselves the strange novelties of civilized life in Sydney. Among others, we are told, "a powerful chief named Tippahee, accompanied by his five sons, came to Port Jackson, and, on seeing the different arts and manufactures carried on by the settlers, was so affected by the conviction thus forced upon him of the barbarous state of ignorance in which his own country was shrouded, that he burst into tears and exclaimed, in the bitterness of his heart, 'New Zealand no good!'"[1] When Tippahee returned to his island home, which was in the extreme north of New Ulster, in the Bay of Islands, at which the English vessels generally touched, he took with him a young Englishman named George Bruce. Bruce, the first European resident in New Zealand, married a native wife, and lived happily among her kindred for many years, doing much, it would seem, to prepare for the closer relations that were soon to spring up between the two races.

These relations were from the first marked by some ugly incidents. In December 1809, a trading-ship, the *Boyd*, with seventy persons on board, left Sydney for England, and, as she intended to go round by New Zealand, and there call for some spars to be

[1] Martin, vol. iii. p. 118.

sold at the Cape of Good Hope, the captain consented to take with him four or five natives of Wangaroa, who were anxious to return home. On the passage some extra work had to be done, and the captain ordered the New Zealanders to share it with the sailors. One of them, known as George, refused on the plea that he was ill, and that, he being a chief's son, the labour was degrading to his rank. "The captain," it is recorded, "treated both representations with ridicule, and had him twice tied up to the gangway and severely flogged, at the same time lessening his allowance of food. In reply to the taunting assertion that he was no chief, George merely remarked that they would find him to be such on their arrival in his country; and so well did he disguise the revengeful passions excited by the treatment he had received, as to persuade the captain to put in at Wangaroa, where his tribe resided, as the best place for procuring the spars, although it was not known that the harbour had ever before been visited by any European vessel. On arriving, the crafty savage landed alone, and, after a brief interview with some of his tribe, returned to the ship and invited the captain to come on shore and point out the trees that would best suit his purpose. Three boats were accordingly manned, and the captain landed and proceeded with his party towards a wood. They had no sooner entered it than they were attacked by the savages, and every one of them was put to instant death. George and his associates disguised themselves in the clothes of the victims—it being now dark—and went off in the boats to the *Boyd*. They got on board by a stratagem, and then slaughtered indiscriminately every man, woman, and child, excepting five seamen, who had escaped to the shrouds, a woman and two children, and a cabin-boy whom George preserved in gratitude for kindness he had received from him during the voyage. When morning dawned upon the ill-fated vessel, the sailors who had taken refuge in the rigging still maintained their dreary watch, until Tippahee, the chief who had visited New South Wales, came alongside in his canoe, and, informing them that he had just arrived from the Bay of Islands to trade for dried fish, offered them his protection. The men descended, entered his canoe, and were safely landed by him, although closely pursued by the Wangaroa tribe. But on shore the savages soon overtook them, and, forcibly detaining the old chief, murdered the others before his face. The ship was thoroughly ransacked, the muskets and ammunition being deemed invaluable. The father of George, eager to try a gun of which he had taken possession, burst in the head of a cask of gunpowder, filled the pan, snapped the lock over the cask, and was himself, with thirteen of his companions, blown to atoms."[1]

Thus a partial retribution fell upon the Wangaroa natives for their barbarous action. It must be remembered, however, that they alone were not guilty. The captain of the *Boyd* was as foolish, and with less excuse, in stirring up the evil passions of the New Zealanders by his treatment of the chief's son, as was the chief in setting fire to the powder cask. Englishmen, accustomed to think that all inferior races may be treated with any harshness

[1] Martin, vol. iii. pp. 118, 119.

and injustice, sometimes forget that a single spark of cruelty may kindle the overpowering wrath of a whole race of savages, and then proceed to rival those savages in the ferocity of the punishment they accord to wrong-doing which they have themselves provoked. That is the painful and humiliating moral of the story of our relations with New Zealand.

Many mischiefs sprang from this disaster of the *Boyd*. Tippahee, who had done all he could in aid of the English, was soon afterwards attacked in his island-home by some whalers who supposed that he was the author of the massacre. Many of his subjects, of both sexes and all ages, were murdered, and their gardens were destroyed. He himself was wounded; and soon afterwards he was killed in battle with the Wangaroa people, who resented the small part he had been able to take on the side of the English. His people, formerly friends of the English, but now their enemies with good reason, next murdered some white sailors who came in their way. And so the dismal work went on.

In this same year, however, efforts began to be made for bringing about a better state of things. Mr Marsden, a clergyman in New South Wales, induced the Church Missionary Society of London to organize a machinery for the conversion of the New Zealanders, urging that the missionaries sent out should be teachers of agriculture, mechanical arts, and other branches of civilization, as well as of Christianity. The suggestion was adopted, and in 1814 the first missionaries arrived in New Zealand, soon to be followed by others, and they were able to send home flattering reports of the success of their work. They made many converts, at any rate, in the northern districts, to which for some time their operations, as well as the visits of the whalers and traders, were confined. Some tribes resented their interference, and regarded their appropriation of lands for churches, schools, and houses, as the beginning of an aggressive movement that would end in the extinction of all native rights; and the stoutest of all their opponents, the same George who had caused the massacre of the crew and passengers of the *Boyd*, proposed to extirpate them, alleging that " he feared that the introduction of Europeans would eventually lead to the destruction of his countrymen, or that they would be reduced to the miserable condition of the Australian aborigines, whom he had seen lying intoxicated in the streets of Sydney, and begging their food from door to door, suppliants for the necessaries of life from those who had possessed themselves of their country and its resources."[1] But most of the Maoris were not so far-seeing. Equally impulsive in their appreciation of kindness and in their resentment of injuries, they listened readily to the good-hearted men who came to instruct them, not merely in religion, but also in everyday civilization.

The missionaries were better teachers, at any rate, than many of the traders who, having gradually got into the way of calling at friendly ports for timber and other native produce, now also began to settle down in the country. At first, and in most districts, they were welcomed more heartily than the missionaries. "When the first straggling ships came here," says one of them, "the smallest bit of iron was a

[1] Martin, vol. iii. p. 124.

prize so inestimable that I might be thought to exaggerate were I to tell the bare truth on the subject. The excitement and speculation caused by a ship being seen off the coast were immense. Where would she anchor? What iron could be got from her? Would it be possible to seize her? The oracle was consulted; preparations were made to follow her along the coast, even through an enemy's country, at all risks; and when she disappeared she was not forgotten, but would continue long to be the subject of anxious expectation and speculation. After this regular trading began. The great madness then was for muskets and gunpowder. A furious competition was kept up. Should any tribe fail to procure a stock of these articles as soon as its neighbours, extermination was its probable doom. After the demand for arms was supplied, came a perfect furor for iron tools, instruments of husbandry, clothing, and all kinds of Pakeha manufactures."[1] The Pakehas, or foreigners, who brought these articles, were gladly received by the New Zealanders, who, having very rough notions as to the rights of property, generally tried first to steal the coveted commodities, and, if they failed therein, made the best bargain they could with the traders.

It is more than likely that the merchants were not very honest in their dealings with these natives, and that they did them far more harm than good by their intercourse. Their ways of trade were often lawless, fraud being met by fraud, and theft by violence; and the things in which they traded were some of them altogether obnoxious. The rum and muskets and

[1] "Old New Zealand," by a Pakeha Maori, pp. 94, 95.

gunpowder which they brought into the country tended greatly to demoralize the people, and to encourage and give deadly issue to the feuds that were always frequent between different tribes. The flax, gum, and other commodities that they took in exchange for these stores were the fruits of wholesome labour, whereby the natives were greatly benefited; but, in these old times, there was one article of commerce which, though not produced in great quantities, was a source of terrible degradation. Some adventurous trader having taken away a few of the heads which it was customary for the New Zealanders to sever from the bodies of their slain enemies, to be dried and kept as treasures, these barbarous trophies became attractive to the vulgar curiosity-hunters in Australia and in Europe; and in the end traffic in heads became a regular branch of Pakeha trade. The thing itself was bad and disgusting enough; but when the price paid for the heads ran high enough to become a premium upon murder, the traffic became indeed degrading. We are told of plenty of this horrible work. "The skippers of many of the colonial trading schooners," it is said by an eye-witness of the traffic, "were always ready to deal with a man who had 'a real good head,' and used to commission low Pakehas to 'pick up heads' for them. It is a positive fact that the head of a live man was sold and paid for beforehand, and afterwards honestly delivered 'as per agreement.'"[1]

[1] "Old New Zealand," p. 59. The author tells (pp. 54-56) how, soon after his arrival, he came by accident upon a collection of heads, ready cured for the market and exposed for sale, under the charge of one of the disreputable whites who engaged in the traffic. "One had undoubtedly been a warrior; there was something bold

All respectable Pakehas of course abstained from this most loathsome branch of New Zealand trade, which lasted till about the year 1830; but there was much evil in even their best intercourse with the natives. When they could make profit out of the bad passions of the people, they too often used their opportunities. Sometimes we find them in league with the natives for carrying out their most revolting practices. Of this one instance will suffice. "In December 1830," we are told, "a Captain Stewart, commanding the brig *Elizabeth*, on promise of ten tons of flax, took a hundred New Zealanders from Kapiti, or Entry Island, in Cook's Straits, to Takou, in Banks's Peninsula, concealed in his vessel. He then enticed on board the chief of Takou, his brother, his two daughters, and some others who came unsuspicious of any ambush. On entering the captain's cabin the door was locked upon the unhappy chief,

and defiant about the look of the head. Another was the head of a very old man, grey, shrivelled, and wrinkled. I was going on with my observations when I was saluted by a voice from behind with 'Looking at the eds, sir?' It was one of the Pakehas formerly mentioned. 'Yes,' said I, turning round just the least possible thing quicker than ordinary. "Eds has been a getting scarce,' says he. 'I should think so,' says I. 'We an't 'ad a 'ed this long time,' says he. 'The devil!' says I. 'One of them 'eds has been hurt bad,' says he. 'I should think all were rather so,' says I. 'Oh, no,' only one on 'em,' says he; 'the skull is split, and it won't fetch nothing,' says he. 'Oh, murder! I see now,' says I. "Eds was *werry* scarce,' says he, shaking his own 'ed. 'Ah!' said I. 'They had to tattoo a slave a bit ago,' says he, 'and the villain ran away, tattooin' and all!' says he. 'What!' said I. 'Bolted afore he was fit to kill,' says he. 'Stole off with his own head!' says I. 'That's just it,' says he. '*Capital* felony,' says I. 'You may say that, sir,' says he. 'Good morning,' said I, and walked away pretty smartly."

his hands were tied, a hook with a cord attached was stuck through the skin of his throat, under the side of his jaw, and the line fastened to some part of the cabin, in which state of torture he was kept for two days, until the vessel arrived at Kapiti, when he was put to death. All the men and women who accompanied the chief were massacred. As a crowning enormity, the 'ship's coppers' are even stated to have been employed in cooking the remains of the victims for the cannibals, whose brutal ferocity was not yet satiated."[1] These circumstances, with many others of almost equal enormity, showing that some of the Pakehas abstained from no wrong-doing which could increase their influence with friendly tribes and promote their trading enterprises, were reported to Viscount Goderich, then Colonial Secretary, in 1831. "It is impossible," he said, in a despatch to Sir Richard Bourke, the Governor of New South Wales, who had declared his inability to prevent the vicious practices, "to read, without shame and indignation, the details which these documents disclose. The unfortunate natives of New Zealand, unless some decisive measures of prevention be adopted, will, I fear, be shortly added to the number of those barbarous tribes, who, in different parts of the globe, have fallen a sacrifice to their intercourse with civilized men who bear and disgrace the name of Christians. When, for mercenary purposes, the natives of Europe minister to the passions by which these savages are inflamed against each other, and introduce them to the knowledge of depraved acts and licentious gratifications of the most debased inhabitants of our

[1] Martin, vol. iii. pp. 125, 126.

great cities, the inevitable consequence is a rapid decline of population, preceded by every variety of suffering. Considering what is the character of a large part of the population of New South Wales and Van Dieman's Land, and what opportunities of settling themselves in New Zealand are afforded them by the extensive intercourse which has recently been established, adverting also to the conduct which has been pursued in these islands by the masters and crews of British vessels, I cannot contemplate the two probable results without the deepest anxiety."

That that anxiety was well-founded the later history of New Zealand abundantly proves. The efforts of the British Government and the authorities of New South Wales, to which New Zealand gradually became a sort of appendage, were only successful in checking the worst exhibitions of misconduct on the part of the Pakeha traders among the Maoris. These Pakehas became more numerous and more influential. All along the shores of the northern island they made their settlements and extended their operations. Land they rarely sought to buy, and thus they were not regarded as aggressors by the natives, and escaped much jealousy that attended the progress of the missionaries among all who did not yield to their religious influences. Two parties, indeed, grew up in New Zealand, and gained strength during the thirty years or so previous to the formation of a regular colony. Both parties abandoned some of their primitive barbarism under English teaching; the one taking their lessons from traders whose instruction, advantageous in some respects, was pernicious in most; the others being guided by missionaries, who, seeking to do only good, and succeeding to a great extent, also did serious harm by favouring their converts, and encouraging them in professions of authority over their heathen neighbours, and in schemes of aggression which, thought by the missionaries to be helpful to the spread of Christianity, have produced very different fruit.

The appearances were greater than the reality, yet during this period the New Zealanders were, in many respects, greatly improved by their contact with the Englishmen. "At Waimati," said Mr Charles Darwin, the eminent naturalist, who visited New Zealand in 1835, "there are three large houses where missionaries reside, and near them are the huts of the native labourers. On an adjoining slope fine crops of barley and wheat were standing in full ear, and in another part fields of potatoes and clover. There were large gardens with every fruit and vegetable which England produces, and many belonging to warmer climates. Around the farm-yard there were stables, a thrashing-barn, with its winnowing machine, a blacksmith's forge, and, on the ground, ploughshares and other tools. In the middle was that happy mixture of pigs and poultry, lying comfortably together, as in every English farm-yard. At the distance of a few hundred yards, where the water of a little rill had been dammed up into a pool, there was a large and substantial water-mill. This is very surprising when it is considered that five years ago nothing but the fern flourished here."[1]

[1] Darwin, "Researches Into the Natural History of Various Countries," p. 425.

If this more complete civilization existed only in small districts, its effects were wide spread. Native warfare became much less frequent than it had been in former times, and many chieftains were encouraged to cultivate the arts of peace; although it was impossible to utterly eradicate habits that had become a second nature to them. A characteristic anecdote is related by Mr Darwin. "A missionary," he says, "found a chief and his tribe in preparation for war; their muskets clean and bright, and their ammunition ready. He reasoned long on the inutility of the war, and the little provocation which had been given for it. The chief was much shaken in his resolution, and seemed in doubt. But at length it occurred to him that a barrel of gunpowder was in a bad state, and that it would not keep much longer. This settled the matter."[1]

Exaggerated views of the Maori character, both in its good and in its bad aspects, having in later times been promulgated, it will be well to adduce the truthful opinion arrived at by one who had long opportunities of observation during the time of Paheka influence. "They are," he says, "neither so good nor so bad as their friends and enemies have painted them, and, I suspect, are pretty much like what almost any other people would have become if subjected to the same external circumstances. For ages they have struggled against necessity in all its shapes. This has given to them a remarkable greediness for gain in every visible and immediately tangible form. Without the aid of iron, the most trifling tool or utensil could only be procured by an enor-

[1] Darwin, p. 419.

mously disproportionate outlay of labour in its construction, and, in consequence, it became precious to a degree scarcely conceivable by people of civilized and wealthy countries. This great value, attached to personal property of all kinds, increased proportionately the temptation to plunder; and where no law existed, or could exist, of sufficient force to repress the inclination, every man, as a natural consequence, became a soldier, if it were only for the defence of his own property and that of those who were banded with him, his tribe or family. From this state of things regular warfare arose, as a matter of course. The military art was studied as a science, and brought to great perfection, as applied to the arms used, and a marked military character was given to the people. The necessity of labour, the necessity of warfare, and a temperate climate, gave them strength of body, accompanied by a perseverance and energy of mind perfectly astonishing. With rude and blunt stones they felled the giant kauri, toughest of pines; and from it, in process of time, at an expense of labour, perseverance, and ingenuity astounding to those who know what it really was, they produced, carved, painted, and inlaid, a masterpiece of art and an object of beauty—the war-canoe, capable of carrying a hundred men on a distant expedition, through the boisterous seas surrounding their island. As a consequence of their warlike habits and character, they are self-possessed and confident in themselves and their own powers, and have much diplomatic *finesse* and casuistry at command. Their intelligence causes them theoretically to acknowledge the benefits of law, which they see established among us; but their hatred of restraint causes them practically to abhor and resist its full enforcement amongst themselves. Doubting our professions of friendship, fearing our ultimate designs, led astray by false friends, possessed of that 'little learning' which is, in their case, most emphatically 'a dangerous thing;' such are the people with whom we are now in contact; such the people to whom, for our own safety and their preservation, we must give new laws and institutions, new habits of life, new ideas, sentiments, and information—whom we must either civilize, or, by our mere contact, exterminate."[1]

[1] "Old New Zealand," pp. 91-93.

CHAPTER XXVII.

NEW ZEALAND COLONIZATION.

THE OLD PAKEHA POPULATION—THE NEW ZEALAND COMPANY—
ESTABLISHMENT OF BRITISH SOVEREIGNTY IN NEW ZEALAND,
AND ITS CONSTRUCTION AS A REGULAR COLONY—ITS PROGRESS
—LAND-QUARRELS WITH THE NATIVES—THEIR ATTEMPTED
PROTECTION BY THE GOVERNMENT—THE INFLUENCE OF THE
MISSIONARIES—LATER GROWTH OF THE COLONY. [1839-1867.]

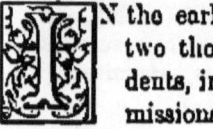N the early part of 1839 there were about two thousand Pakehas, or English residents, in New Zealand, some of them as missionaries and their dependants, but most of them as traders of one sort or another. They were scattered along the shore, and in various inland parts, though chiefly in the northern island, or New Ulster, and especially in its most northern districts. Kororarika, in the Bay of Islands, was the locality most frequented by them; and there, in 1838, a sort of republic had been formed, with laws of its own making, for mutual assistance and protection in dealings with the natives. The report of this organization seems to have encouraged some English adventurers in the adoption of schemes, previously advanced, for establishing in New Zealand a regular colony.

The schemes had taken shape in the founding, in 1837, of a New Zealand Association, designed to carry out plans very similar to those that already had been tried and had failed in South Australia. In both cases the guiding genius was Mr Edward Gibbon Wakefield; and here the proposal was at once to buy up from the natives large tracts of land to be sold to private adventurers, to whom special inducements were to be offered for extending English civilization over the whole country, —all which, it was expected, would in a short time pass from its native owners and become English property. The association, being refused a charter, was dissolved; but in 1838 it was revived as the New Zealand Company, which, its proposals being again rejected by the Government, proceeded to put them in force without authority. It had many supporters, and Colonel Wakefield, the son of the projector, went out with a party of pioneers. He reached Cook's Straits in August 1839, and in the course of two months went through the form of buying land, on both sides of the channel, which formed in all a territory as large as Ireland, for about £1500 worth of muskets, gunpowder, tomahawks, pocket-handkerchiefs, tobacco, Jews' harps, and other articles; being at the rate of about sixpennyworth of goods for every thousand acres. The chieftains of whom it was bought had, of course, no right to sell it; but, if this was known to the leaders of the enterprise, it was not understood by most of the colonists who were induced to join in the work, and who, soon after landing, found themselves involved in serious difficulties with the natives on account of their aggressions.

They had difficulties also with the English Government. In June 1839 instructions were sent out by

Lord Normanby, then Colonial Secretary, to the Governor of New South Wales, authorizing him to regard all British residents in New Zealand as his subjects, and, both on their behalf and in the interests of the natives, to treat with the latter for the purchase of land. These instructions, designed especially as a curb upon the ill-planned projects of the New Zealand Company, were wise and generous. "The Queen," it was there said, "disclaims, for herself and for her subjects, every pretension to seize on the islands of New Zealand, or to govern them as a part of the dominion of Great Britain, unless the free and intelligent consent of the natives, expressed according to their established usages, shall be first obtained." Careful directions were given with a view to securing this end, and to the observance of sincerity, justice, and good-faith in all dealings with the natives. "Nor is this all," it was added. "They must not be permitted to enter into any contracts in which they might be ignorant and unintentional authors of injuries to themselves. You will not, for example, purchase from them any territory, the retention of which by them would be essential or highly conducive to their own comfort, safety, or subsistence. The acquisition of land by the Crown for the future settlement of British subjects must be confined to such districts as the natives can alienate without distress or serious inconvenience to themselves. To secure the observance of this will be one of the first duties of their official protector."[1]

The English Government cannot be blamed for the troubles that began in that early day, and have lately

[1] "Parliamentary Papers," 1840, pp. 37-42.

become very grievous, through the greed of private speculators, and the jealous, violent patriotism of the New Zealanders. In accordance with the instructions issued by Lord Normanby, Captain Hobson was sent to New Zealand as lieutenant-governor. He reached Kororarika, in the Bay of Islands, on the 29th of January 1840, and there established the rule of English law in lieu of the self-governing regulations of its British residents. In February he had a conference with forty-six chiefs of the islands and neighbouring mainland, and submitted to them a treaty by which they recognised the sovereignty of Queen Victoria, on condition of having all their local rights and privileges respected. "Send the man away!" said one chief, with whom many sympathized. "Do not sign the paper. If you do, you will be reduced to the condition of slaves, and be obliged to break stones to make roads. Your land will be taken from you, and your dignity as chiefs will be destroyed." But other chiefs thought differently, and urged so eloquently the value of alliance with Great Britain that all were convinced, and the treaty was signed. "You must be our father!" said the leader of this friendly party to Captain Hobson. "You must not allow us to become slaves! you must preserve our customs, and never permit our lands to be wrested from us!" Captain Hobson afterwards visited the principal parts of New Ulster, and sent a deputy on a like tour through New Munster. Everywhere he received the submission of the principal chiefs. Thus British sovereignty was commenced in New Zealand.

On the 16th of November 1840 the colony of New

Zealand was established by charter, and Captain Hobson was appointed its first governor. He was empowered to grant "waste and uncleared lands" to European settlers, "provided that nothing shall affect or be construed to affect the rights of any aboriginal natives of the colony, to the actual occupation or enjoyment in their own persons, or in the persons of their descendants, of any lands now occupied or enjoyed by such natives." Captain Hobson was also enjoined "to promote education among the native inhabitants; to protect them in their persons, and in the free enjoyment of their possessions; by all means to prevent and restrain all violence and injustice which may in any manner be practised or attempted against them; and to take such measures as may appear necessary for their conversion to the Christian faith, and for their advancement in civilization."

No colony ever began better in theory; but in practice the generous principles propounded were found utterly untenable. The native chiefs, in yielding submission to the English Crown, thought they were only conferring on it magisterial powers, and intended to keep their territorial rights intact. In the treaty nothing had been said about "waste lands," and the natives considered that there were no "waste lands" at all in the country. Every acre, whether cultivated or left desolate, had some individual claimant, or was regarded as the common property of the members of some tribe; and, though at first they offered no objection to small appropriations of land on the coast, especially when they knew that the monster pretensions of the New Zealand Company were repudiated by the Government, their jealousy was aroused as soon as larger allotments began to be made. This was soon the case. The New Zealand Company had caused a tide of emigration, which was strengthened as soon as the country was known to be formally annexed to the Crown; and however zealously Captain Hobson sought to act upon his instructions and respect all native rights, he could not bring himself to send back the English settlers, or prevent them from acquiring property which, even if it seemed to be fairly bought, was soon declared by the natives to have been wrongfully taken possession of. In other respects, too, his instructions were found to be inconsistent. He was to respect all native rights; he was also to extend civilization. Among the rights most dear to the natives were some, like cannibalism or the practice of human sacrifices, which no civilized institutions could tolerate; and in the efforts made to suppress them great offence was given to many of the people who, it had been expected, would be the most faithful supporters of English rule. On these and kindred points it is not here necessary to enter into details; but they must be borne in mind as explaining the ill-will which, if suppressed at first, was destined to break out in the deplorable occurrences of our own day.

There was not, however, much show of ill-will in the beginning of the colony's history. It progressed rapidly. In the four years ending with May 1843, the New Zealand Company sent out 8796 colonists, and others came by other channels. The population numbering about 2000 in 1839, had increased to 11,948 in 1844, and to 20,396 in 1849. It has continued to increase very rapidly. In 1858 it amounted to 59,254, in 1864 to 173,618, and in 1867 to 218,668.

Nine little colonies, now the centres of as many provinces, have grown up in New Zealand. Auckland, to which the centre of government was transferred from the Bay of Islands, is the most northern of these, and from its official associations as well as from the excellent position of its harbour, and its consequent facilities for trade, was for a long time the richest and most populous. Below it, on the western side of New Ulster, the settlement of New Plymouth, or Taranki, "the garden of New Zealand," was founded in 1841 by some adventurers from the west of England. Wellington, occupying the southern part of the island, begun a year earlier, was the chief scene of the operations of the New Zealand Company, and prospered in spite of the serious difficulties that attended its early history, owing to disputes with the natives concerning land-claims, which the Government could only settle by giving offence both to settlers and to natives. Napier, the northern port of this section, afterwards became the capital of the province of Hawke's Bay, stretching up to Auckland on the eastern side. Nelson, forming the northern portion of New Munster, was another settlement of the New Zealand Company, dating from 1841, and for some time it was the only centre of colonization in the middle island. Its eastern half was afterwards converted into the separate province of Marlborough. The southern district—from which the portion known as Southland was subsequently detached—was colonized in 1847 under the name of Otago; and Canterbury, occupying the centre of New Munster, was inaugurated in 1850. These two latter settlements, after long struggling against misfortunes, and vainly attempting to become model religious colonies, the one Presbyterian, the other Episcopalian, have recently been made the most prosperous of all, owing to the discovery in them of profitable gold-fields.

The history of these nine settlements, diverse and complicated, but monotonous in its series of quarrels concerning land between settlers and natives, need not be recounted. Each settlement gradually grew from a sea-port in which the colonists first made sure their footing, and thence, step by step, encroached upon the inland possessions of the Maoris, and so aroused their hatred, to be long suppressed, or only exhibited in occasional and partial outbursts of fury, but to be in no way lessened by time.

The discontent of the natives was restrained by two causes, the prudent behaviour of the Government and the powerful influence of the missionaries. Captain Hobson found it impossible to hinder the aggressive action of the colonists; but he was zealous in his endeavours to see that, at any rate, partial justice was done to the natives, whereby he earned the vehement opposition of most of his white subjects. He died in 1842, but his policy was continued, as far as the difficult circumstances allowed, by his successor, Captain Fitzroy, and by the third governor, Captain, now Sir George, Grey, who ruled from 1845 to 1853, and who had a hearty coadjutor in Mr, now Sir Edward, Eyre, who was appointed lieutenant-governor of New Munster. But governors could not do much.

The chief pacificators of the Maoris were the missionaries. Their disinterested and persevering labours had made many converts before New Zealand became a colony in 1840, and after that date they carried on their work so zealously that nearly all the natives were in the end made Christians in name. The religious influence was not very deep, but in outward show it was very great, and it was not all superficial. The worst vices of the Maoris have been nearly eradicated, and the worst barbarities in which they now indulge bear no comparison to those which were the rule in former times. For many years it seemed not only as if their heathen customs had been altogether rooted out, but as if they had been taught the harder lesson of patient submission to the aggressive policy of the English settlers. Here and there there were violent outbursts of vindictive fury; but generally, and in most districts, the natives were induced to give way, if not without murmuring, at any rate without open resistance. It was no slight achievement to persuade them meekly to abandon their homesteads and go farther into the forests, making no bolder complaint than appeared in such pathetic chants as this:—

"The sun shines, but we quit our land; we abandon for ever its forests, its groves, its lakes, its shores.
All its fair fisheries here, under the bright sun, we renounce for ever.
It is a lovely day; fair will be the children that are born to-day; but we quit our land.
In some parts there is forest; in others, the ground is skimmed over by the birds in their flight;
Upon the trees there is fruit; in the streams, fish; in the fields, potatoes; fern-trees in the bush; but we quit our land."

THE PROGRESS OF THE COLONY. 347

The fertility and beauty of New Zealand, "the Britain of the South," might well endear it to its native possessors. But for some time very slender use was made by the English colonists of its natural resources. Until the gold-fields were discovered, the trade and enterprise of the colony did not even keep pace with its growth of population; but then the new emigrants who arrived appeared to have infused a new energy into the whole community. In 1852 the imports were only worth £359,444, the exports £145,972. In 1863 the imports amounted in value to £7,024,674, and the exports to £3,485,405. More than two-thirds of the latter, £2,432,479, consisted of gold and gold-dust. The other staple was wool, of which 12,585,980 pounds, worth £830,495, were exported. In 1866 the total exports, amounting to £4,520,074, included £2,898,412 worth of gold, and £1,354,152 worth of wool, representing 22,810,776 pounds. In 1858 the sheep in the colony from whom the wool was obtained numbered only 1,523,324. In 1864 they were 4,937,273, and in 1867, 8,418,579. Between 1858, when the gold-fields were first opened, and 1860, the metal extracted from them and exported amounted in value to £98,455. In 1861 it was £752,657; since then it has averaged nearly £2,500,000 a year—the ten years' yield up to September 1868 being £16,404,673. In 1867 about one-third of the white population was in the northern island, and two-thirds were in the southern,—about a quarter each in Auckland, Canterbury, and Otago, and the remaining quarter in the six other provinces.

CHAPTER XXVIII.

NEW ZEALAND WARFARE.

THE RIVAL RACES IN NEW ZEALAND—THE MAORI WARS OF 1843 AND THE FOLLOWING YEARS—THE SUBSEQUENT CONDITION OF THE MAORIS—THEIR CIVILIZATION—THEIR NUMBERS—THE RENEWAL OF HOSTILITIES—THE KING-MOVEMENT AND ITS ISSUE—HOSTILITIES IN 1860 AND 1861—THE WAR OF 1863-1865—NATURE OF THE STRIFE—LATER GUERILLA WARFARE—THE PAI-MARIRE OR HAU-HAU SUPERSTITION—THE FUTURE OF NEW ZEALAND. [1843-1869.]

DURING some three hundred years, if not for a much longer time, the Maoris were in undisturbed possession of New Zealand. They cultivated their fields and caught their fish and game, and enjoyed themselves in their own barbarous way. Endless warfare prevailed between rival tribes and clans, and it was often attended by hideous atrocities; but in spite of this and other drawbacks, a fine race of savages grew up, almost superior to any other savage race of which we know. Then the Pakehas came among them, some as missionaries, others as traders; and though their numbers were few, their influence was rapidly felt among nearly the whole community of natives. Civilization, partly good and partly bad, but equally powerful whether good or bad, began a rapid disintegration of the barbarous elements; and, though many held aloof in sullen wrath, the great majority of the Maoris were attracted to European institutions, like iron to the loadstone. That preparation for English colonization lasted for about thirty years, and it was followed by regular colonial enterprise, which has lasted for just thirty other years. That it will continue and increase, until "the Britain of the South" becomes worthy of its title, cannot be doubted, and the only question to be solved is as to the length of time that must elapse before the natives are altogether driven out, and the whole of Maori-land becomes Pakaha-land; but there are some features in the struggle now going on, and apparently approaching its end, which are well worth noting.

That New Zealand should cease to be a mere haunt of lawless savages, however noble may be some characteristics of their savage life, and should become the great centre of civilized enterprise and civilizing agency for which its natural features and its place in the South Pacific Ocean make it specially adapted, is a change of which the wisest and most far-seeing philanthropy cannot but approve, however much we may deplore some of the conditions of the change. Even the natives themselves are conscious of the necessity, and, while loth to give up the struggle, know that it cannot be carried on for very much longer. "As the Pakeha fly has driven out the Maori fly," they sing, in one of their plaintive chants; "as the Pakeha grass has killed the Maori grass; as the Pakeha rat has slain the Maori rat; as the Pakeha clover has starved the Maori fern; so will the Pakeha push back and destroy the Maori." The destroying work has proceeded with equal rapidity during the periods in which the doomed race has quietly succumbed to its destiny, and during those in which it has striven desperately to avert the evil, or, at any rate, to punish its authors.

With one exception, there was not much resistance shown till 1861. The exception was in 1843 and the four following years. In 1843 Colonel Wakefield, having had a dispute about land with some chiefs, had determined to take the law into his own hands, and had accordingly gone into their district on the banks of the Wairau, in Nelson, with armed followers, and handcuffs and leg-irons for making captives of the chiefs. The natives resenting this procedure, he had fired upon them, and thus caused a small battle, ending in the defeat of the English intruders, with serious loss of life. "So manifestly illegal, unjust, and unwise were the martial array and the command to advance," said Lord Stanley (the present Earl of Derby), who was then Colonial Secretary, "that the authors of that order must be held responsible for all that followed in natural and immediate sequence upon it. The natives only exercised the rights of self-defence and of mutual protection against an imminent, overwhelming, and deadly danger. Revolting to our feelings as Christians, and to our opinions as members of a civilized State, as was the ultimate massacre, it is impossible to deny to our savage antagonists the benefits of the apology which is to be urged in their behalf. They who provoke an indefensible warfare with barbarous tribes are hardly entitled to complain of the barbarities inseparable from such contests."[1]

The effect of this catastrophe was most disastrous.

[1] "Report of Select Parliamentary Committee," 1844, pp. 172-174.

Exaggerated reports of it were spread over both the islands, and the irons seized from the English aggressors were exhibited both as tokens of what they meant to do with the Maoris, if they could, and as trophies of the prowess by which they had been, and might again and again be, successfully resisted. Tribes that had hitherto submitted quietly to British rule now gave visible signs of their discontent, and the tribes that had always been inimical, now had a powerful argument in favour of violent opposition. An open feud between Maoris and Pakehas began, never to be thoroughly healed.

It found expression in several acts of hostility during the few years ensuing. It extended so far north that, in March 1845, Kororarika was invaded and destroyed, the missionaries' quarter alone being spared. "The natives carried on their work of plunder," said Bishop Selwyn, who witnessed it, "with perfect composure; neither quarrelling among themselves, nor resenting any attempt on the part of the English to recover portions of their property. Several of the people of the town landed in the midst of them, and were allowed to carry off such things as were not particularly desired by the spoilers."[1]

Here and elsewhere the Maoris showed remarkable moderation in their resistance of the colonists. Violent in their opposition to those who sought to dispossess them of what they reasonably regarded as their lawful property, they did no harm to friendly missionaries and traders, and even allowed them to mix freely with their armies, and use all the conciliatory arts that they possessed. Praiseworthy modera-

[1] "Annals of the Diocese of New Zealand," p. 108.

tion also was shown by Governor Fitzroy and his successor Governor Grey. They were forced to obtain from England military reinforcements for the protection of the colonists, but they used them with a prudence which gave great offence to the more hotheaded and vindictive of these colonists. By help of friendly natives peace was made with many hostile tribes; and those which still carried on the war were gradually, and without unnecessary severity, driven out of the fastnesses which they occupied as centres of guerilla warfare during 1845, 1846, and 1847.

The result was a pacification which then and for fourteen years after was thought to be final. The natives confined themselves to their tribal wars, and these became rarer every year. The old grudges were not forgotten by them, but they found profit in intercourse with the colonists. "They are fond of agriculture," said Sir George Grey in 1849, "take great pleasure in cattle and horses, like the sea and form good sailors, are attached to Europeans and admire their customs and manners, are extremely ambitious of rising in civilization, and of becoming skilled in European arts. They are apt at learning, in many respects extremely conscientious and observant of their word, are ambitious of honours, and are probably the most covetous race in the world. They are also agreeable in manners, and attachments of a lasting character readily spring up between them and the Europeans." Civilized ways took the place of barbarism, and Christianity, which satisfied its teachers, superseded the mild polytheism or nature-worship which had formerly been dominant. Civilization, however, enervating a race which seemed only fit for the wild habits of a barbarism which was not altogether barbarous, caused a more rapid dying out of the people than the sword would have been likely to effect, and close and impartial observers assure us that the Christianity was only superficial.

The native population of New Munster, or the Middle Island, never very numerous, is already nearly extinct, having dwindled from about 15,000 to about 2000, most of whom are old people, between 1848 and 1868. In New Ulster, or the Northern Island, the natives were estimated at 105,000 in 1848, and at 36,000 in 1868. But this residue seems to consist of the most vigorous and determined representatives of the race, men willing to gain all they can by English intercourse, but resolved to receive from it nothing that is not gain. These are the people with whom in recent times we have been brought into fierce conflict, and among them, at any rate, Christianity has developed no spirit of meekness or self-abandonment. All that it has taught them is to cherish a love of independence; and for ways of asserting that independence they go back to the traditions of their forefathers, only substituting the Christian musket for the heathen tomahawk.

Quaint illustration of the temper, at its best, in which the Maoris entered upon the present contest appears in the parable with which an old chief in Taranaki justified his participation in the rebellion, if it is to be called by that name, which was then beginning. Planting a long fern-stick in the ground to represent the Deity, he held two shorter ones in his hands, which, he said, represented the Maori and the Pakeha. "Before the Pakeha came," he proceeded, "we thought ourselves the nearest to God, and standing nearly equal with Him;" and he planted the Maori stick close to the one representing the Godhead. "But when the Pakehas came, we thought that they stood higher than we did, that they were next to the Godhead;" so he put the Pakeha stick near to the tall one, and removed the Maori stick to a distance and sunk it deep in the earth. "But now we have learnt that the Maori and the Pakeha issue from one and the same source, from God; that they both have good and evil qualities, and are alike before Him;" so he planted the Maori stick beside the Pakeha stick, at the same distance from the stick of the Godhead. "Pakeha and Maori are equal," he exclaimed. "They have equal rights, and it is proper that the Maoris should have their king, just as the Pakehas have theirs."

The first idea of setting up a native king was wisely conceived. Its chief promoter was Wirimu Tamihana, better known as William King, a zealous Christian, and accounted one of the most diligent leaders of civilization and English influence; and his purpose, or at any rate that avowed by him, was to bring the various tribes under the authority of some one who could put a stop to the disastrous tribal wars and help on the progress of his subjects, without offering any resistance to the recognised English authorities. "The river of blood was open," he said, "and I therefore sought for some plan to make it cease. I applied my thoughts to seek for some plan by which the Maori tribes should cleave together, so that the people might become one, like the Pakehas. I looked at your books, where Israel cried to have a king to themselves, to be a judge over them." The result was the setting up of a young man named Potatau, as King of the Maoris, in 1857. His authority was tolerated by the Government, and accepted by most of the native chiefs, and the consequence was a great lessening of the internal strife and rapid development of Maori strength to be applied either in good ways or in bad.

Unfortunately bad ways soon opened up. In 1860 a quarrel began at Waitara, in the province of Taranaki, owing to the sale of some land by a native, contrary to the wishes of his chief, Wirimu Tamihana. The settler's title was investigated and reported to be good, and the land was bought; but when surveyors were sent to define its boundaries, they were stopped and driven back by the chief and his followers. They returned with a party of soldiers to protect them, and found the natives in armed possession of the land. A scuffle ensued; and soon it grew into a war. Taranaki was ravaged by the Maoris; and the English troops were not strong enough to follow them into the mountain fastnesses to which they retired. Before a sufficient force could be brought from Auckland, the whole machinery of the Maori kingdom was applied to the fomenting of a general rebellion, and it spread over the whole northern island. "In 1862," we are told, "the movement presented the following features:—an elected king, a very young man of no force of character, surrounded by a few ambitious chiefs, who formed a little mock court, and by a body-guard who kept him from all vulgar contact, and even from the inspection of Europeans, except on humi-

liating terms; entirely powerless to enforce among
his subjects the decisions of his magistrates; but
with an army, if it might be called so, of 5000 to
10,000 followers, scattered over the country, but
organized so that large numbers could be concen-
trated on any one point on short notice; large accu-
mulated supplies of food, of arms, and ammunition;
a position in the centre of the island from which a
descent could be made in a few hours on any of the
European settlements; the Queen's law set at utter
defiance, her magistrates treated with supercilious
contempt; her writs torn to pieces and trampled
under foot; Europeans who had married native
women driven out of the King's districts, while their
wives and children were taken from them, unless
they would recognise and pay an annual tribute to
the King."

Perhaps there was fault on the part of the Colonial
Government in insisting on the obnoxious land-pur-
chase in Waitara in 1860. Perhaps the King-movement had all along been a mere device for preparing
a formidable rebellion, and ought not to have been
tolerated at starting. But on both these points it
is not easy to attach reasonable blame to the local
authorities. All that is clear is that the colonists
who had long thought their position secure, found
themselves surprised by a powerful organization
which they had no means of at once putting down.
They were forced to make an ignominious truce with
the insurgents in 1862, which was followed by a full
and insolent outburst of war in 1863.

The colonists had feebly prepared for meeting

[1] Fox, "The War in New Zealand," pp. 30, 31.

future dangers. The Maoris needed no preparation. In April 1863 they renewed their ravages in Taranaki. In May they threatened to invade Auckland. Their march was interrupted by General Cameron, at the head of a small body of troops, who bravely repulsed them in the open field and hunted them through the Waikato district, but was powerless in his attempts to follow them to their hiding-places and bring them into subjection. Thus three-quarters of a year were spent. The general character of the strife is shown in the closing episode of the campaign in Waikato. "On the 30th of March 1864," we are told, "Brigadier-General Carey was informed that the natives were entrenching themselves at Orakau, about three miles from his quarters. After reconnoitring their position he returned, and, collecting a force of about a thousand men, with three guns, he made a night march, appearing before the pah at early daylight, and having so arranged the arrival of his detachments from different posts that from the first they surrounded the enemy's position, and rendered escape impossible. The pah proved to be a place of great strength, with the usual ditches and parapets of more than usual depth and height, surrounded by a strong post and rail fence, and outlying connected rifle-pits. At first General Carey attempted to storm the works and take them by a rush; but, after three assaults, he wisely desisted and determined to approach the defences by sap. The number of natives inside is supposed to have been about three hundred, commanded by Rewi, the great fighting general of the King-party. During the afternoon a reinforcement of a hundred and fifty or two hundred rebels appeared in sight, evidently intending to relieve the place. They advanced to the edge of a bush, about nine hundred yards in the rear of our outposts, but there they stopped and commenced firing harmless volleys, at the same time endeavouring to encourage their friends by dancing the war-dance and yelling. In the meantime reinforcements kept arriving on our side, which brought up our number to over two thousand men, who were so disposed that the escape of the beleagured Maoris seemed to be absolutely impossible. All that day and the following night heavy firing was kept up on both sides. Not less than 40,000 rounds of cartridges were served out to our troops. By the morning of the 2d of April the sap was pushed close up to the works, and hand-grenades were thrown into the entrenchments. The Armstrong guns were brought into play, silencing the fire of the enemy to a great extent. General Cameron now arrived on the ground, but did not interfere with the direction of operations. As it was well known, however, that there were many women and children inside, he sent an interpreter to tell them that if they would surrender their lives would be spared. Their reply was, 'This is the word of the Maori; we will fight for ever, and ever, and ever.' They were then urged to send out the women and children. They answered, 'The women will fight as well as we.' Then the firing recommenced. Our troops were now getting desperate. Three attempts at a hand-to-hand encounter were made, but without success. It was now four o'clock of the third day, during which the Maoris had had no food but a few raw potatoes, and not a drop of water; while the shower of grape, hand-grenades, and rifle-balls, poured with more and more effect into their entrenchments. Suddenly, on that side of the works which was supposed to be closely invested by a double line of the 40th Regiment, the whole Maori force was seen to be escaping. Before they knew that the Maoris were out, it is said, they jumped over their heads, and broke away for a neighbouring swamp and scrub. Here they might all have escaped in a body but for a small corps of cavalry and artillery, which got a-head and met them just as they emerged from the swamp and scrub, and did great execution. The natives afterwards acknowledged a loss of two hundred. Our casualties amounted to sixteen killed and fifty-two wounded."[1]

Of that sort was nearly all the fighting; a vast expenditure of energy being required to bring about a very small result, which left the enemy almost as strong as ever. There were more battles—one of them, at Te Ranga, being more than ordinarily successful—in 1863; and in 1864 there was a lull in the contest. In 1865 it was revived; but so formidable was the action of the English troops, aided by friendly natives, that, before the year closed, peace was supposed to be restored. The peace, however, was only followed by a course of guerilla warfare, maintained by about a thousand rebels, by which the colony is still afflicted. It will probably continue till the rebel portion of the natives, if not the whole body of them, is exterminated. In the second half of 1868 and the first half of 1869 it is reckoned that about two hundred and sixty insurgents, out of something over a thousand in arms,

[1] Fox, pp. 97-102.

were put to death. The losses are supplied, in part at any rate, by fresh recruits from the neutral or secretly disaffected tribes; but as their supply of strong men is limited, and, by reason of the gradual dying out of the natives through causes with which the war has nothing to do, the strife can hardly last for many years longer; though the increasing atrocity of disposition shown by those who carry on the fight makes it likely that these final years of conflict will be attended by horrors wholly disproportioned to the extent of the war and the relative strength of the combatants.

A dying outburst of savage fury and fanaticism appears in the latest development of the King-movement, known as the Pai-Marire or Hau-Hau superstition. It began in March 1864, when Captain Lloyd of the 57th Regiment, with a detachment of a hundred men, was defeated on the Taranaki hills, he and eight others being killed. "The rebels drank the blood of those who fell," we are told, "and cut off their heads, burying for the time the heads and bodies in separate places. A few days afterwards, according to the native account, the angel Gabriel appeared to those who had partaken of the blood, and, by the medium of Captain Lloyd's spirit, ordered that his head should be exhumed, cured in their own way, and taken throughout the length and breadth of New Zealand, and that from henceforth this head should be the medium of man's communication with Jehovah. These injunctions were carefully obeyed, and immediately the head was taken up it communicated in the most solemn way the tenets of this new religion, namely:—The followers shall be called 'Pai Marire.' The angel Gabriel, with his legions, will protect them from their enemies. The Virgin Mary will constantly be present with them. The religion of England, as taught by the Scriptures, is false. The Scriptures must all be burnt. All days are alike sacred, and no notice must be taken of the Christian Sabbath. Men and women must live together promiscuously, so that their children may be as the sand of the sea-shore for multitude. The priests have superhuman power, and can obtain for their followers complete victory by uttering vigorously the word 'Hau.' The people who adopt this religion will shortly drive the whole European population out of New Zealand. This is only prevented now by the head not having completed its circuit of the whole land. Legions of angels await the bidding of the priests to aid the Maoris in exterminating the Europeans. Immediately the Europeans are destroyed and driven away, men will be sent from heaven to teach the Maoris all the arts and sciences now known by Europeans."

"These were the first developments of the Pai Marire or Hau-Hau fanaticism. Its emissaries were sent into every part of the islands, and their creed, which was framed on the convenient principle of embodying something from most other creeds, spread like wild-fire; its votaries apparently adding new articles to it to meet the growing furor of their disciples. A large infusion of Judaism, some leading features of Mormonism, a little mesmerism, a touch of spiritualism, occasional ventriloquism, and a large amount of cannibalism, are the characteristic features which it exhibits. Its rites are bloody, sensual, foul, and devilish; the least reprehensible and most orderly consisting in running round a pole stuck in the ground, howling and uttering gibberish, till catalepsy prostrates the worshippers, who sometimes lie senseless on the ground for hours. Their bitterest hatred and most refined cruelties are reserved for the missionaries, who are accused of robbing them of their lands by tribes which never sold, gave away, or were deprived of an acre."[1] It may be hoped that the very viciousness of this new religion will cause its ready abandonment by all but the most degraded of the Maoris; and that then, if a wise policy be adopted by the colonial authorities, their subjection to English rule, under which they can be quietly left to die out, will be made easy.

That the Maoris should speedily die out is now the best hope for New Zealand. Foolish and dishonourable conduct pursued towards them in former times has rendered their existence as an independent and prosperous section of the population now impossible; and perhaps their wasting away is in great measure due to causes for which neither colonists nor missionaries are in any way responsible. In the rocky peninsula which forms the extreme north of the northern island there are still some 9000 or 10,000 natives who live apart both from their own kinsmen and from the English community, save in the carrying on of a humble trade with them, and for the peaceable progress of these

---

[1] Fox, pp. 127-129, 139, 140. Much information about Hau-Hauism, Kingism, and the whole condition of the Maoris, is contained in a bulky New Zealand Blue-Book (part L) which has been published while this volume is going to press.

there is the best chance, though only a poor one. Of the 28,000 said to be in the interior of the northern island, only 3000 or fewer are in open hostility to the colonists; but the sympathy that binds them all together, and renders them now obnoxious to Englishmen, must hasten on their decay. Not till they have disappeared will New Zealand be able to enter without hindrance upon the bright future in store for it.

CHAPTER XXIX.

ENGLISH AUSTRALASIA.

THE RELATIVE ADVANTAGES OF OUR AUSTRALASIAN COLONIES—
WESTERN AUSTRALIA—QUEENSLAND—NEW SOUTH WALES—
VICTORIA—SOUTH AUSTRALIA—TASMANIA—NEW ZEALAND.

HARDLY more than eighty years have passed since, in May 1787, the first cargo of convicts, with their keepers and attendants, was sent out from England to begin the colonization of New South Wales. The only object of that enterprise, highly applauded by a few philanthropists and other enthusiasts, but ridiculed and blamed by nearly everybody else, was to get rid of some obnoxious members of society, and to see whether they could be made better use of in the far-off wastes of the antipodes than in crowded and pestilential prisons at home. Yet out of it has grown an empire five and twenty times as large as Great Britain and Ireland, and which, though still in the first stage of its growth—the whole vast area having less than half the population of London—already has a commercial value to the mother-country hardly less than that of India, and greater than that of all the other English dependencies put together. When the difficulties in the way of the first attempts at orderly settlement are considered—and in the presence of its convict population those difficulties were great indeed—its present prosperity is truly marvellous. What prosperity may be attained hereafter perhaps it is hardly possible for the most sanguine onlooker to anticipate.

In only one of the seven colonies already formed, and that one the nearest to England in actual distance, though the most remote from it in general characteristics, is the prospect uninviting. The immense territory of Western Australia has few attractions for British enterprise. Least favoured by nature, its comparatively scanty resources have never been duly made use of by the arts of man. The scene, at starting, of grievous blunders in colonization, it has profited little by the subsequent efforts to improve it through help of convict labour; and it can hardly be expected to attain much importance till the whole Australian continent has become so well peopled, and is so well provided with means of transit and intercommunication, that its deficiencies can easily be supplied from richer districts, and the wealth of those districts can give a new value to its more barren regions. Its northern provinces and coast districts, however, deserve more attention than they have yet received; and perhaps the day is not far distant when they will be parted off from it and associated with the contiguous parts of Queensland in a new and flourishing colony. To these districts, now appended to South Australia, the independent name of North Australia has already been given. Its harbours offer special facilities for trade with the neighbouring Indian Archipelago, and the rich pasture-lands in the interior wait only to be turned to profit by prudent adventurers.

Thriving Australia, however, still means little more than the coast-line of the eastern half of the island, and much of this has as yet been but slightly used. We are only now beginning to prove the value of Queensland as a great field for cotton cultivation, whence even greater profit may be derived than from the inland pasture-grounds which are already vieing with the highlands of New South Wales and Victoria in production of wool, the other great staple material for clothing. To supply the requirements of this younger trade, new ports will have to grow up along the north-eastern shore, and the enterprise developed in them will become the parent of fresh energy in the almost boundless plantation grounds and squatters' runs that adjoin them.

If cotton is to rival wool as a source of wealth to Queensland, coal is already beginning to rival wool in making the fortune of New South Wales. Gold has lately usurped too much of the energy that can find suitable employment in producing wool in Victoria; but here, in the end, the gold trade must help the wool trade, and both must contribute mightily to the further growth of the southern colony, which has already grown with a rapidity and vigour unsurpassed in the history of the world. Copper is joined with wool in promoting the prosperity of South Australia, which also has another great source of profit in its luxuriant farm-lands, making it the principal granary of the whole Australian island. Thus, if wool is a common source of wealth to all the Australian colonies, each has a second staple of its own, enabling it to assert its independence in the race of advancement in which all are alike engaged.

The early Australasian voyagers were not far wrong in supposing that Van Dieman's Land was a part of Australia. The narrow straits that divide them, separate islands almost identical in character, or differing from one another only so far as an outlying peninsula must necessarily differ from the neighbouring mainland. From tropical Queensland there is an even gradation of climate down to temperate Tasmania; and here, as in the northern districts, wool is the main source of wealth. If the southern colony has made less progress than the other offshoots of New South Wales, it is due alone to the excess of the convict element in its social constitution—a source of weakness that time and the in-coming of fresh colonists will speedily remove.

From the other portions of Australasia New Zealand stands quite apart. If, as is likely, all the others soon unite, after the fashion of the North American colonies, in a grand Australian confederation, the south-eastern group of islands can have no place therein. New Zealand has, in its iron, its coal, and its agricultural capabilities, greater, though less showy, sources of wealth than its gold; but the gold will have done good service if it brings into the islands settlers ready to develop its other resources. The "Britain of the South" must justify its title by manufacturing industry of the sort that has made England great.

CHAPTER XXX.

THE END OF THE STORY.

THE VALUE OF OUR COLONIES—THE POLITICAL AND COMMERCIAL ADVANTAGES DERIVED AND DERIVABLE FROM THEM—THEIR IMPORTANCE AS FIELDS OF EMIGRATION.

"N effect of peace in fruitful kingdoms, where the stock of people, receiving no consumption nor diminution by war, doth continually multiply and increase, must, in the end," wrote Lord Bacon, in 1606, in a document addressed to James I., setting forth the advantages of English emigration to Ireland, "be a surcharge or overflow of people more than the territories can well maintain; which many times, insinuating a general necessity and want of means into all estates, doth turn external peace into internal troubles and seditions. Now, what an excellent diversion of this inconvenience is ministered to your Majesty in this plantation of Ireland, wherein so many families may receive sustentation and fortune, and the discharge of them out of England and Scotland may prevent many seeds of future perturbation; so that it is as if a man were troubled for the avoidance of water from the places where he hath built his house, and afterwards should advise with himself to cast those floods, pools, or streams, for pleasure, provision, or use. So shall your Majesty in this work have a double commodity, in the avoidance of people here, and in making use of them there."

Through the last two centuries and a half the wisdom of that quaintly expressed opinion has been fully proved, if not in the colonization of Ireland, yet in other work of the sort recommended by Lord Bacon. During that period, as we have seen, England has gradually acquired a vast colonial territory, which, if capable of almost boundless development in the future, has already proved of great advantage to her, both " in the avoidance of people here, and in making use of them there." The good issues of the "double commodity," indeed, have been far more numerous and far more various than Bacon could have conceived. Our "plantations," as colonies were formerly styled, have yielded and continue to yield a perennial harvest of benefits, political, commercial, and social, to the mother-country.

The political benefits were most apparent in the first period of our colonial history. The successive migrations by which, during the seventeenth century, the United States of America and the West Indian Islands were stocked with enterprising settlers, though fortunately they did not relieve England of all her "unquiet spirits," did "prevent many seeds of future perturbation." Many of the most violent Cavaliers, and as many of the most violent Roundheads, crossed the Atlantic, and thus, without weakening the strife between the champions and opponents of Stuart rule and misrule, rid it of many confusing elements, and left a freer battle-ground for fighting out the great fight of constitutional and religious liberty which has mainly conduced to the later greatness of our country. Had all the forces been retained within the narrow limits of the kingdom, the contest would necessarily have been attended with vastly greater misery to those who had to struggle through it, and the final issue might have been very different. And her colonies have continued, though in less degree, to be of the same use to England. In each generation wise or unwise enthusiasts, violent thinkers and actors of all sorts, have, to use Bacon's simile, been drained, like baneful floods, from ground in which they were or might have become only obnoxious and pestilential elements, and have been turned into channels that have changed barren wastes into fertile gardens. This has been notably the case with our Australian colonies. Our sometime convict settlements have received injury as well as benefit from their extensive peopling with troublesome and dangerous criminals; but many of those criminals have in their new homes been converted into honest and enterprising men, who, in helping themselves, have famously helped on the progress of their new homes; and the conversion would have been much more thorough and universal had it been more wisely conducted. This is a theme of encouraging reflection to philanthropists; and, in these days in which it is rightly considered better to prevent people from becoming criminals than to allow them to fall into vice and then to punish them for being vicious, it should suggest a far wider field for reformatory enterprise than now generally finds favour.

Another, and perhaps a yet more evident, political benefit derived and still more derivable from our colonies is in their value as vast military and naval schools. War is altogether hateful; but, until all the world consents to turn swords into ploughshares and spears into pruning-hooks, we must be prepared to fight in case of need, and our colonies have always furnished the best of all training-grounds for warfare. Happily they can be made full use of without actual fighting. In India, in Canada, in the Cape, and in Australia, as well as in the two small colonies of Malta and Gibraltar, which are almost exclusively military settlements, capacity for enduring hardship, variety of resource, and fitness for all the stern necessities of war, are excellently learnt by soldiers whose present use is important enough as guardians of the strongholds of English power and influence. In this much has been done; but more remains. We have as yet but feebly copied the machinery by which ancient Rome so long gave strength to her vast possessions. We have taken good soldiers from some of our subject races; but we have only here and there, though always with good result, shifted them from their own neighbourhoods to others in which they can be more useful. Sikhs in China, Kaffirs in the West Indies, perhaps even Maoris in Canada, would materially conduce to the defence of our various possessions and the binding of them all into one great British dominion.

Our colonies, however, and the trades begotten by them, are yet more valuable as nurseries for seamen than as schools for soldiers. In this respect the advantages are too transparent to need any arguments. The hundreds of thousands of hardy mariners who man our trading ships form a race from which our vessels of war can be supplied, in time of need, with ready-made crews.

"Whatever gives colonies to France," said Talleyrand, and that which he wished for France has been attained by Great Britain, "supplies her with ships and sailors, manufacturers and husbandmen. Victories by land can only give her mutinous subjects, who, instead of augmenting the national force by their riches or numbers, contribute only to disperse and enfeeble that force; but the growth of colonies supplies her with zealous citizens, and the increase of real wealth and effective numbers is the certain consequence."

And that value is far greater from a commercial than from a political point of view. It is impossible to over-estimate the benefits which, in this way, England has received from her colonies. English commerce was great before English colonization began. Famous merchants, like Sir Thomas Gresham and others, before and after his day, sent their ships and went themselves to every port and mart of size in Europe, and there made interchange of commodities, whereby both they and their country were enriched. Of the wealth of the world a large portion flowed into and through that country in the sixteenth century, as it does in the nineteenth; "but," as a shrewd merchant quaintly said in 1638, "England being naturally seated in a northern corner of the world, and herein bending under the weight of too ponderous a burthen, cannot possibly and for ever find a vent for all those commodities that are to be seen daily exported and brought within the compass of so narrow a circuit, unless there can be, by the policy and government of the State, a mean found to make this island the common emporium and staple of all Europe."[1] The emporium of a good deal more than all Europe this island has become through our colonies and the enterprise which has led to their formation, but which, without them, would have been sorely crippled. New commodities of every sort, from tobacco to cotton, have been brought into use; old commodities as various, from sugar to silk, have been vastly increased in quantity through the energy of Englishmen in our colonial plantations, and thereby those who have remained at home have been enriched no less than those who have gone abroad. Our little kingdom, which, four centuries ago, was little more than a collection of farms, growing food enough to nourish its two or three millions of inhabitants, and not always able to do that without great privation to many, and with only a sufficient number of small and clumsy manufactories to supply those inhabitants with coarse clothing, and the bare necessaries of life, has now become the great workshop and market of the world, bringing a thousand precious wares from its vast colonial possessions, rendering them far more precious by its manufacturing art, exchanging a portion of them for the valuable produce of other nations, and distributing the rest among its own inhabitants and the people of its colonies; and, with the profits of its merchandise, able to buy food enough to supplement its own agricultural resources in nourishing a population of thirty millions and more.

 A wonderful growth in British commerce has arisen

[1] Lewis Roberts, "The Merchants' Map of Commerce."

through the growth of British colonization. Three
hundred years ago England was rising out of the
insignificance which seemed reasonably to belong to
it by reason of its small territorial extent, and beginning to deserve the title, tauntingly given to it, but
really high praise, of "a nation of shopkeepers." Two
hundred years ago it was receiving the first-fruits
of its colonial enterprise in America and the West
Indies, and of trade which was nearly akin to colonial
enterprise in India. One hundred years ago those
sources of profit, though yet far from maturity, had
attained gigantic proportions, and the advantages
derived from them were of corresponding magnitude.
The progress made during the past century has
eclipsed in grandeur all that preceded it. In 1761
the entire exports from Great Britain to all parts of
the world amounted to £16,038,913; the corresponding imports to £10,292,541. The value of exports to
North America and the West Indies was £3,330,371,
or more than a fifth of the whole; the value of the
imports thence was £3,726,261, or more than a third.
The exports to the East Indies were worth £845,797;
the imports from thence were worth £840,987; the
former being about a twentieth, the latter about a
twelfth. In 1865 the total exports amounted to
£271,134,969; the total imports to £165,862,402.
The United States of America, no longer British
colonies, but none the less direct outcomes of
British colonization, received from us goods worth
£21,773,250, and sent us goods worth £21,235,963.
The exports to the colonies still owned by us were
valued at £72,865,067, including £37,395,372 to
India, £10,283,113 to Australia, £6,350,148 to British

North America, £6,867,270 to the West Indies and British Guiana, £3,707,615 to Ceylon, and £2,445,485 to the Cape colonies; the imports were valued at £48,222,862, including £18,254,570 from India, £13,352,357 from Australia, £4,705,079 from British North America, £2,686,091 from the West Indies and British Guiana, £685,308 from Ceylon, and £1,700,156 from the Cape colonies.[1] Our export trade with our colonies and with the United States is nearly six times, our import trade nearly five times, as great as they were with all the world a hundred years ago.

But even those figures do not fairly estimate the commercial value of our colonies. From them, still reckoning the United States as the noblest of England's offspring, we receive large supplies of flour, the main necessary of life, and nearly all our stores of sugar, coffee, and other articles, which, by reason of their abundant supply, have ceased to be luxuries. From them, too, we receive very nearly all the cotton, and the chief proportion of the wool, which are the

[1] The statistics for 1865 are given as representing a truer average than the last three years, in which many branches of trade and some colonies have suffered heavily by the panic of 1866. But it is hardly necessary to say that no single year can give a precise view of the general state of each colony's commerce. Thus the exports to India were valued at £19,876,197 in 1863, at £26,213,669 in 1864; the imports thence at £27,544,284 in 1863, and at £44,971,263 in 1864. In 1863 the exports to Australia were worth £18,111,206, the imports thence £11,680,066, the former being nearly twice as much as, the latter considerably less than, the amounts for 1865. As regards British North America both exports and imports were almost exactly the same in 1865 as in 1863; but the West Indies received from us in 1863 less than half as much (£3,062,410), and sent us more than twice as much (£6,469,920) as in 1865.

mainstays of our manufacturing energy, without which our coal and iron would be comparatively useless, and England would fall back into the insignificance that it emerged from when our colonies began to be formed.

And yet those colonies seem only to be in the first stages of their development. In nearly all of them vast tracts of land are still unused, or to a great extent neglected, and in most of their busiest portions there is room for much fresh enterprise. They have an aggregate area of about 4,300,000 square miles, being nearly thirty-five times as large as Great Britain and Ireland; but their entire population amounted in 1862 to only about 150,000,000, less than five times that of the United Kingdom; and of this population fourteen-fifteenths, or 143,271,210 persons, were in India, whose 1,000,000 or so square miles constitute only a fourth of the whole area. India, having a hundred and fifty persons to the square mile, is not much less crowded than Great Britain; and a few smaller dependencies, especially Ceylon and Barbados, in each of which there are a thousand to the square mile, are more crowded—the crowding being by inhabitants who are not Englishmen. All those colonies in which subject races are few or altogether wanting are peopled very sparsely indeed. Even the West Indies, with their great negro population, excluding British Guiana, have, in the aggregate, but eighty to the square mile, and British Guiana has hardly more than two. In the Canadian Dominion, excluding the almost uninhabited Hudson's Bay Territory, there are only about twelve to the square mile, and British

Columbia has nearly fifty square miles for each inhabitant. To each square mile there are in Cape Colony about two and a half persons, and in Natal, about twenty-four—these being chiefly Kaffirs; in Victoria there are only seven; in Tasmania only four; in New Zealand, less than two; and in New South Wales, less than one; while, in South Australia, there are two and a half square miles, in Western Australia three, in Queensland eighteen, for each person. In all our colonies there are not more than five million English residents. It has been estimated that they could easily maintain a hundred million, when they would still be only one-fourth as populous as Great Britain now is.

Any other than a very gradual approximation to that vast increase of population, of course, were it at all possible, would be altogether inexpedient. Waste lands cannot be at once rendered fit for use by any but a very scanty population. They have to be cultivated and improved step by step. Western Australia does not furnish the only painful illustration on record of the ill effects of too hasty effort in the way of colonization; but in nearly all our colonies there is ample room, if not pressing need, for a far greater number of colonists than they possess; and this being so, it is surely strange that there should not be a far larger migration to them than now occurs from the over-crowded population of the mother-country. Nearly every calling in Great Britain, from the lowest to the highest, is over-manned. About £7,000,000 are annually spent by the nation, besides all the outlay of private charity, in the relief of the million or more poor persons who, unable to maintain themselves, or hindered from doing so by their own misdeeds, are thus a heavy burthen on the other millions, who, for the most part, find it very difficult to provide themselves with the necessaries of life, and the rapid growth of population makes the burthen and the difficulty greater every year. Philanthropists and statesmen, no less than the sufferers themselves, are seriously at fault. for not duly considering the value of our colonies for what Lord Bacon called "the double commodity in the avoidance of people here, and the making use of them there." If the administrators of our poor laws, and the dispensers of private charity understood their duty they would do vastly more than they have hitherto done in lessening the load of domestic pauperism by means of emigration to colonies in which there is room and need for millions of fresh settlers.

Useless paupers, however, would be as useless in the colonies as they are at home. Men and women who have been rendered apathetic and witless by the degradation of poverty have small prospect of advancement in regions where everything depends upon capacity for hard work and readiness in using that capacity in any labour that circumstances require. And the same remark applies, with equal force, to those other paupers of a higher social grade, who, by training or natural deficiency, are unable to maintain their ground in the struggle for independence that arises in every sphere of occupation, from those of the field-labourer and the artizan to those of the merchant and the candidate for professional employment. In the colonies, even more than at home, none but those who have power and will to work can expect to make progress. But as every calling is overcrowded with such, it is eminently desirable, both in their own interests and in those of the nation, that their ranks should be thinned and the colonies should be aided by the transference of some of them to new scenes of enterprise. England can spare a goodly number of them, and is constantly breeding more than she herself can give work to, and the colonies require all they can receive, for generations to come, of immigrants who will have to toil as manfully as at home, but who may fairly expect far richer gains than they could expect from their toil at home, and who may derive an additional satisfaction in their good fortune by knowing that their gains involve no loss to their neighbours.

Each colony has its special needs and its special facilities for advancement; but in nearly all—in all but the few that are already well supplied with an enterprising population—there is room for hard-working settlers of every grade. In the great emigration-fields of British North America and Australia, however, there is most, and for the present boundless, room for farm labourers and their employers, and for artizans and their directors. Where vast tracts of land wait only to be tilled, and to have their useless vegetation replaced by wholesome cultivation, where new roads and canals have to be constructed, and where, as the produce is multiplied, the towns require fresh building of houses, increased development of manufactories and augmentation of all the resources for rendering available and transmitting to near and distant marts the fruit of agricultural and other labours, it is evident that all who can supply these demands will be most welcome and will profit most by their enterprise.

That enterprise, if rightly directed, cannot fail of success. It must benefit the individuals who engage in it, and confer equal benefit on the countries that receive them and the country that sends them forth. The noblest outcome of English colonization appears in the vast empire of the United States of America. But offspring as noble are now growing, and whether they continue to own formal allegiance to their mother-country, or in the end become independent nationalities, they cannot fail to be of inestimable advantage to the little island that gave them birth. And no political divergence can break the bonds of Anglo-Saxon friendship, or retard the progress of that best endowed race of men which, emerging from its English cradle, promises to spread the civilizing influences of its birth over the fairest and broadest portions of both hemispheres, and, in spite any turmoils that may be incident to its development, to continue its good work

"Till the war-drum throbs no longer, and the battle-flags are furl'd
In the Parliament of man, the Federation of the world."

APPENDIX.

I.—AREA AND POPULATION OF THE BRITISH COLONIAL POSSESSIONS.

The following table is based upon the latest returns. In some cases, where precise surveys and reckonings have not been made, the figures are only approximate. The last column shows the date of each census or estimate of the population.

	AREA.	POPULATION.			DATE.
	Sq. Miles.	Males.	Females.	Total.	
WEST INDIES.					
Jamaica,	6,400	213,521	227,743	441,264	1861
Turk's Islands,	..	2,129	2,244	4,372	1861
Bahamas,	2,921	17,446	17,821	35,287	1861
Leeward Islands { Antigua,	183	17,060	20,065	37,125	1861
Dominica,	291	11,839	13,226	25,065	1860
St. Christopher's,	108	11,457	13,003	24,460	1861
Montserrat,	47	3,447	4,198	7,645	1858
Nevis,	50	4,626	5,296	9,922	1861
Virgin Islands,	57	2,907	3,144	6,051	1861
Windward Islands { Barbadoes,	166	70,799	81,928	152,727	1861
Grenada,	133	15,413	16,487	31,900	1861
St Vincent,	131	15,695	16,760	31,755	1861
Tobago,	97	7,433	7,977	15,410	1861
St Lucia,	250	12,962	14,173	26,135	1858
Trinidad,	1,754	46,074	38,364	84,438	1861
British Guiana,	76,000	79,644	68,382	148,026	1861
Honduras,	13,500	13,789	11,846	25,635	1861
NORTH AMERICA.					
Canada { Western,	310,020	..	..	1,396,090	1856
Eastern,		..	..	1,257,480	
Nova Scotia and Cape Breton,	19,671	165,484	165,373	330,857	1861
New Brunswick,	27,037	129,948	122,099	252,047	1861
Prince Edward Island,	2,173	40,590	39,977	80,857	1861
Newfoundland,	40,200	64,268	58,370	122,638	1857
Bermuda,	24	4,902	6,549	11,451	1861
British Columbia { White,	200,000	8,000	350	8,350	1863
Aboriginal		..	..	30,000 to 40,000	
Vancouver Island { White,	16,000	..	..	8,000	1863
Aboriginal		..	..	10,000	

Area and Population of the British Colonial Possessions—continued.

	AREA.	POPULATION.			DATE.
	Sq. Miles.	Males.	Females.	Total.	
AFRICA.					
Cape { White, Coloured, }	104,961	290,966	278,192	{ 167,430 / 578,719 }	1865
Natal { White, Coloured, including 6000 Coolies, }	16,145	9,272 / 113,634	7,930 / 119,203	17,202 / 232,837	1869
Gambia,	21	3,985	2,954	6,939	1861
Sierra Leone,	468	21,203	20,588	41,791	1863
Gold Coast,	6,000	..	..	151,346	1858
Lagos,	..	16,708	15,837	32,545	1863
St Helena,	47	3,774	3,086	6,860	1861
BRITISH INDIA.					
White / Native	} 1,094,618	{ .. / ..	.. / ..	125,945 / 145,000,000 }	1861
EASTERN COLONIES.					
Ceylon { White, Coloured, }	24,700 {	7,838 / 1,167,488	6,476 / 1,042,188	14,314 / 2,209,626 }	1863
Mauritius,	708	206,110	107,359	313,462	1861
Seychelles & other dependencies,	..	4,893	4,162	9,055	1861
Hong Kong,	29	84,797	32,674	117,471	1867
Labuan,	45	2,703	643	5,346	1863
AUSTRALASIA.					
New South Wales,	823,437	227,106	184,192	411,388	1865
Queensland,	678,006	60,215	39,097	99,312	1868
Victoria,	86,375	380,234	296,356	676,590	1868
South Australia,	383,323	89,991	82,869	172,860	1867
Western Australia,	978,000	14,539	8,194	22,733	1868
Tasmania,	26,215	..	..	96,454	1867
New Zealand,	106,260	131,929	86,739	218,668	1867
" Natives,	..	31,607	24,503	55,970	1804
Auckland Islands,	..	..	..	151	1851
OTHER POSSESSIONS.					
Malta, exclusive of Troops, etc.,	115	69,717	71,125	130,842	1861
Gibraltar,	1¾	7,139	8,323	15,462	1863
Heligoland,		..	..	2,030	1856
Falkland Islands,	7,600	365	227	592	1863

II.—OUR EMIGRATION-FIELDS.

The following notes respecting the immigration capacities and needs of our principal colonies are drawn chiefly from the "Colonization Circular" of Her Majesty's Colonial Land and Emigration Commissioners, published in July 1869.

The United States and the British North American and

Australasian Colonies are our great emigration fields. India, Ceylon, and the other colonies which are well supplied with a native population, offer, of course, few facilities for general emigration, though in them there is considerable room for competent settlers who can promote their trade and give an impetus, beneficial to themselves as well as to others, to other appliances for aiding the residents in augmenting the resources of the various countries. In the development of the manufacturing arts, in constructing railways and other means of transit, enterprising merchants, engineers, and the like, have shown how much can be done in these colonies, and especially in India. Here, too, there is room for professional men, whether lawyers or doctors; but not for the great majority of those who may seek to advance themselves by emigration. The same may be said of our West Indian colonies. Most of them are yet sparsely peopled; but experience seems to prove that in them manual labour can best be done, if not by the resident negroes, by emigrants from India, who are better adapted than Englishmen for the West Indian climate.

No such objection applies to the United States, to which the great majority of British emigrants go in search of prosperity that they cannot hope to attain at home; or to our own vast colonies in the more northern section of the American continent.

"The following remarks," it is said in the "Colonization Circular" referred to, "of the late Mr Buchanan, Chief Agent for Immigration at Quebec, are stated in a communication from the Deputy Minister of Agriculture, dated 27th of March 1869, to be still applicable:—'The classes which may be recommended to emigrate to Canada are (1) persons with capital seeking investment; (2) produce farmers; (3) agricultural labourers; (4) male and female servants; and (5) boys and girls over 15 years of age. Families with fixed incomes will find in Canada, with much less difficulty than in the mother-country, a suitable house, good society, and every facility for educating and starting their children in life. Persons possessing small capitals (say from £200 to £500) are advised to purchase or rent a farm with some little improvement upon it, instead of going into the bush at once. Parties desirous of investing may obtain from seven to eight per cent. for their money on mortgage with perfect security.' A small capitalist, Mr Buchanan adds, would act wisely, if, instead of buying land before becoming acquainted with its character and the kind of labour required in a new country, he were to place his money in the Savings' Bank, take lodgings for his family in some neighbourhood affording a good prospect of employment, and work at wages for a year or so, thus gaining the knowledge and experience necessary to realise independence. Such a course is not deemed degrading in Canada, and is sure to result in ultimate good. Let it be borne in mind that all persons belonging to Canada, whether they be possessed of £100 or £1000, must fail unless they come determined to labour themselves; and it may be asserted without fear of contradiction, that the family who pursues this plan will, at the end of a few years, be far in advance of him, no matter what his capital may be, who has not taken to the axe and the hoe. Improved farms may be purchased at from five dollars to fifty dollars per acre, according to situation and extent of improvement; or rented, with or without the option of purchase, at from one dollar to four dollars per acre. The emigrant should not invest all his capital in land, but reserve sufficient to enable him to stock and work it. The classes who should be warned against emigration are clerks, shopmen, or persons having no particular trade or calling, and unaccustomed to manual labour. To emigrants of this class Canada affords but little encouragement at present. With regard to females above the grade of domestic servants, Mr Buchanan adheres to his statements and opinions expressed in a special report, dated the 16th May 1862, that there exists but a very limited demand for that class of women, and that the present introduction of such a class into Canada would be attended with consequences far from advantageous.'"

Of the same sort is the advice from competent authorities in the other provinces of the Canadian dominion. "There will be a large demand for labour," says the Immigration Agent of New Brunswick, in a report dated the 22d of February 1869, "in the coming season. Already there have been portions of the Great Intercolonial Railway placed under contract, and labourers and mechanics will consequently be in great demand. There has been a falling off in shipbuilding, but all other branches of industry are in a healthy state. Farming was carried on with great advantage last year; and the prospect for those willing to undertake the cultivation of the soil promises to be remunerative. One hundred acres of Government land can be had for 20 dols. currency; or it can be paid for by labour on the roads, say 10 dols. for three successive years; then the land is granted by deed to the settler and his heirs. Agricultural labourers, dairywomen, female servants, and boys and girls over fifteen years of age, will find ready and remunerative employment. To these classes New Brunswick offers great inducements. With land so easily procured, and remunerative wages for all kinds of labour, the country offers great inducements to all who are disposed to labour for a living. The many thousands of emigrants who landed in the country but a few years ago, and who have become the owners of productive farms, and are living in comfort, and in many cases in affluence, should induce those who are intending to emigrate, to look favourably upon our young and growing country."

In Nova Scotia, too, it was said by the Deputy Provincial Secretary of the colony in December 1866, "a good class of farmers who have sufficient means wherewith to purchase small farms, already under cultivation, would do well in the western parts of the province. Fruit-growers in particular could make money; but this is no place for paupers. What is required is more capital and industry, and there is a good opening for the expenditure and employment of both."

In Newfoundland there are fewer attractions for emigrants. "This colony," according to the report of its Colonial Secretary in October 1866—and his remarks are still applicable—"has very little demand for labour, except during the fishing season, which may be said to last from May till October. During that period every able-bodied operative is fully employed, and it is upon the success or otherwise of that fishery that the condition of the people during the ensuing winter in a great measure depends, as, unfortunately, there is very little to be had by the people in the shape of employment during the winter, there being but very few manufactories or other sources of employment at those times when the fishery cannot be prosecuted. The seal-fishery in March employs a large number of the young and able-bodied men of the colony for a period ranging from one month to six weeks and two months. The taking of herring and salmon commences earlier than the cod-fishery, which cannot be said to be fully engaged in earlier than in the month of June. Agriculture is progressively increasing."

More auspicious in climate than some of our settlements in North America and its eastern islands, and equal in resources to the best of them, are the younger colonies of British Columbia and Vancouver's Island, now united under one Government, in the far west. "The climate of Vancouver Island," we are told, "is excellent, and has been compared to the climate of the milder parts of England or to that in the south of France. Indeed, it is said to be preferable to that of England, as it has more fine steady weather, is far less changeable, and on the whole milder. The days in summer are warm, but not oppressive, and free from glare: the evenings are cool, with a gentle sea breeze. Heavy rains generally fall in December or January. The winter is a little cold, but not severe. There are occasional frosts and falls of snow, but they rarely last long." "British Columbia, also, may compare favourably with most colonies, more particularly with those on the American continent in similar latitudes. It is remarkably healthy both in summer and winter, there being nothing like malaria or ague either in the hottest summer weather or the dampest localities. On the western and eastern side of the Cascade Range the climate is quite different. The western is heavily timbered, and subject to heavy rains in spring and autumn; while on the eastern side the country consists of rolling grassy plains, lightly timbered, the summer heat more intense, the rain light. Tomatoes and melons ripen readily in the open air, and the winters are comparatively mild."

Both the island and the mainland wait to be made use of by enterprising colonists, whose enterprise takes healthier shape than in search for gold. "The population of British Columbia is chiefly migratory, consisting of mining adventurers from California and other parts of the world, and including considerable numbers of Chinese. The settled white population may be estimated at about 8000. Settlement is however rapidly in progress, and farms are being taken up and cultivated throughout the colony. In addition to its gold mines, which are as yet the principal source of wealth to the colony, the natural resources of the country have thus been summed up in evidence given before the House of Commons: 'Its minerals are most valuable; its timber the finest in the world for marine purposes; it abounds with bituminous coal well fitted for the generation of steam; from Thomson's River and Colville Districts to the Rocky Mountains, and from the 49th parallel, some 350 miles north, a more beautiful country does not exist.' It is in every way suitable for colonization. The soil has proved extremely fertile, and cereals have been everywhere raised to great advantage. Grazing and dairy farming, though carried on to a limited extent, have been highly profitable and successful. During the year 1865 a valuable silver lead mine was discovered in the Shuswap District, at a place called Cherry Creek. The ore on assay has been found to yield as much as 2000 ounces of silver to the ton. Preparations are being made to mine here on an extensive scale, and it is generally supposed that the silver mines of the country will prove one of its most valuable sources of wealth and prosperity. Silver has been found in various other parts of the country. Excellent anthracite coal has also been discovered on Queen Charlotte's Island, and great expectations have been formed of the result of the labours of the company who have undertaken to work the mine."

The West African colonies, by reason of their unhealthy climate, are of no value as emigration-fields. All the progress that can be made by them will be by wise education and employment of their own natives, and of those negroes who go to it from the United States and the West Indies.

Nor does Cape Colony at present invite fresh settlers. The climate is healthy and the soil is various and fertile; but those already resident in it seem sufficient for all the work that has to be done, until fresh enterprise opens up new fields of labour. And from Natal, yet more favourable in climate and soil than the Cape, we have the same report. "There is no demand for artizans," wrote the Colonial Secretary in February 1869, "or field and house servants, at the present time. All British field and domestic servants have to compete in the labour market with the numerous coloured inhabitants working for small wages. Small British farmers, who have been accustomed to labour themselves, and have a little capital, might find it profitable to emigrate to Natal, where they can purchase or rent small farms near markets, and live at little cost for necessaries."

Of that latter sort are the emigrants for whom there is most room in all our leading colonies, but hardly anywhere as much as in Australia. Farmers and farm-labourers, mechanics and engineers, are the men most needed by all the Australian colonies. With slight variations, arising from the special conditions of the various settlements, the reports of the immigration agents in each are to the same effect.

"To Queensland, the youngest of them," says the Executive Council of the Colonial Government, "as a general rule, and with the exception of a few professional men, only two classes of men should emigrate, viz.: (1) Capitalists large or small; (2) Labourers, that is, men or women accustomed to work with their hands. All others will be doomed, not only to almost certain disappointment, but also to severe hardships."

In Victoria, it was reported in February 1869, "the provisions of the Land Act, by which the land within certain areas has been thrown open to lease, and which has been extensively taken up, have tended very considerably to enhance the demand for agricultural labour, and will year by year increase it, as persons whose labour has been hitherto available become proprietors themselves, and employers of labour. At present, in many parts of the colony, this description of labour is said to be wanted. It is advisable for persons desirous of emigrating to any of the Australian colonies, to bear in mind that men without or with small families are likely to find employment soonest, and are the most sought after. Clerks, shopmen, and men not accustomed to manual labour are not advised to emigrate, the supply being greater than the demand, especially as so many colonial-born youths fit for these occupations are now competing for employments of this description. The emigration of needlewomen, housekeepers, governesses, and others of the class who have not been accustomed to domestic service, is not encouraged. The description of female emigrants most required are general servants, who can cook and wash, etc., housemaids, good cooks, and industrious strong girls who can cook a little, milk a cow, make butter, and are accustomed to other farm and dairy work."

From New South Wales and South Australia, from Tasmania and New Zealand, similar advice is sent home. In Tasmania, "female domestic servants who thoroughly understand household work are in constant demand, at wages varying from £20 to £30 per year. Agricultural labourers always find employment at high wages, with rations of meat, flour, tea, and sugar, and dwellings rent free. Tailors, shoemakers, and brassfounders are of artizan labourers the most in demand at present." In New Zealand, "good female domestic servants are wanted throughout the colony. Young men of no particular profession and without capital fail to procure employment; and those brought up to mercantile pursuits are equally unsuccessful."

Concerning Queensland, the Australasian colony in which there is most room for the enterprise of settlers able to buy or lease land and stock it for agriculture or pasturage, the following observations are especially worth extracting:—" The colony possesses numerous harbours, of which Moreton Bay is the principal. Anchorage may be found in almost any part of it, under shelter of the numerous shoals. It is about forty miles long north and south by seventeen miles wide, and receives the waters of five navigable rivers, viz., the Arrowsmith, the Logan, the Brisbane, the Pine, and the Cabulture. Most of these rivers have, however, a bar entrance. Besides Moreton Bay, there are Keppel Bay, Hervey's Bay, Port Curtis, Port Bowen, Port Denison, Cleveland Bay, Rockingham Bay, Port Albany (near Cape York), and several other smaller harbours on the eastern sea-board of Queensland. The principal harbour at the head of the Gulf of Carpentaria is at Investigator Road. There are already settlements at or near all the above-named ports. The upland plains and downs of the interior afford excellent cattle and sheep pasturage throughout the year. The agricultural capabilities of Queensland are also great. Wheat, maize, and other cereals, potatoes, cotton, the sugar cane, tobacco, indigo, coffee, rice, and almost all the English and tropical fruits, are successfully cultivated in suitable situations. In the uplands beyond the mountain range the wheat is of the finest quality, sometimes weighing above 60 lbs. to the bushel, and yielding about 30 bushels to the acre. The average yield of maize is 40 bushels, and of potatoes about three tons to the acre. East of the main range of mountains the climate and soil are reported to be peculiarly adapted to the growth of the finest kinds of cotton; and owing to the absence of frosts the plant is perennial, and not an annual, as it is in America. It is estimated that some millions of acres are well suited to the production of cotton. To encourage its cultivation the local legislature have offered a premium in land-orders to the extent of £10 for every bale weighing 300 lbs. of colonial grown clean cotton exported to Great Britain before October 1868. For the succeeding two years the premium is reduced to £5, and half these premiums are payable on the exportation of the common descriptions of cotton. Temporary privileges have also been granted to encourage the cultivation of sugar and coffee. To encourage immigration land-orders are granted to the value of £30 to each adult emigrant direct from Europe who may pay his own passage, or the passage of any member of his family. A land-order of the value of £15 is granted on account of a child between one and twelve years old. Besides its agricultural and pastoral resources, the colony is stated to possess much mineral wealth. Gold has been found in several localities, though no systematic search has yet been made for it; also copper and tin in a very pure state. Coal of good quality is abundant, and is accompanied as usual with iron ores. Provision has also been made by the legislature for promoting education by means of primary and grammar schools, and in the towns ample means exist for public worship for all denominations."

With these observations may be compared some remarks by Mr Brough Smyth upon Victoria, in which, though the best peopled of the Australian colonies, there is ample room for fresh enterprise, especially in agriculture. "It is the most southerly part of the island continent of Australia, and consequently enjoys a comparatively cool climate. Though the country is generally low and level, there is a great range (an extension of the Australian Cordillera) extending from the sources of the River Murray to Wilson's Promontory, the highest peaks of which attain an elevation not far short of 6000 feet; and there is also a great spur running westward at a distance of 40 or 50 miles from the coast, which, in some places, is very high. The ranges running at right angles to the main dividing range are not very lofty. Gipps Land, which lies to the east, and is bounded by the great dividing range on the north and west, and by the sea on the south and south-east, has a cool and rather moist climate. There snow lies on the high lands during a great part of the year,

and cool and refreshing streams flow from the icy reservoirs in
the great range all through the year. The country south of the
great spur, extending westwards from Melbourne to the 141st
meridian, consists of plains broken by schist ranges and
volcanic hills of inconsiderable height. The river basins are
mostly at right angles to the sea, and consequently the sea
breezes penetrate far inland. That part of Victoria north of
the main spur has a warmer climate, and near the Murray the
vine yields a grape as rich and as luscious as can be found in
any part of Europe. The estimated area of the colony is
55,571,840 acres, or 86,831 square miles. In other words,
Victoria is nearly as large as England, Scotland, and Wales
united. It contains, in addition to almost inexhaustible
mineral wealth, fine soils, suitable for wheat, barley, oats,
potatoes, the grape, olive, fig, date, coral tree, sugar, millet,
and tobacco; and in certain favoured situations the tea plant
would grow remarkably well. There are some parts also
suitable for cotton and rice. The mean temperature for the
year, as deduced from a long series of meteorological observations, is 58°. In autumn and winter the northerly winds
exceed the southerly, and in spring and summer the southerly
winds exceed the northerly. In summer the north winds are
dry and often hot, but at night the wind most often changes to
the south-west or south; and from either of these points it is
always cool and refreshing. The climate is indeed delicious.
Probably in no part of the world is it possible to find fewer
impediments to labour or recreation, as regards the weather,
than in Victoria. Though the summer is invariably marked
by a few days of great heat, yet, even in that season, there are
many days when the weather is pleasant and cool, and nothing
can exceed the climate experienced in this colony during the
autumn, winter, and spring. A cloudless sky, a bright sun,
and a refreshing breeze, are characteristic of the greater
number of days in each of those seasons; and while the
salubrity of the climate is shown by the absence of those
diseases which yearly sweep off so many of the inhabitants of
England, it is yet equally favourable to the growth of fruits
and vegetables of colder countries. The apple, pear, peach,
nectarine, apricot, almond, gooseberry, currant, and fig, and
the cabbage, cauliflower, turnip, carrot, parsnip, asparagus, pea,
bean, water melon, rock melon, and tomatoes, may be seen all
growing together luxuriantly, in the same plot of ground;
while the borders blossom with the fuschias, geraniums, and
other common flowers of the English garden. Already the
wines made in Victoria have taken a high place in the estima-
tion of the European connoisseurs, and the cultivation of the

grape will, it is certain, form a source of great wealth. Already large vineyards have been planted, and, while the quality of the wine is such as to command a ready sale at a high price, the yield per acre is large; the average being about 250 gallons per acre. From the nature of her soils, and the favourable character of her climate, it is not too much to say that Victoria will be as remarkable for the growth of wine and oil as for the extraordinary yield of gold."

The quantity of land available for settlement, and its cost in the leading colonies, are shown in the two following tables—

COLONIAL PUBLIC LANDS ALIENATED AND REMAINING FOR ALIENATION AT THE DATE OF THE LAST RETURNS.

Colony.	Amount alienated.	Estimated Amount remaining for Alienation.	Open for Settlement and mostly Surveyed.	Date of Return.
NORTH AMERICAN COLONIES.	*Acres.*	*Acres.*	*Acres.*	
Canada, Upper	71,468,342	56,118,106	} 10,000,000 {	31 Dec. 1845
,, Lower	19,089,357	115,313,448		1858
New Brunswick	7,000,000	9,000,000	500,000	1858
Nova Scotia	5,405,678	5,641,041	55,000	1856
Cape Breton	813,548	1,277,438	777,438	1860
Prince Edward Island	2,432	2,000	1,965	1854
AUSTRALIAN COLONIES.				31 Dec. 1867
New South Wales	9,483,151	159,143,089	159,143,089	
Queensland	957,635	Above 535,000,000	No accurate return.	} 1867
Victoria	9,517,015	46,087,094	5,500,000	30 June 1868
Tasmania	5,763,087	16,014,933	718,255	1868
Western Australia	1,459,348	612,913,220	None.	31 Dec. 1868
South Australia (exclusive of northern territory.)	3,670,204	241,549,704	400,605	1868
New Zealand	2,790,275	Varies, as the Government make from time to time large purchases from the natives.	46,000,000 in Middle Island and 6,000,000 in Northern Island.	} 1860
OTHER COLONIES.				
Cape of Good Hope	57,994,196	61,687,802	Not stated.	1867
Natal	7,446,302	4,352,596	2,476,848	1858
British Guiana	Say 2,000,000	Say 45,000,000	Say 45,000,000	1858

Summary of Modes of Sale, and Prices, in the Principal Land-Selling Colonies.

Colony.	Mode of Sale.	Price per Acre.
North American Colonies—		
Canada (West),	Auction and fixed price.	Certain township lots if sold for cash 2s. 11d. sterling, if on credit, 4s. 2d. per acre. For all other lands upset price 6s. currency, 4s. 2d. sterling.
Canada (East),	Ditto.	According to situation, 10d. to 2s. 6d. sterling.
Nova Scotia,	Fixed price.	1s. 9d. sterling.
New Brunswick,	Fixed price for actual settlement.	£4. 3s. 4d. sterling for 100 acres.
Prince Edward Island,	Auction.	5s. to 70s. according to situation.
Newfoundland,	Auction. Lands not sold after second auction may be bought at the upset price.	Upset price, 2s. currency, 1s. 8d. sterling.
British Columbia,	Auction. Afterwards upset price to be fixed price.	Upset price, for country lands, 4s. 2d. If town lots (66 by 132 feet), upset price £20.
Vancouver Island,	Ditto.	Upset price, 4s. 2d.
Australian Colonies—		
New South Wales,	Auction. Country lands not sold at auction may afterwards be bought at the upset price.	Upset price, £1 sterling.
Queensland,	Ditto do.	Ditto, in "Agricultural Reserves," selected without competition.
South Australia,	Ditto do.	Ditto.
Victoria,	(1) By selection at fixed price. (2) By auction.	£1 lots leased for 7 years at 2s. an acre. Upset price not less than £1 an acre. Prompt payment.

Summary of Modes of Sale, and Prices, in the Principal Land-Selling Colonies—*continued.*

Colony.	Mode of Sale.	Price per Acre.
Australian Colonies *Continued—*		
Western Australia,	Fixed price for agricultural lands. Auction for town, suburban, and mineral.	10s. Upset price for town and suburban to be fixed by Governor, for mineral lands, 20s.
Tasmania,	Auction and private sales at £1 per acre.	Upset price to be fixed by Government not less than 10s. per acre.
New Zealand [Crown lands],	Auction for town and suburban lands. Fixed price generally for country lands.	Fixed price in 4 provinces, 10s. In the remaining 5, from 5s. to 40s.
Other Colonies—		
British Guiana,	Fixed Price.	10 dollars.
Trinidad,	Auction.	Upset price— Arable land, £1. Swamp land, 10s.
Other West India Colonies.	Ditto.	Upset price, £1.
Honduras,	Auction.	Minimum upset price, 20s.
Cape of Good Hope,	Ditto, subject to a quit-rent.	No fixed upset price.
Natal,	Auction.	Upset price, 4s. sterling.
Ceylon,	Ditto.	Upset price to be fixed by Governor, but not to be less than 5s. sterling.

APPENDIX.

The rates of wages and the price of food are, of course, valuable indexes of the value of our colonies as emigration fields. In the spring of 1869 a quartern loaf of bread cost from 4d. to 5d. in Canada, about 6d. in New Brunswick, from 3d. to 4d. in Nova Scotia and Prince Edward's Island, from 1s. to 1s. 6d. in British Columbia and Vancouver Island, about 1s. 2d. in Cape Colony, and 1s. in Natal; from 6d. to 8d. in New South Wales, about 4d. in Victoria, about 8d. in Queensland and South Australia; from 6d. to 8d. in Tasmania, and about 1s. in New Zealand. Beef and mutton cost respectively about 5d. and 6d. in Canada, 3d in New Brunswick, 4d. and 3d. in Nova Scotia, 3d. and 4d. in Prince Edward's Island, 1s. 6d. or 2s. and 1s. in British Columbia and Vancouver Island ; about 4d. and 3½d. in Cape Colony and Natal, 5d. and 3d. in New South Wales, 5d. and 4d. in Victoria, rather less in Queensland and South Australia, and rather more in Tasmania and New Zealand. These, of course, were the prices in the chief towns ; they varied according to circumstances in the country districts, being lower in some parts, and very much higher, sometimes three or four times as high, in the gold districts. The following table shows the principal wages' rates, with similar variations :—

TABLE OF THE PRINCIPAL WAGES' RATES.

(Per day, without board, unless otherwise stated.)

Trade or Calling.	Canadian Dominion.	Cape Colony and Natal.	New South Wales.	Victoria.	Queensland.	South Australia.	Tasmania.	New Zealand.
Bakers	3/ to 2/6‡ or 5/	5/ to 4/	£73 ‡	5/ to 10/	7/ to 10/	5/ to 5/½	5/ to 7/6	5/ to 6/
Blacksmiths	4/ to 6/	5/ to 8/	£50 to £70‡	8/ to 12/	10/ to 11/	7/ to 8/	8/ to 8/	6/ to 8/
Butchers	1/6 to 2/6‡ or 4/ to 4/6	8/ to 4/	£70 to £78‡	5/ to 10/	7/ to 10/	8/ to 6/½	5/ to 7/6	5/ to 6/
Carpenters	6/ to 7/	6/ to 6/	£50 to £70‡	8/ to 10/	8/ to 18/	7/ to 9/	7/ to 8/	6/ to 8/
Coopers	4/ to 6/	6/ to 6/	12/	8/ to 10/	15/	7/6 to 8/	8/	6/ to 8/
Dairywomen	15/ to 20/*‡	...	£30 to £35‡‡	£25 to £30‡	...	3/ to 1/6‡	£20‡‡	£12 to £40‡
Dressmakers & Milliners	2/ to 3/‡	2/ to 3/‡	3/ to 5/‡	3/ to 10/‡	2/ to 4/‡	3/ to 4/‡	£25‡‡	...
Grooms	50/ to 60/*‡	...	£35 to £40‡	£30 to £50‡‡	£40 to £50‡	3/ to 4/‡	£30 to £35‡‡	...
Labourers—								
Agricultural	40/ to 60/*‡	60/ to 80/*‡	£25 to £30‡	£35 to £40‡	8/ to 7/	3/ to 5/	3/ ‡	£50 to £100‡
Common, Town	3/ to 4/	...	6/ to 7/	6/ to 7/	4/ to 5/	4/6 to 5/6	4/ to 5/	6/ to 8/
" Country		6/ to 8/	£20‡‡	2/ to 3/‡	4/ to 6/	6/ to 7/	4/ to 5/	4/ to 6/
Painters and Glaziers	5/ to 7/	5/ to 9/	9/	7/ to 10/	9/ to 12/	7/ to 9/	7/ to 8/	6/ to 9/
Shepherds	60/*	1s.*‡	£30 to £35‡‡	£25 to £35‡‡	£30 to £35‡‡	£25 to £40‡‡	£15 to £40‡‡	£30 to £50‡‡
Servants, Female Domestic	20/ to 25/*‡	10/ to 20/*‡	£20 to £25‡‡	£25 to £30‡‡	£15 to £25‡‡	£20 to £25‡‡	£20‡‡	£15 to £30‡
Tailors	4/ to 6/	6/ to 7/	£3 ‡‡	7/6 to 9/6	5/ to 7/6	7/ to 9/	4/ to 10/	6/ to 10/
Watchmakers & Jewellers	...	...	7/ to 10/	10/ to 14/	...	10/ to 14/	5/ to 6/	8/ to 10/

* Per month. † Per year. ‡ With board and lodging, which in the Australian colonies generally consists of a dwelling, with a weekly allowance of 10 lbs. of meat, 10 lbs. of flour, 2 lbs. of sugar, and 4 oz. of tea.

III.—OUR COLONIAL GOLD-FIELDS.

The following information is taken chiefly from the *Colonization Circular* for 1869:—

1. *Victoria.*—About one-third of the colony, or an area of nearly 30,000 square miles, is supposed to have gold under its surface; but of this area only a tenth has, as yet, been laid open to miners, and less than one three-hundredth, or about 600,000 acres, has been actually opened up. Many of the parts require more elaborate mechanical working and more scientific skill than are possessed by ordinary gold-seekers. The whole colony, with the exception of the immediate vicinity of Melbourne, is divided, for mining purposes, into seven principal districts. "Miners' Rights," or licences, are granted for any number of years not exceeding fifteen, at the rate of £5 a year, and about 600,000 have hitherto been issued. "In each of the seven mining districts there is a legislative body termed a Mining Board. These boards are empowered to make bye-laws, applicable to the district generally, with respect to mining affairs and occupation under business licences. Each of these boards consists of ten members, four of whom retire from each board annually by rotation, when their places are supplied by the election of four others to fill the vacancies, or by the re-election of the retiring members. The members of the mining boards are elected by ballot, and each male holder of a 'Miner's Right' is entitled to a vote. Each district has its separate Court of Mines, which is a Court of Record, and is presided over by a District Judge. One of the judges of the Supreme Court is appointed to act as Chief Judge of the Court of Mines. The Courts of Mines have jurisdiction to hear and determine all suits cognizable by a court of law or by a court of equity which may arise concerning any Crown land claimed under 'Miners' Rights,' leases, or licences, mining partnerships, boundaries, contribution to calls, and generally all questions and disputes which may arise between miners in relation to mining upon Crown lands. The duties of the wardens, of whom one is in each division, are mostly of a judicial character, and they generally act as police magistrates. As wardens they hear and determine all suits cognizable by a court of law, which the Courts of Mines are empowered to hear, and they may proceed summarily to settle

any dispute concerning any Crown land, share, or interest in any claim. The mines of the colony are placed under a Mining Department, whose head has a seat in the Legislative Assembly and in the Cabinet."

The following table shows the divisions and population, in December 1867, of the Victoria gold-fields:—

Mining Districts.	Alluvial Miners.		Quartz Miners.		Total.
	Europeans.	Chinese.	Europeans.	Chinese.	
Ballarat District, including Ballarat, Boninyong, Smythesdale, Creswick, Gordon, Steiglitz, Blackwood, and Blue Mountain (South)	10,684	3,053	2,194	8	16,139
Beechworth District, including Beechworth, Stanley, Yackandanah, Sandy Creek, Indigo, Buckland, Jamieson, Gaffney's Creek, Wood's Point, Big River, and Mitta Mitta	3,580	3,504	2,624	5	9,713
Sandhurst District, including Sandhurst, Kilmore, Heathcote, Wangara (North and South), and Raywood	4,781	1,418	3,693	..	9,897
Maryborough District, including Maryborough, Amherst, Avoca, Dunolly, Tarnagulla, Korong, Redbank, and Saint Arnaud (North and South)	5,464	2,116	1,909	16	9,505
Castlemaine District, including Castlemaine, Fryer's Creek, Hepburn, Taradale, Maldon, St Andrews, Kyneton, and Blue Mountain (North)	4,957	3,324	2,020	19	10,820
Ararat District, including Ararat, Pleasant Creek, Barkly, and Raglan	2,070	1,573	782	..	4,425
Gipps Land District, including Omeo, Mitchell River, Crooked River, Jericho, Donnally's Creek, and Stringer's Creek	1,671	640	743	..	3,054
Total	33,407	15,629	13,970	47	63,053

APPENDIX.

The quantity of gold obtained in Victoria, since its first discovery in 1851, is thus stated:—

Year.	Exported.	Value at 60s. per oz.	Average yearly earnings per man per annum.		
	Ozs.	£	£	s.	d.
1851	145,146	580,584	30	1	7·60
1852	2,218,782	8,875,128	303	11	8·66
1853	2,676,345	10,705,380	202	15	0·81
1854	2,150,730	8,602,920	130	16	4·08
1855	2,751,538	11,006,140	100	7	2·75
1856	2,985,991	11,943,964	103	11	0
1857	2,762,460	11,049,840	83	7	9·59
1858	2,528,478	10,118,912	63	12	3·59
1859	2,280,050	9,128,800	72	10	11·27
1860	2,156,660	8,626,640	70	9	8
1861	1,967,420	7,869,680	74	15	11
1862	1,658,207	6,633,878	67	14	5·11
1863	1,620,572	6,507,488	70	8	0·42
1864	1,544,694	6,178,776	74	1	9·29
1865	1,543,801	6,175,204	74	4	2·09
1866	1,479,194	5,916,776	80	8	8
1867	1,433,697	5,734,748	57	1	7
	33,910,952	135,643,808	—		

The average earnings from 1851 to 1858 are, in the estimate, calculated for the entire population of the gold-fields. Since 1859 they are reckoned only for those actually engaged in gold-mining. This statement is very noteworthy, as showing that, though some fortunate persons are greatly enriched by the pursuit, ordinary adventurers cannot count upon obtaining as much remuneration as is procured by farm servants and town labourers, and this under conditions that add considerably to the cost of food and all the necessaries of life. In 1868, however, the average yield per head (£104, 18s. 8d.) was higher than in previous years.

2. *New South Wales.*—In this colony the annual charge for a gold-mining licence is 10s. Its principal gold-fields, nearly all alluvial, are (1) Ophir or Summerhill Creek, about forty miles long, with its tributaries Lewis Ponds Creek and Emu Swamp Creek, each about fifteen miles long, in the county of Roxburgh; (2) Turon River, fifty miles long, with several tributaries; (3) Meroo River, about forty miles long, with Louisa Creek for its chief tributary, connected with a wide extent of country, especially rich in auriferous deposits; (4) Tamboroura Creek, twenty miles long; (5) Lachlan gold-

field, near the river of that name; (6) Abercrombie River, sixty miles long, emptying into the Lachlan; (7) Cudgegong River, also near the Lachlan; (8) Arauen River and its tributaries, stretching up to the Buffalo Range; (9) Murrumbidgee and Adelong; (10) Burrangong and other rich gold-fields in the south; (11) Liverpool Plains, Hanging Rock, and Peel River, in the north; (12) New England, also in the northern district.

The following are the details of the New South Wales gold exports, the exact produce not having been recorded:—

Year.	Quantity exported.	Value.	Year.	Quantity exported.	Value.
	oz.	£	Bt. forwd.	2,944,268	10,647,036
1851	144,120	489,336	1860	483,012	1,876,043
1852	902,873	3,600,175	1861	488,293	1,889,208
1853	648,052	1,781,171	1862	609,568	2,715,037
1854	237,910	773,209	1863	605,722	2,361,049
1855	64,284	209,250	1864	721,777	2,951,671
1856	42,463	138,007	1865	682,521	2,647,663
1857	253,564	848,850	1866	742,270	2,924,891
1858	254,907	994,060	1867	461,775	2,170,175
1859	435,095	1,608,078	1868*	1,333,747	11,299,880
Forward,	2,944,268	10,047,036	Total	8,162,451	31,483,254

*The first nine months only.

3. *Queensland.*—Several important gold-fields have been discovered, the first great impetus resulting from the finding of a nugget, which weighed nearly a hundredweight, at Gympie Creek, in September 1867. Other fields now being worked are at Cape River, Boulderscome, Moriniah, Rosewood, Calliope, Ridgelands, Crocodile and Canal Creek. The total yield in 1868 was 166,000 ounces, worth £664,000.

4. *New Zealand.*—This colony is second only to Victoria in wealth of gold. The Otago gold-fields of Tuapeka, Mount Benger, Dunstan, Wakatipu, Wokomai, and Mount Ida, supposed to cover in all an area of two and a half million acres, yielded, up to the end of September 1868, £9,036,750. Those in Westland are next in value, their yield to the same period being worth £4,293,832. The gold obtained from Nelson before the same date amounted to £2,674,202, that from Auckland to £180,209, that from Marlborough to £131,458, and that from Southland to £88,132. The recent discovery of the Thames gold-field in Auckland promises to vastly increase the importance of that province as an auriferous district.

5. *British Columbia and Vancouver Island.*—Gold was found in the former of these colonies in 1850, though with slight result till the opening of the Big Bend field in the summer of 1865. The auriferous value of Vancouver Island was proved by the opening of the Locke mines, eighteen miles from Victoria, in 1864. The British North American gold-fields, however, are by no means so extensive or useful as the Australasian.

INDEX.

ABERCROMBIE, Sir Ralph, Canada invaded by, 93.
Acadie, or New France. *See* Canada and Nova Scotia.
Adelaide River, North Australia, 315, 316.
Adelaide, South Australia, 260, 261, 265, 267, 269, 272, 308.
Africa, Colonies in Western, 153, 154.
Albany, Western Australia, 302, 304.
Alexander, Sir William, Nova Scotia granted to (1621), 85, 97.
Antigua, its colonization and history, 55, 56.
Arthur, Sir George, first governor of Tasmania, 235, 238.
Auckland, New Zealand, 344, 347, 355, 357.
Australia, 198-232, 243-322, 864-366.
Australia Felix, 230, 245, 308.
Australia, South. *See* South Australia.
Australia, Western. *See* Western Australia.
Australian Aborigines, 199, 203-205, 280-282, 304, 309-312, 314, 319, 328.
Aysone, Sir George, his invasion and capture of Barbados in 1651 and 1652, 22-24.

BACON, Lord, on colonization, 368.
Bahamas, the, first visited by Columbus, 15; their colonization by the English, and present condition, 54.
Baird, Sir David, in Cape Colony, 160.
Ballarat Gold-Fields, Victoria, 279, 281, 284, 285-287, 290, 291.
Barbados, discovered by the Portuguese, 19; robbed of its Indian inhabitants by the Spaniards, 19, 20; visited by the English in 1605 and 1625, 20; colonized by Sir William Courteen in 1625, 20; its early troubles, 21; made a Royalist stronghold by Lord Willonghby of Parham in 1650, 22, 23; conquered for the Commonwealth by Sir George Aysone in 1652, 22-24; furnished with white slaves from England in 1657 and other years, 24, 25; its prosperity in the middle of the seventeenth century, 22, 25, 26; Lord Willoughby's second government, 26; its later progress, 26-28; its slave-laws, 27; its present condition, 60.
Barker, Captain, the Australian explorer, 261.
Bass, the Australian discoverer, 214, 215, 234, 243.
Bass's Straits, 215, 243.
Bathurst, Australia, 217, 278, 290, 291, 305.

Batman, John, his early settlement in Victoria, 215, 216, 218
Bay of Islands, the, New Zealand, 324, 338, 344, 351.
Bendigo Gold-Fields, Victoria, 279, 281, 291.
Bermudas, the; their discovery and colonization, 53; their progress and present condition, 54.
Blaxland, the Australian explorer, 305.
Bligh, Captain, governor of New South Wales, 213.
Borneo, Sir James Brooke's rule in, 194-197.
Botany Bay, 203, 205, 206, 209, 211.
Bourke, Sir Richard, governor of New South Wales, 227, 228, 249, 250, 332.
Bowen, Sir George, governor of Queensland, 296.
Boyd, massacre of the crew of the, in New Zealand, 324-326.
Bradford, Canada West, 126.
Brazil, the fabled Island of, 1-3.
Brisbane, Sir Thomas, governor of New South Wales, 219, 226.
Brisbane, Queensland, 292, 295, 296.
Bristol, early voyages of exploration from, 1, 3-7.
British Columbia, its early history, 136; its establishment as a colony (1857), 137, 148; its gold and other wealth, 137, 148, 151, 152; its union with Vancouver Island, 137; its present condition and resources, 385, 386.
British Guiana, its history and present condition, 57, 58.
Brooke, Rajah, in Borneo, 194-197.
Bruce, George, the first English resident in New Zealand, 324.
Buccaneers, the, of the West Indies, 32-40, 44.
Buckley, his adventures among the natives of Victoria, 246, 249.
Burke, Robert O'Hara, the Australian explorer, 317-320.
Burra Burra Copper Mines, South Australia, 266, 267, 271.
Bushrangers, in Australia, 220, 228; in Tasmania, 235-237.

Cabot's discovery of America, 4-6, 68.
Calvert, Sir George, his colonization of Newfoundland, 70.
Cameron, General, in New Zealand, 357, 358.
Canada, discovered by Jacques Cartier (1534), 82; colonized by the French (1608), 83, 84; Champlain's government (1608-1635), 84-86; conquered by Sir David Kirk in 1629, and restored to France in 1633, 86; early history of, 87-89; its condition in the 18th century, 90-91; wars with America and England, 91-96; conquered by the English (1759), 93-96; its early condition as an English colony, 106, 107, 109; its first war with the United States (1775-1776), 107-109; the relations of its French and English inhabitants, 109-113; political disputes, 113-116; formation of the provinces of Upper and Lower Canada (1791), 115; the "Reign of Terror" (1807-1811), 116; its second war with the United States (1812-1814), 116-119; further political troubles, 119-121; insurrections in Upper Canada (1837-1838), 121-124; the Earl of Durham's visit to the colony (1838), 123; Mr Charles Poulett Thomson's and Sir Charles Metcalf's administrations, 124; union of the two provinces (1839), 124; the

INDEX. 403

Canadian Confederation (1867), 125, 188, 189; its purchase of the Hudson's Bay Territory, 128; growth of population, 115; development of the principal towns, 125-127, 147; its natural features and resources, 144-149; its value as an emigration field, 383, 384.
Canterbury, New Zealand, 344, 347.
Cape Breton, colonized by the French, 91; captured by the English in 1745, and restored to the French in 1748, 91; re-captured by the English in 1758, 93, 100; its later history, 101; its present condition and resources, 141, 142.
Cape Colony, its history under the Dutch, 150-160; its annexation by England (1795-1815), 160, 161; the first Kaffir war (1811), 162-165; the origin of Graham's Town, 165; the Dutch Insurrection (1815), 167; the second Kaffir war (1818), 166, 167; the third Kaffir war (1834-1836), 167-170; the fourth Kaffir war (1846-1852), 171, 172; the progress of the colony, 170, 173; its condition and resources, 173, 174, 387.
Cape Coast Castle, 153, 154.
Cape Town, 160, 172.
Carey, General, in New Zealand, 357-359.
Carlisle, the Earls of, owners of Barbados, 20-22.
Carpentaria, the Gulf of, 294, 318, 321.
Cartier, Jacques, discovery of Canada by, in 1534, 81.
Cathay, the fabled riches of, 1-3.
Ceylon, its ancient prosperity, 187, 188; its Portuguese and Dutch occupation, 188; its conquest by the English, 188; its present condition and resources, 188-191.
Champlain, Samuel, his colonization and government of Canada, 82-86.
Charlotte-town, Prince Edward's Island, 141.
Clarke, Dr., discovery of gold in Australia by, 278.
Coal in Cape Breton and Nova Scotia, 141-142; in British Columbia and Vancouver Island, 148; in Queensland, 298; in New South Wales, 297, 298.
Cod-fisheries, Newfoundland, 68-80.
Collins, Captain, his attempted settlement in Port Phillip, 244.
Collins, Colonel, in Cape Colony, 162.
Colombo, 188.
Columbus, his discovery of America, 2, 4, 15; his exile in Jamaica, 20, 32.
Convicts in New South Wales, 208-214, 216, 220, 224-226, 228; in Tasmania, 234-240; in Western Australia, 303, 304.
Cook, Captain, his visits to New Zealand and Australia, 200-206, 208, 292.
Cooper's Creek, Australia, 317, 318, 319.
Copper, South Australian, 265-267, 271, 272.
Corn: British North American, 147; South African, 173, 182; South Australian, 271.
Cotton, Jamaica, 43; Queensland, 296, 389.
Courteen, Sir William, his colonization of Barbados, 20.
Cunningham, Allan, explorations in Australia by, 306.

INDEX.

Dampier, William, as a buccaneer, 89, 199; his visits to Australia, 199, 200.
Darling Downs, Australia, 292, 294, 806.
Darling River, Australia, 229, 245, 271, 306.
Darling, Sir Ralph, governor of New South Wales, 226.
Darwin, Mr Charles, in New Zealand, 334.
Derby, the Earl of, on New Zealand warfare, 350.
Dorado, El, 57, 58.
D'Oyley, Colonel, governor of Jamaica, 37-39.
Drake, Sir Francis, his piracies and public warfare against Spain in the West Indies and elsewhere, 9, 18, 19, 32; his visit to the site of British Columbia, 136.
Dundonald, the Earl of, his visit to Trinidad, 59, 60.
D'Urban, Natal, 180.
D'Urban, Sir Benjamin, governor of Cape Colony, 167.
Durham, the Earl of, in Canada, 109-113, 122-124.
Dyaks, the, of Borneo, 194-197.

Emancipists in Australia, 214, 220-222, 302.
Emigration-fields, British, 377-380, 382-395.
Entry Island, New Zealand, 331, 332.
Erie, Fort, 118, 119.
Esquimault, Vancouver Island, 151.
Evans, the Australian explorer, 305.
Eyre, Sir Edward, the Australian explorer, 308-318; his services in New Zealand, 345.
Eyre, Lake, Australia, 321, 322.

Fairwell, Lieutenant, his settlement in Natal, 178, 179.
Falkland, Lord, his share in colonizing Newfoundland, 70.
Fawkner, John Pascoe, his early settlement in Victoria, 245, 246, 257.
Fisheries, Newfoundland, 68-80.
Flinders, Captain, the Australian discoverer, 214-216, 234, 243.
Food, price of, in the principal colonies, 394.
Franklin, Sir John, governor of Tasmania, 232.
Freemantle, Western Australia, 302.
Free Town, Sierra Leone, 154.
Furs, Canadian, 87, 89, 92, 130, 134.

Gambia, 154, 155.
Gardiner, Captain Allen, in Natal, 179, 180.
Gawler, Colonel, governor of South Australia, 263, 264.
Geelong, Victoria, 249, 257, 284.
George Town, British Guiana, 58.
George Town, Tasmania, 234, 238.
Gilbert, Sir Humphrey, his attempted colonization of Newfoundland, 7, 69.
Gipps, Sir George, governor of New South Wales, 250.
Glenelg, Lord, on the Kaffir wars, 168, 169.
Gold Coast, 158-165.

INDEX. 405

Gold Mines of California, 137; of British Columbia, 187, 151, 152, 386, 400; of Cape Colony, 173; of New South Wales, 277, 278, 290-292, 308, 399; of Victoria, 278-282 285-287, 306-308; of Queensland, 389, 399 ; of New Zealand, 347, 399.
Graham, Colonel, in Cape Colony, 162-165.
Graham's Town, 165, 168, 173.
Gregory, A., the Australian explorer, 320.
Grey, Sir George, governor of South Australia, 264, 265; his explorations in West Australia, 308; his services as governor of New Zealand, 345, 352.
Guiana, 57, 58.

Habitans, the French, in Canada, 110-113, 116.
Hamilton, Canada West, 125, 126, 147.
Hargreaves, Mr E. H., gold discovered in Australia by, 278.
Hawkins, Sir John, his slave-trading expeditions to the African coast and the West Indies, 16-19.
Head, Sir Francis, governor of Canada, 122.
Helpman, Lieutenant, the Australian explorer, 315.
Henty, Thomas, his early settlement in Victoria, 244, 245.
Heredia Godinho de, his discovery of Australia, 198.
Hindmarsh, Sir John, first governor of South Australia, 262, 263.
Hobarton, Tasmania, 234.
Hobson, Captain, the first governor of New Zealand, 341-343, 345.
Hong Kong, 192, 193.
Hottentots, the, 156-161, 166, 167, 170.
Hovell, the Australian explorer, 306.
Howitt, Alfred William, the Australian explorer, 320.
Hudson, Henry, in America, 60, 128.
Hudson's Bay Company, the, 128-187.
Hudson's Bay Territory, the, its extent and character, 128, 129, 148; early settlements and trade in, 131-134, 144; its Indian natives, 135, 136; its surrender to Canada, 152.
Hughes, Captain, in South Australia, 271, 272.
Hume, Hamilton, the Australian explorer, 306.

India, British, its history and commerce, 7, 184-186; its value as an emigration-field, 376, 388.
Indians, North American, their early relations with the French and English, 61, 87-89, 92.
Ipswich, Queensland, 205.

Jamaica, discovered by Columbus in 1494, 29; his residence in it, 29, 30; captured and almost depopulated by the Spaniards, 30, 31; first visited by the English (1605), 31; captured for Cromwell by General Venables (1655), 81, 86; its first English colonists, 81; its connection with the Buccaneers, 82-40, 44; its progress in the 17th century, 89, 40; its losses by earthquakes and hurricane in 1692 and 1698, 40-42; its commercial importance in 1728, 43, 44; its progress in the 18th century,

11, 13; its condition as a slave colony, 45-51, 65; the insurrection of 1760, 47, 49; the Consolidated Slave Act of 1792, 49; the insurrection of 1832, 50, 51; the abolition of slavery in 1834, 52; its natural beauties and resources, 60, 63; its degradation and its causes, 64-66; the chances of its amelioration. 66, 67.
Jay, John, " the younger," his voyage in search of Cathay, 4.

Kaffirs, the, in South Africa, 161-178, 175-180.
Kapunda Copper Mines, South Australia, 265, 266.
King, Captain, his account of South Australia, 260.
Kingston, Canada, 140, 147.
Kingston, Jamaica, 64, 65.
Kirk, Sir David, his share in colonizing Newfoundland, 70; his invasion of Canada, 86.
Kororarika, New Zealand, 338, 344, 851.

Labrador, 5, 6, 139.
Labuan, 197.
Lachlan River, Australia, 217, 306.
Lagos, 155.
Landesborough, William, the Australian explorer, 320.
Lane, Sir Ralph, the first governor of Virginia, 7.
Launceston, Tasmania, 238.
Lawson, the Australian explorer, 305.
Leichhardt, Dr, the Australian explorer, 294, 318.
London, Canada West, 126, 147.
Lushington, Lieutenant, the Australian explorer, 306.

Macarthur, John, " the father of New South Wales," 213, 214, 222, 223.
Macartney, the Earl of, in Cape Colony, 160.
M'Donald, Sir Richard, governor of South Australia, 270, 271.
M'Kinlay, John, the Australian explorer, 320.
M'Leay, Alexander, in South Wales, 253, 254.
M'Nab, Lieutenant-Colonel, his suppression of the Toronto insurrection in 1837, 122.
Macquarie, General, governor of New South Wales, 213, 214, 217, 219.
Macquarie River, 217, 300.
Malabars, the, of Ceylon, 190.
Malacca, 191.
Manoa, the Golden City of, 57.
Maoris, the, of New Zealand, 200-202, 324-363.
Marlborough, the Earl of, first owner of Barbados, 20.
Marlborough, New Zealand, 844.
Maroons, the, of Jamaica, 81, 82, 40, 45-47.
Marsden, Mr, and later missionaries in New Zealand, 327, 328, 334, 335, 339, 346, 348, 851, 352, 353, 362.
May, Henry, his visit to the Bahamas, 53.
Melbourne, 219, 248, 249, 256, 257, 258, 278, 280, 281, 282-284.

Metcalf, Sir Charles, governor of Canada, 124.
Mississippi, French and English quarrels concerning the, 88, 89, 91.
Mitchell, Sir Thomas, the Australian explorer, 230, 245, 246, 294, 303.
Montmorency Falls, Canada, 145.
Montreal, 82, 83, 87, 90, 96, 107-109, 112, 118, 127, 145, 146, 147.
Moonta Copper Mines, South Australia, 271.
Moors, the, of Ceylon, 190.
Moreton Bay, Queensland, 292-294.
Morgan, Sir Henry, the buccaneer, 37-39.
Mount Alexander Gold Fields, Victoria, 273.
Murchison, Sir Roderick, the gold discoveries in Australia anticipated by, 278.
Murray, Lieutenant, his discovery of Port Phillip, 243.
Murray River, Australia, 230, 245, 271, 306-308.
Murrumbidgee River, Australia, 234, 256, 306.

Napier, New Zealand, 344.
Natal, its early history and Kaffir inhabitants, 175-177; Dutch intercourse with it, 177, 178; its colonization by Lieutenant Fairwell (1828), 178, 179; its second colonization (1835), 179; its later history, 180; its present condition and resources, 181-183, 387.
Nelson, New Zealand, 344.
New Brunswick, its early history, 100; its progress, 101-104; its present condition and resources, 143, 144; its value as an emigration field, 384, 385.
Newcastle, New Brunswick, fire at, in 1825, 102-104.
Newcastle Coal-Field, New South Wales, 202.
Newfoundland, discovered by John Cabot in 1497, 5, 68; early fishing expeditions to, 6, 68, 69; Sir Humphrey Gilbert's attempted colonization of, in 1583, 7, 69; the first regular settlements in, 69, 70; the quarrels between the fishers and the colonists, 71, 72; French and English struggles for possession of the island, 72-75; its progress since 1715, 75-77; the cod-fisheries, 76, 78-80; seal-hunting, 77, 78.
New South Wales, Captain Cook's visits to the site of the colony, 205-206; its appropriation as a convict settlement, 208; the first planting of convicts at Port Jackson under Captain Phillip (1787-1792), 209, 210; its convict population, 210-212; its early governors, 211, 213; General Macquarie's government, (1810-1821), 213, 214, 218; progress of the colony from 1787 to 1821, 209, 213, 217, 218, 219; from 1821 to 1839, 220, 223, 226, 229; Sir Thomas Brisbane's government (1822-1825), 219, 226; its bush-rangers, 220; its reformed convicts, 220-222; John Macarthur and the wool-trade, 218, 228; its free and convict population in 1829, 224-226; Sir Ralph Darling's government (1826-1831), 226; political reforms, 226, 227; Sir Richard Bourke's government (1831-1838), 227, 228, 250; Sir George Gipps's government, 250; squatters in, 251-256; its progress from 1839 to 1851, 256; its political re-organization, 250;

Sydney in 1846, 258, 259; progress of the colony after the separation of Victoria from it, 289, 290; the gold discoveries, 277, 278; their effect, 277, 290-292; the establishment of Queensland as an independent colony, 292, 293; later progress of New South Wales, 297; its coal, 297; condition and prospects of the colony, 298, 366.

New Westminster, British Columbia, 151.

New Zealand, its early inhabitants, 323; Captain Cook's visits, 200-202, 206; early English intercourse with it, 324; the massacre of the crew of the *Boyd* (1809), 325-327; missionary work in it, 327, 328, 333-335, 346; the first traders and their influences, 327, 328-333; the character of the Maoris, 335-337; the beginning of English colonisation, 338; the New Zealand Company, 339, 340, 342, 343, 344; establishment of the colony (1839, 1840), 339-342; Captain Hobson's rule as first governor (1840-1842), 341-345; growth of the white population, 843, 344, 347; the nine provinces of New Zealand, 344, 345; its commercial progress, 347; the gradual displacement of its Maori inhabitants, 346, 348-350, 853; Colonel Wakefield's aggression in 1843 and its consequences, 350-352; Sir George Grey's government, 345, 352, 353; rise of the King-movement, 353-356; the disturbances of 1860, 358; warfare between 1862 and 1869, 355-360; the Hau-Hau superstition, 360-362; the dying out of the Maoris, 362, 363; its present condition and prospects, 363, 367.

Niagara, 90, 117, 146.
Nicholson, General, first governor of Nova Scotia, 97.
Norfolk Island, 233.
North Australia, 315-317, 366.
Nova Scotia, colonised by the French (1604), 82, 83, 97; conquered by the English (1614), 85, 97; retaken by the French (1667), 97; finally transferred to the English (1713), 89, 97; its early French inhabitants—their expulsion in 1755 and return, 97-100; its progress as an English colony, 100, 101; its present condition and resources, 141-143, 385.

Osborne, Captain Henry, first governor of Newfoundland, 75.
Otago, New Zealand, 344, 347.
Ottawa, Canada West, 127, 147.
Oxley, the Australian explorer, 217, 292, 306.

Parametta, New South Wales, 217.
Penang, 101.
Perth, Western Australia, 302.
Phillip, Captain Arthur, first Governor of New South Wales, 209, 210, 214.
Pitch Lake of Trinidad, 59.
Port Elizabeth, 171, 173.
Port Essington, 313.
Port Jackson, 209, 217, 219, 298.

INDEX.   409

Port Macquarie, 219.
Port Natal, 176, 180.
Port Phillip, 216, 219, 243, 306.
Port Phillip District. *See* Victoria, Australia.
Port Royal, Jamaica, a buccaneer haunt in the 17th century, 37, 39, 40; destroyed by an earthquake in 1692, 40-42, 64.
Portland Bay, Victoria, 245.
Prince Edward's Island, its history, 105; its present condition, 140, 141.

Quebec, 82, 83, 85, 86, 90, 93-96, 106, 108, 112, 127, 145, 147.
Queensland, Its early exploration, 292-294; Its separation from New South Wales and establishment as a separate colony, (1859) 295; Its progress and prospects, 295, 296, 297, 360, 387-389.

Raffles, Sir Stamford, capture of Singapore by, 191.
Raleigh, Sir Walter, his attempted colonization of Virginia, 7, 8; and his expeditions to Guiana, 57, 58.
Red River Settlement, the, 136, 148.
Ristigouche River, New Brunswick, 144.
Rockhampton, Queensland, 296.

Sable Island, North America, 82.
Saint Christopher, or St Kitts, first colonized by the English, 20, 21.
Saint George's Sound, Australia, 302.
Saint Lawrence, Gulf and River of, 81, 82, 87, 90, 107, 139, 144-146.
Sandhurst, Victoria, 284.
Sarāwak, 195, 196.
Saskatchewan, the site for a new colony, 148.
Seal-hunting, Newfoundland, 77, 78.
Selwyn, Bishop, in New Zealand, 351.
Shirley, Sir Anthony, his visit to Jamaica, 31.
Sierra Leone, 153-155.
Singapore, 191, 192.
Singhalese, the, 189.
Slaves, African, in Barbados, 25, 27, 28; in Jamaica, 31, 39, 40, 44-52, 65; in Antigua, 55; in Cape Colony, 158-161, 170, 171.
Slaves, Caribbean, in the West Indies, 19, 20, 29, 30.
Slaves, English, in Barbados, 24, 25.
Smith, Sir Harry, in Cape Colony, 168, 169, 171, 172.
Somers, Sir George, his visits to the Bermudas, 53.
Somerset, Lord Charles, governor of Cape Colony, 165.
South Australia, its discovery, 260, 261; its colonization on the Wakefield scheme (1836) 261, 262; its first governors, Captain Hindmarsh and Colonel Gawler, and its early troubles (1836-1841), 262-264; its improved condition under Captain Grey (1841-1845), 264-266; and Sir Henry Young (1848-1854), 267-270; its copper and lead mines, 265-267, 271, 272; effects of the gold discoveries, 267-270; its progress under Sir Richard M'Donald (1853-1862), 270, 271; its wool trade, 265, 272; its

wheat trade, 265, 273; its wine trade, 273, 274; its present condition, 274, 275, 366.
Southland, New Zealand, 344.
Spanish Town, Jamaica, 89.
Squatters, Australian, 252-256.
Stuart, John M'Douall, the Australian explorer, 813-318.
Sturt, Captain, the Australian explorer, 229, 260, 261, 300-308, 313, 314.
Stockenstrom, Mr, in Cape Colony, 163, 164.
Straits Settlements, the, 191, 192.
Strzelecki, Count, his discovery of gold in Australia, 277.
Sugar, Jamaica, 48.
Swan River, Western Australia, 299-302.
Sydney, New South Wales, 209, 213, 217, 218, 224-226, 244, 258, 259, 289, 291, 298, 305.

TABANARI, New Zealand, 344, 355, 356, 357.
Tasmania, its discovery, 193; Captain Cook's visit to it, 208; its insularity proved by Bass and Flinders, 215; its adoption and early progress as a convict settlement, 234, 235; its bushrangers, 235-238; its reformation and growth, 238, 240; its governors—Sir George Arthur, 235-238; Sir John Franklin. 239; its progress and present condition, 240-242, 367, 388.
Te Ranga, New Zealand, 359.
Thomson, Mr Charles Poulett, governor of Canada, 124.
Timber, British North American, 140-142, 144-147.
Toronto, 118, 122, 125, 126, 146, 147.
Torrens, Lake, Australia, 309, 314, 321, 322.
Trinidad, its history and present condition, 56-60.
Tufton, Sir William, governor of Barbados, 21.

UNITED STATES OF AMERICA, the, their commencement and early history, 7, 8, 10-13; their Canadian wars, 91-90, 107-109, 116-119.

VANCOUVER ISLAND, its early history, 136, 137; its formation as a colony (1849), 137, 149; its union with British Columbia (1866), 137; its condition and resources, 148-152, 385.
Van Dieman's Land. See Tasmania.
Vaughan, Lord John, governor of Jamaica, 89.
Veddas, the, of Ceylon, 189.
Venables, General, conquest of Jamaica by, in 1655, 81, 86.
Verazzano, Giovanni, exploration of North America by, 61.
Victoria, or the Port Phillip District, Australia, its discovery, 243; its colonization attempted (1803), and early settlements in, 244, 245; Mitchell's visits to, 230, 243, 246; William Buckley's wanderings in, 246-248; its formal occupation under Sir Richard Bourke, 249; its early progress as a province of New South Wales, 249-251, 256, 257; Melbourne in 1836, 257, 258; its establishment as an independent colony (1851), 276, 277; the gold discoveries, 278, 279; their effects on the colony, 279-282;

its recent progress, 282, 283; the growth of Melbourne, 283, 284; the Ballarat outbreak (1854), 285-287; political changes in Victoria, 287, 288; its present condition, 366, 387, 889, 390.
Victoria, Hong Kong, 192, 193.
Victoria, Vancouver Island, 148, 150, 151.
Victoria Lake, South Australia, 260, 261.
Victoria River, North Australia, 294.

Wages, rates of, in the principal colonies, 395.
Waikato, New Zealand, 357-359.
Waimati, New Zealand, 334.
Waitara, New Zealand, 355, 356.
Wakefield, Colonel, in New Zealand, 339, 350.
Wakefield Scheme of Colonization, the, in South Australia, 261-264; in New Zealand, 339, 340, 342, 343, 344.
Walker, Frederick, the Australian explorer, 320.
Wallaroo Copper Mines, South Australia, 271, 272.
Wangaroa, New Zealand, 325, 326, 328.
Warner, Sir Thomas, colonizer of Antigua, 55.
Wellington, New Zealand, 344.
Wentworth, the Australian explorer, 305.
West Indies, our colonies in the, 15-67. (*See names of Islands.*)
Western Australia, its early explorations, 229; its unfortunate colonization (1829-1832), 300-302; its subsequent progress, 302-305; its convicts, 303, 304; its present condition, 365.
Willoughby of Parham, Lord, governor of Barbados, 22-26; his reconquest of Antigua, 55.
Wills, William John, the Australian explorer, 317-320.
Wolfe, General James, his capture of Cape Breton, 93; his siege of Quebec and death, 98-99.
Wool, South African, 173, 181; Australian, 213, 217, 223, 224, 229, 252-256, 265, 272, 295; New Zealand, 347.

Yorke's Peninsula, South Australia, 271, 272.
Young, Sir Henry, governor of South Australia, 270.

Commercial Printing Company, Edinburgh.

NEW BOOKS.

"Mit Gott für König und Vaterland."

BISMARCK'S BOOK.

In one vol., large 8vo, 16s.,

THE LIFE OF COUNT BISMARCK:
PRIVATE AND POLITICAL.
WITH DESCRIPTIVE NOTICES OF HIS ANCESTRY.

By DR GEORGE HESEKIEL.

Translated by KENNETH R. H. MACKENZIE, F.R.A., F.A.S.I.,

Translator of "Lepsius's Letters from Egypt," and Co-Translator of "Humboldt's Correspondence with Varnhagen von Ense," &c.

WITH UPWARDS OF

One Hundred Illustrations by DIEZ, GRIMM, PIETSCH, *and others.*

PRELIMINARY ANNOUNCEMENT.

This work contains a complete and trustworthy account of the personal and political career of Count Otto von Bismarck, the distinguished Premier of Prussia. It has been carefully prepared from authentic documents by Dr George Hesekiel, the well-known German author, and is profusely illustrated by eminent German artists.

In its English form, the translator has endeavoured to preserve the spirit of the German original, and render it an acceptable and standard historical work. Some notes of an explanatory character have also been added where it appeared advisable, with notices of the principal noble families whose members were coadjutors or opponents of Bismarck. The arrangement of the work comprises an account of Schönhausen, the birth-place and family mansion of Count Bismarck. In the second part, an historical sketch of his ancestry is presented, together with a description of the armorial bearings of the family. Then follows the history of his early youth and education, with the commencement of his political life at Frankfurt and Paris. The later portions of the work contain his political and private correspondence—almost forming an autobiography—and refer to those measures which have rendered him so celebrated throughout the European continent. The stirring events of the Danish and Austrian campaigns, culminating in so remarkable a triumph for Prussia and North Germany, will be found in the concluding part.

Dr Hesekiel has approached the subject with a spirit of candour, mingled with due admiration for the acts of this remarkable man.

In fcap. 8vo, cloth, price 2s. 6d.,

A HANDY BOOK OF REFERENCE AND QUOTATION.

MOTTOES AND APHORISMS FROM SHAKESPERE.

A Selection of nearly TWO THOUSAND SEVEN HUNDRED Mottoes and Aphorisms from Shakespere, with a copious Index of upwards of NINE THOUSAND References to words and ideas. The whole is numbered and arranged alphabetically, so that any word or idea can be traced at once, and the correct quotation (with the name of the play, act, and scene) given without going further. This is not simply a key to Shakespere, but a book which it is believed will be found generally useful for quotation and reference.

LONDON: JAMES HOGG & SON, York Street, Covent Garden, W.C.

In fcap. 8vo, cloth, price 2s. 6d.,

THE RULES OF RHYME:
A GUIDE TO VERSIFICATION.
WITH A COMPENDIOUS DICTIONARY OF RHYMES.

By TOM HOOD.

This guide to English Versification will give the strict rules and correct rhymes for that style of composition, touching upon the peculiar requisites of song-writing, and the necessities of comic and burlesque verse. The Dictionary of Rhymes will distinguish between such words as are admissible in serious verse; such as, being archaic and Shakesperean, will be only available for exceptional use; and those which will simply answer the purpose of comic verse. Classical measures will be examined, with a view to their adaptability to English verse, taking into consideration the relations of quantity and accent.

In one vol., crown 8vo,

THE NATURAL HISTORY ANECDOTE-BOOK:
ILLUSTRATIVE OF
INSTINCT AND SAGACITY IN THE ANIMATED KINGDOM.

With numerous Woodcuts of Animals, Birds, Insects, Reptiles, &c.

In this book will be found a most varied and interesting collection of Anecdotes in Natural History—perhaps the most comprehensive collection ever drawn together. Besides affording instructive, and in many instances humorous, reading on one of the most pleasant subjects to which the attention of both old and young can be profitably directed, the aim has been to show how much less within the power of all—in a way and in quarters not generally thought of—to shed abroad the cheering influences which sympathy and kind, acts cannot fail to impart. In no better way, it was considered, could this be effected than by drawing together well-authenticated instances of the Remarkable Habits, the Natural Peculiarities, and the Mysterious Existences, traceable in greater or lesser degrees through all classes of Animal Creation.

THE SHORT OR EASY WORD SERIES.
Demy square 16mo,
THE SWALLOWS OF LEIGH FARM:
A STORY FOR CHILDREN.
By the Editor of "The Book of Children's Hymns and Rhymes."
WITH TWELVE ILLUSTRATIONS.

PICCIOLA;
Or, The Prison Flower, and the Lessons it Taught.
By the Rev. F. W. BOUVERIE,
Author of "Short Stories for Short People," &c.
WITH ILLUSTRATIONS.
Others of this Series in preparation.

LONDON: JAMES HOGG & SON, York St., Covent Garden, W.C.

New Work by the Rev. Prebendary Jackson.

CURIOSITIES OF THE PULPIT AND PULPIT LITERATURE:

Memorabilia, Anecdotes, &c., of celebrated Preachers from the Fourth Century of the Christian Era to the present time.

BY THOMAS JACKSON, M.A.,

Prebendary of St. Paul's Cathedral, and Rector of Stoke Newington, London.

In the novel and attractive black and gold binding, gilt top, price 6s.

New Work by the Rev. T. Pelham Dale, M.A.

A LIFE'S MOTTO.

Illustrated by Biographical Examples.

"Whatsoever thy hand findeth to do, do it with thy might."

I. AUGUSTINE, BISHOP OF HIPPO—*Faith's great Victory over Heathenism.*
II. BERNARD, THE MONK—*Faith amidst the dark Clouds of Mediæval Superstition.*
III. WESLEY, THE METHODIST—*Faith arousing the slumbering Church.*
IV. JOHN NEWTON, THE CONVERTED SLAVE-DRIVER—*Faith victorious over blaspheming Atheism.*
V. CHARLES SIMEON: THE DESPISED EXALTED—*Faith patient in Well-doing.*
VI. HENRY KIRKE WHITE—*Faith not striving lawfully.*
VII. EDWARD IRVING, THE ENTHUSIAST—*Faith in Credulity.*
VIII. HENRY MARTYN AND CHARLES FREDERICK MACKENZIE, THE MARTYR MISSIONARIES—*Faith loving not Life unto Death.*
IX. AN EPILOGUE OF CONTRASTS.

With a Frontispiece by J. D. WATSON.

In the novel and attractive black and gold binding, gilt top, price 5s.

The Christian Life of the Present Day.

NEW AND CHEAPER EDITION.

THE PATH ON EARTH TO THE GATE OF HEAVEN,

Essays of Counsel and Encouragement for the Christian Life of the Present Day.

By the REV. FREDERICK ARNOLD, of Christ Church, Oxford.

With a Frontispiece.

In the novel and attractive black and gold binding, gilt edges, price 3s. 6d.

LONDON: JAMES HOGG & SON, York St., Covent Garden, W.C.

BOOKS RECENTLY PUBLISHED.

NEW WORK BY H. R. FOX BOURNE.

FAMOUS LONDON MERCHANTS.

With Portraits of George Peabody, Sir Richard Whittington, Sir Thomas Gresham, Sir Hugh Myddelton, Sir Joseph Child, Paterson, Founder of the Bank of England, Coutts, the Banker, and 17 other Illustrations.

By H. R. FOX BOURNE,

Author of "Merchant Princes of England," &c.

In the novel and attractive black and gold binding, gilt edges, price 3s. 6d.

CAPTAIN PENNY, THE VETERAN WHALER.

ADVENTURES IN THE ICE:

A comprehensive Summary of Arctic Exploration, Discovery, and Adventure, including Experiences of Captain Penny, the Veteran Whaler, *now first published.*

With Portraits of Sir John Franklin, Captain Penny, Dr Elisha Kent Kane, Dr Isaac I. Hayes, and 14 other Illustrations.

By JOHN TILLOTSON.

In the novel and attractive black and gold binding, gilt edges, price 3s. 6d.

THE WORLD'S PROGRESS.

PIONEERS OF CIVILIZATION.

By the Author of "Lives of Eminent Men," &c.

CHAP.	CHAP.
I. THE SOLDIER PIONEER.	IV. PEACEFUL PIONEERS.
II. PIONEERS OF ENTERPRISE AND DARING.	V. TRADING PIONEERS.
	VI. SETTLING PIONEERS.
III. EXPLORING PIONEERS.	VII. THE PIONEERS OF FAITH.

With Portraits of Dr Livingstone, Captain Clapperton, William Penn, Captain Cook, Lord Robert Clive, Captain Flinders. Rev. Henry Martyn, and 10 other Page Illustrations.

In the novel and attractive black and gold binding, gilt edges, price 3s. 6d.

LONDON: JAMES HOGG & SON, York St., Covent Garden, W.C.

www.ingramcontent.com/pod-product-compliance
Lightning Source LLC
Chambersburg PA
CBHW051741300426
44115CB00007B/646